Spiritual Emergency

This **New Consciousness Reader** is part of a series of
anthologies of original and classic writing by renowned experts
on the quest for human growth and the
transformation of the spirit.

Other books in this series include:

Healers on Healing, edited by Richard Carlson, Ph.D.,
and Benjamin Shield

Also by Christina and Stanislav Grof:

Beyond Death
The Stormy Search for the Self (March 1990)

Also by Stanislav Grof:

Realms of the Human Unconscious
The Human Encounter with Death
LSD Psychotherapy
Beyond the Brain
The Adventure of Self-Discovery
Ancient Wisdom and Modern Science (as editor)
Human Survival and Consciousness Evolution (as editor)

SPIRITUAL EMERGENCY

When Personal Transformation Becomes a Crisis

EDITED BY

STANISLAV GROF, M.D.
and **CHRISTINA GROF**

JEREMY P. TARCHER, INC.
Los Angeles

All proceeds from the sales of this book will go to the Spiritual Emergence Network.

"Self-Realization and Psychological Disturbances" is reprinted from *Re-Vision* journal, 8(2):21−31, 1986. Originally published in *Synthesis* magazine, no. 3−4, pp. 148−171, 1978. Based on a chapter from *Psychosynthesis: A Manual of Principles and Techniques*, originally published by Viking Press; reprinted with permission of the Berkshire Center for Psychosynthesis.

"Transcendental Experience in Relation to Religion and Psychosis" is reprinted by permission from *The Psychedelic Review*, no. 6, 1965, pp. 7−15.

"Spiritual Emergence and Renewal" is reprinted from *Re-Vision* journal, 8(2):33−38, 1986.

"When Insanity Is a Blessing: The Message of Shamanism" originally appeared under the title "Suffering Kills, Suffering Enlivens: Sickness and Self-Healing" in *Dreamtime and the Inner Space: The World of the Shaman* by Holger Kalweit. Boston: Shambhala Publishing, 1988.

"Kundalini: Classical and Clinical" is reprinted from *Kundalini, Evolution and Enlightenment*, John White, ed. Garden City, N.Y.: Anchor Books/Doubleday, 1978.

"The Challenges of Psychic Opening: A Personal Story" is reprinted from *Re-Vision* journal, 8(2):55−60, 1986.

Library of Congress Cataloging in Publication Data

Spiritual emergency: when personal transformation becomes a crisis/
  edited by Stanislav Grof and Christina Grof.
    p.   cm.
  Bibliography.
  1. Spiritual life. 2. Psychiatric emergencies. I. Grof,
Stanislav, 1931−   . II. Grof, Christina.
BL624.S677   1989   89-34831
291.4 ' 2—dc20   CIP
  ISBN 0-87477-538-8

Jeremy P. Tarcher, Inc.
9110 Sunset Blvd.
Los Angeles, CA 90069

Distributed by St. Martin's Press, New York

Manufactured in the United States of America

10   9   8   7   6   5   4   3   2   1

First Edition

We dedicate this book with appreciation to our beloved teachers who have guided us during our own journeys; to the many fellow adventurers who, over the years, have told us their personal stories; and to the visionaries throughout the ages who have forged the trails and provided the maps.

CONTENTS

INTRODUCTION

To your tired eyes I bring a vision
of a different world,
so new and clean and fresh
you will forget the pain and sorrow
that you saw before.
Yet this a vision is
which you must share
with everyone you see,
for otherwise you will behold it not.
To give this gift is how to make it yours.

A Course in Miracles

The central theme explored in this book in many different ways by various authors is the idea that some of the dramatic experiences and unusual states of mind that traditional psychiatry diagnoses and treats as mental diseases are actually crises of personal transformation, or "spiritual emergencies." Episodes of this kind have been described in sacred literature of all ages as a result of meditative practices and as signposts of the mystical path.

When these states of mind are properly understood and treated supportively rather than suppressed by standard psychiatric routines, they can be healing and have very beneficial effects on the people who experience them. This positive potential is expressed in the term *spiritual emergency,* which is a play on words, suggesting both a crisis and an opportunity of rising to a new level of awareness, or "spiritual emergence." This book is meant to be an educational reader for people undergoing such crises, for their relatives and friends, for the ministers whom they might consult, and for the therapists who treat them. We hope that it will help turn such crises into opportunities for personal growth.

The concept of spiritual emergency integrates findings from many disciplines, including clinical and experimental psychiatry, modern consciousness research, experiential psychotherapies, anthropological field studies, parapsychology, thanatology, comparative religion, and mythology. Observations from all these fields suggest strongly that spiritual emergencies have a positive potential and should not be confused with diseases that have a biological cause and necessitate medical treatment. As we will see in this book, such an approach is fully congruent with ancient wisdom as well as modern science.

The focus of this book is primarily, although not exclusively, on experiences that have an explicitly spiritual content or meaning. Throughout the ages, visionary states have played an extremely important role. From ecstatic trances of shamans, or medicine men and women, to revelations of the founders of the great religions, prophets, saints, and spiritual teachers, such experiences have been sources of religious enthusiasm, remarkable healing, and artistic inspiration. All ancient and preindustrial cultures placed high value on nonordinary states of consciousness as an important means of learning about the hidden aspects of the world and of connecting with the spiritual dimensions of existence.

The advent of the Industrial and Scientific Revolution dramatically changed this situation. Rationality became the ultimate measure of all things, rapidly replacing spirituality and religious beliefs. In the course of the Scientific Revolution in the West, everything even remotely related to mysticism was disqualified as left over from the Dark Ages. Visionary states were no longer seen as important complements of ordinary states of consciousness that can provide valuable information about the self and reality, but as pathological distortions of mental activity. This judgment has been reflected in the fact that modern psychiatry tries to suppress these conditions instead of supporting them and allowing them to take their natural course.

When medical strategies were applied to psychiatry, researchers were able to find biological explanations for some disorders with psychological manifestations. Many conditions were found to have organic bases such as infections, tumors, vitamin deficiencies, and vascular or degenerative diseases of the brain. In addition, medically oriented psychiatry found means of controlling the symptoms of those conditions for which no biological causes were found.

These results were sufficient to establish psychiatry as a subspecialty of medicine, although no organic basis has yet been found for the majority of problems psychiatrists treat. As a result of this historical development, people who have various emotional and psychosomatic disorders are automatically referred to as patients, and the difficulties they are having are referred to as diseases of unknown origin, even if clinical and laboratory findings in no way substantiate such labels.

Furthermore, traditional psychiatry makes no distinction between psychosis and mysticism and tends to treat all nonordinary states of consciousness by suppressive medication. This development has created a peculiar schism in Western culture. Officially, the Judeo-Christian religious tradition is presented as being the basis and backbone of Western civilization. Every motel room has a copy of the Bible in the drawer of the bedside table, and in their speeches, high-ranking politicians make references to God. However, if a member of a religious community had a powerful spiritual experience similar to those that many important figures in Christianity's history have had, the average minister would send that person to a psychiatrist.

During the last few decades, this situation has been changing very rapidly. The 1960s brought a wave of interest in spirituality and consciousness exploration that manifested itself in many different ways, from a renaissance of the ancient and Oriental spiritual practices to experiential psychotherapies and self-experimentation with psychedelic drugs. At that time, many people became deeply involved in meditation and other forms of spiritual practice, either under the guidance of a teacher or on their own.

Since such techniques are specifically designed to facilitate spiritual opening, spirituality became for many people a matter of personal experience rather than something they heard or read about. Since the 1960s, the number of those who have experienced mystical and paranormal states has been steadily increasing. As indicated by anonymous polls conducted by the minister and writer Andrew Greeley and by George Gallup, a remarkable proportion of the population now admits having had such experiences. Although there are no reliable statistical data available, it seems that the number of difficulties associated with spiritual experiences is also increasing from year to year.

Rather than concluding from the apparent increase of mystical and visionary experiences that we are in the middle of a global epidemic of mental disease, we should reevaluate the relationship between psychiatry, spirituality, and psychosis. We are now realizing to our surprise that, in the process of relegating mystical experiences to pathology, we may have thrown the baby out with the bath water. Step by step, spirituality is making a comeback into modern psychiatry and into science in general.

The popularity of the Swiss psychiatrist C. G. Jung, whose pioneering work represents a milestone in the new appreciation of spirituality, is rapidly increasing among mental-health professionals, on college campuses, and in lay circles. The same is true for transpersonal psychology, a new discipline that bridges science and the spiritual traditions. Convergence between revolutionary advances in modern science and the worldview of the mystical schools has been the subject of many popular and professional books that have found large audiences. The healthy mystical core that inspired and nourished all great spiritual systems is now being rediscovered and reformulated in modern scientific terms.

More and more people seem to be realizing that true spirituality is based on personal experience and is an extremely important and vital dimension of life. We might be paying a great price for having rejected and discarded a force that nourishes, empowers, and gives meaning to human life. On the individual level, the result seems to be an impoverished, unhappy, and unfulfilling way of life, as well as an increased number of emotional and psychosomatic problems. On the collective scale, the loss of spirituality might be a significant factor in the current dangerous global crisis that threatens the survival of humanity and of all life on this planet. In view of this situation, we feel that it is important to offer support to people undergoing crises of spiritual opening and to create circumstances in which the positive potential of these states can be fully realized.

However, it also seems necessary to issue a word of caution. Episodes of nonordinary states of consciousness cover a very wide spectrum, from purely spiritual states without any pathological features to conditions that are clearly biological in nature and require medical treatment. It is extremely important to take a balanced approach and to be able to differentiate spiritual emergencies from genuine psychoses. While traditional approaches tend to pathologize mystical states, there is the opposite danger of spiritualizing psychotic states and glorifying pathology or, even worse, overlooking an organic problem.

Transpersonal counseling is not appropriate for conditions of a clearly psychotic nature, characterized by lack of insight, paranoid delusions and hallucinations, and extravagant forms of behavior. People with chronic conditions and long histories of institutional treatment who require large doses of tranquilizers are clearly not candidates for the new approaches. We feel strongly, however, that in spite of possible misapplications of the category of spiritual emergency, the benefits for those who are truly undergoing a transformation crisis are so significant that it is important to continue our efforts. The matter of discriminating between pathological conditions and transpersonal crises will be examined more closely in our opening essay, "Spiritual Emergency: Understanding Evolutionary Crisis."

Our interest in this area is very personal and is intimately connected with our individual histories. Stanislav began his professional career as a traditional psychiatrist and Freudian analyst. A profound experience in a psychedelic session conducted for training purposes attracted his attention to nonordinary states of consciousness. More than three decades of research on and observations of the nonordinary experiences of others and his own, induced by a variety of means, convinced him that the current understanding of the human psyche is superficial and inadequate to the task of accounting for the phenomena he has witnessed. He also realized that many of the states that psychiatry considers to be manifestations of mental diseases of unknown origin are actually expressions of a self-healing process in the psyche and in the body. It became his lifelong interest to explore the therapeutic potential of these states and the theoretical challenges associated with them.

Christina's interest in the area of spiritual crisis also results from deep personal motivation. She experienced a spontaneous and completely unexpected spiritual awakening during childbirth, followed by years of dramatic experiences that ranged from hellish to ecstatic. After years of searching, she discovered that her difficulties accurately matched the descriptions of "Kundalini awakening," a process of spiritual opening described in Indian sacred scriptures. (Lee Sannella takes a close look at this phenomenon in "Kundalini: Classical and Clinical," included in Part Two of this book.)

In 1980, in an attempt to make the situation easier for others in a similar predicament, Christina founded the Spiritual Emergence Network (SEN), a worldwide organization that supports individuals in spiritual crises, provides them with information that gives them a new understanding of their process, and advises them on available alternatives to traditional treatment. SEN's work will be described fully in Jeneane Prevatt's and Russ Park's essay, "The Spiritual Emergence Network (SEN)," in the final section of this book.

The present volume is an integral part of our efforts. Here we present a collection of articles by various authors offering a new understanding of unusual experiences and states of consciousness and exploring their positive potential and constructive ways of working with them. The contributions fall into four broad categories, forming the main sections of the book.

Part One, "Divine Madness," explores the relationship between psychology, spirituality, and psychosis. It opens with our own introductory essay, "Spiritual Emergency: Understanding Evolutionary Crisis," which outlines the subject of this book. It defines the concept of spiritual emergency, describes the different forms it takes, and discusses a new map of the psyche based on modern consciousness research that can provide useful orientation for people in spiritual crises.

Roberto Assagioli, an Italian psychiatrist and the founder of an original psychotherapeutic system called psychosynthesis, was a true pioneer in the field of transpersonal psychology. Like Jung, he emphasized the role of spirituality in human life and formulated many ideas that are very important for the concept of spiritual emergency. His essay, "Self-Realization and Psychological Disturbances," describing the emotional problems preceding, accompanying, and following a spiritual opening, is a document of great historical value and of theoretical, as well as practical, importance.

R. D. Laing has been for many years one of the most stimulating and controversial figures in contemporary psychiatry. Challenging both traditional psychiatry and Western society, he asserts that the sanity of our culture is at best "pseudosanity" and that what is called mental illness is not true madness. Laing's contribution to this anthology, "Transcendental Experience in Relation to Religion and Psychosis," is of particular interest since it expresses his attitude toward mystical experiences and spirituality.

Part Two, "Varieties of Spiritual Emergency," focuses more specifically on the different forms of personal evolutionary crisis. John Weir Perry's "Spiritual Emergence and Renewal" discusses an important type of transformation crisis that reaches to the very core of the personality structure as he observed it during years of intensive psychotherapy with his clients. Perry also summarizes his experiences with an experimental treatment facility in San Francisco, where patients undergoing episodes that would traditionally be seen as psychotic were treated without suppressive medication.

The paper by psychologist and anthropologist Holger Kalweit, "When Insanity Is a Blessing," explores the wisdom of the world's oldest religion and healing art, shamanism. Kalweit shows that certain forms of suffering and sickness have a potential for self-healing and transformation. An obvious fact among tribal cultures of all ages, this knowledge has been lost in modern Western society.

The idea of Kundalini awakening, a dramatic and colorful form of spiritual opening, has become very popular in the West due to the prolific writings of Gopi Krishna, a pandit from Kashmir who had himself undergone a dramatic and challenging spiritual transformation of this kind. In our book, this subject is represented by the essay, "Kundalini: Classical and Clinical," by the psychiatrist and ophthalmologist Lee Sannella, who has the merit of having introduced the Kundalini syndrome to Western professional audiences.

Here he complements the traditional point of view with a medical and scientific perspective on the subject.

In "The Challenges of Psychic Opening," psychic and transpersonal counselor Anne Armstrong describes the emotional turmoil and psychosomatic difficulties that accompanied the opening of her remarkable psychic gift and resulted in dramatic self-healing.

The problems of people who have had "UFO encounters" and experienced other forms of extraterrestrial contacts are so similar to those associated with transformational crises that these experiences can be considered spiritual emergencies. This subject is discussed in Keith Thompson's essay "The UFO Encounter Experience as a Crisis of Transformation."

The third part, "The Stormy Search for the Self," discusses the problems that spiritual seekers might encounter during systematic practice. Mystical literature of all cultures and ages offers many examples of the problems and complications that we can encounter when we embark on a spiritual journey. This theme is discussed by two well-known and highly competent spiritual teachers. Jack Kornfield's essay "Obstacles and Vicissitudes in Spiritual Practice" is based on the Buddhist tradition, with occasional excursions into other belief systems. Richard Alpert, better known under his spiritual name, Ram Dass, describes some of the fruits of his rich and fascinating personal quest, which has extended over the last quarter of a century, in "Promises and Pitfalls of the Spiritual Path."

Part Four, "Help for People in Spiritual Emergency," focuses on the practical problems of assisting individuals in psychospiritual crises. In our own essay on the subject, "Assistance in Spiritual Emergency," we explore the different forms of help that can be offered by family, friends, spiritual teachers and communities, and professional therapists.

More than one-third of the people who undergo a sudden confrontation with death experience a radical and profound spiritual opening that might be very difficult to assimilate. Approaches for assisting this type of crisis are addressed in the essay "Counseling the Near-Death Experiencer" by Bruce Greyson and Barbara Harris, prominent researchers in the field of thanatology. While this essay focuses on professional helpers, the general principles the authors outline will be of use to all who come into close contact with those undergoing any form of spiritual emergency.

Paul Rebillot's contribution, "The Hero's Journey: Ritualizing the Mystery," introduces the mythological perspective and shows its relevance to the problem of spiritual emergency. Drawing inspiration from his own transformative crisis and from Joseph Campbell's classic work *The Hero with a Thousand Faces*, Rebillot has developed a modern ritual where a symbolic healing crisis is experimentally evoked through the use of guided imagery, psychodrama, music, and group play.

The final paper, "The Spiritual Emergence Network (SEN)," is written by Jeneane Prevatt, current director of that organization, and by Russ Park, a doctoral student deeply involved with it. They outline the history and function of this worldwide network founded in 1980 by Christina to support individuals undergoing crises of spiritual opening.

In the epilogue, we have tried to put the problem of spiritual emergency into the context of the crisis modern humanity is facing. We firmly believe that spiritual emergence—transformation of the consciousness of humanity on a large scale—is one of the few truly promising trends in today's world.

The appendix provides suggestions for further reading for those who would like more information on the various issues explored in this book. Also included is an extensive bibliography on spiritual emergency and related subjects.

It is our hope that this selection of essays will provide valuable information for those undergoing psychospiritual crisis and seeking understanding and treatment that supports the positive potential of these states.

STANISLAV GROF
CHRISTINA GROF
Mill Valley, California
August 1989

Part One

DIVINE MADNESS: PSYCHOLOGY, SPIRITUALITY, AND PSYCHOSIS

Stanislav Grof and Christina Grof

SPIRITUAL EMERGENCY: UNDERSTANDING EVOLUTIONARY CRISIS

*The mystic, endowed with native talents . . . and fol-
lowing . . . the instruction of a master, enters the waters
and finds he can swim; whereas the schizophrenic, unprepared, unguided, and ungifted, has fallen or has intentionally plunged and is drowning.*

JOSEPH CAMPBELL, *Myths to Live By*

F eelings of oneness with the entire universe. Visions and images of distant times and places. Sensations of vibrant currents of energy coursing through the body, accompanied by spasms and violent trembling. Visions of deities, demigods, and demons. Vivid flashes of brilliant light and rainbow colors. Fears of impending insanity, even death.

Anyone experiencing such extreme mental and physical phenomena would instantly be labeled psychotic by most modern Westerners. Yet increasing numbers of people seem to be having unusual experiences similar to those described above, and instead of plunging irrevocably into insanity, they often emerge from these extraordinary states of mind with an increased sense of well-being, and a higher level of functioning in daily life. In many cases, long-standing emotional, mental, and physical problems are healed in the process.

We find many parallels for such incidences in the life stories of the saints, yogis, mystics, and shamans. In fact, spiritual literature and traditions the world over validate the healing and transformative power of such extraordinary states for those who undergo them. Why, then, are people who have such experiences in today's world almost invariably dismissed as mentally ill?

Although there are many individual exceptions, mainstream psychiatry and psychology in general make no distinction between mysticism and mental illness. These fields do not officially recognize that the great spiritual traditions that have been involved in the systematic study of human consciousness for millennia have anything to offer. Thus the concepts and practices found in the Buddhist, Hindu, Christian, Sufi, and other mystical traditions are ignored and dismissed indiscriminately.

In this essay, we will explore the idea that many episodes of unusual states of mind, even those that are dramatic and reach psychotic proportions, are not necessarily symptoms of disease in the medical sense. We view them as crises of the evolution of consciousness, or "spiritual emergencies," comparable to the states described by the various mystical traditions of the world.

Before discussing more specifically the concept of spiritual emergency, let us take a closer look at the relationship between psychosis, mental disease, and mysticism, and the historical developments that have resulted in the rejection of classic spiritual and mystical experiences as symptoms of mental illness by modern science and psychiatry.

The worldview created by traditional Western science and dominating our culture is, in its most rigorous form, incompatible with any notion of spirituality. In a universe where only the tangible, material, and measurable are real, all forms of religious and mystical activities are seen as reflecting ignorance, superstition, and irrationality or emotional immaturity. Direct experiences of spiritual realities are then interpreted as "psychotic"—manifestations of mental disease.

Our personal experiences and observations during years of involvement in various forms of deep experiential psychotherapy have led us to believe that it is important to take a fresh look at this situation in psychiatry and in our worldview in general, and reevaluate it in light of both historical and recent evidence. A radical revision of thinking about mysticism and psychosis is long overdue. A clear differentiation between these two phenomena has far-reaching practical consequences for those people who have experiences of nonordinary states of consciousness, particularly those with a spiritual emphasis. It is important to recognize spiritual emergencies and treat them appropriately because of their great positive potential for personal growth and healing, which would ordinarily be suppressed by an insensitive approach and indiscriminate routine medication.

The group of mental disorders known as *psychoses* represents a great challenge and enigma for Western psychiatry and psychology. These conditions are characterized by a deep disruption of the ability to perceive the world in normal terms, to think and respond emotionally in a way that is culturally and socially acceptable, and to behave and communicate appropriately.

For some of the disorders in the category of psychosis, modern science has found underlying anatomical, physiological, or biochemical changes in the brain or in other parts of the organism. This subgroup is referred to as *organic psychoses* and belongs unquestionably in the domain of medicine. However, for many other psychotic states, no medical explanation has been found in spite of the focused efforts of generations of researchers from various fields. In spite of the general lack of results in the search for specific medical causes, these so-called *functional psychoses* are usually put into the category of mental diseases whose cause is unknown. It is this subgroup of psychoses that interests us here.

In view of the absence of a clear consensus regarding the causes of functional psychoses, it would be more appropriate and honest to acknowledge our complete ignorance as to their nature and origin and use the term *disease* only for those conditions for which we can find a specific physical basis. Thus we can open the door to novel approaches to at least some functional psychoses, yielding new perspectives that differ theoretically and practically from the medical view of disease. Alternatives have already been developed, particularly in the context of so-called depth psychologies. These are various psychological theories and psychotherapeutic strategies inspired by the pioneering work of Sigmund Freud.

Although the approaches of depth psychology are discussed and taught in academic circles, the understanding and treatment of functional psychoses in mainstream psychiatry is, for a variety of reasons, dominated by medical thinking. Historically, psychiatry has been able to establish itself firmly as a medical discipline. It has found an organic basis for certain psychotic states and, in some instances, even effective treatments for them. In addition, it has been able to successfully control the symptoms of psychotic states of unknown origin by tranquilizers, antidepressants, sedatives, and hypnotics. It thus might seem logical to extend this trajectory and expect success along the same lines in those disorders for which causes and treatments have not yet been found.

There are additional facts that make a persuasive case for the medical, or psychiatric, perspective. Psychiatry traces psychotic states and behaviors to physical and physiological conditions, whereas depth psychologies attempt to find the causes of mental problems in events and circumstances of the patient's life, usually occurrences in his or her childhood. Thus traditional psychology limits the sources of all contents of the mind to observable aspects of the client's personal history. This is what we call the "biographical model" of psychosis. Psychotic behaviors and states of mind for which causes in biographical history cannot be found would therefore seem to provide evidence for the medical model.

Indeed, there are significant aspects of many psychoses that cannot be accounted for by the psychological method of finding the origins of all mental conditions in the patient's life history. Some of them involve certain extreme emotions and physical sensations that cannot easily be understood in terms of the individual's childhood history or later events. Here belong, for example, visions and experiences of engulfment by the universe, diabolic tortures, disintegration of the personality, or even destruction of the world. Similarly, abysmal guilt feelings, a sense of eternal damnation, or uncontrollable and indiscriminate aggressive impulses in many cases cannot be traced to specific events or conditions in the patient's life. We might then easily assume that such alien elements in the psyche must be due to organic pathological processes directly or indirectly affecting the brain.

There are other types of experiences that present problems for the biographical view, not only because of their intensity but because of their very nature. Experiences of deities and demons, mythical heroes and landscapes, or celestial and infernal regions have no logical place in the world as it is understood by Western science. Therefore it seems obvious to suggest, as the medical perspective does, that they must be products of some unknown physical process of disease. The mystical nature of many experiences in nonordinary states of consciousness puts them automatically into the category of pathology, since spirituality is not seen as a legitimate dimension in the exclusively material universe of traditional science.

Recent developments in psychology, however, have begun to suggest sources for such extraordinary experiences that lie outside both medical pathology and personal life history. Historically, the first breakthrough in this respect was the work of the Swiss psychiatrist C. G. Jung. Jung vastly expanded the biographical model by introducing the concept of the collective unconscious. Through careful analysis of his own dream life, the dreams of his clients, and the hallucinations, fantasies, and delusions of psychotics, Jung discovered that the human psyche has access to images and motifs that are truly universal. They can be found in the mythology, folklore, and art of cultures widely distributed not only across the globe but also throughout the history of humanity.

These archetypes, as Jung called them, appear with astonishing regularity even in individuals whose life history and education lack direct exposure to their various cultural and historical manifestations. This observation led him to the conclusion that there is—in addition to the individual unconscious—a racial or collective unconscious that is shared by all mankind. He saw comparative religion and mythology as invaluable sources of information about these collective aspects of the unconscious. In Jung's model, many experiences that do not make sense as derivatives of biographical events, such as visions of deities and demons, can be seen as the emergence of contents from the collective unconscious.

Although Jung's theories have been known for many decades, they did not initially have a significant influence outside narrow circles of dedicated followers. His ideas were very much ahead of their time and had to wait for additional impetus to gain momentum. This situation started to change during the 1960s, the time of a great renaissance of interest in the further reaches of human consciousness. This era of inner exploration started with clinical experimentation with psychedelic drugs among professionals and personal exposure by a portion of the lay population, which for a while came to be known as the counterculture. Exploration continued with an avalanche of experiential techniques of psychotherapy and spiritual practices of all kinds, from Gestalt therapy to transcendental meditation, among therapists and laypeople in the 1970s and 1980s.

As many began to experience the kinds of images and symbols Jung ascribed to the collective unconscious, as well as episodes of a classic mystical nature, this wave brought strong supportive evidence for Jungian ideas and a powerful validation of the mystical traditions of the world, Eastern as well as Western. During this time, it became obvious to many practitioners involved in these explorations that we needed a new model of the psyche whose important elements would include not only the Freudian biographical dimension but the Jungian collective unconscious and spirituality as well.

When one thinks about the mind in such vastly expanded terms, the contents of the experiences that emerge during various nonordinary states of consciousness are not seen as random and arbitrary products of impaired brain functioning. Rather, they are manifestations of the deep recesses of the human psyche that are not ordinarily accessible. And the surfacing of this unconscious material can actually be healing and transformative, if it occurs under the right circumstances. Various spiritual disciplines and mystical traditions from shamanism to Zen represent rich repositories of invaluable knowledge with regard to these deeper domains of the mind. It has been known for centuries that many dramatic and difficult episodes can occur during spiritual practice and that the road to enlightenment can be rough and stormy.

Thus, the light shed by depth psychology and ancient spiritual legacies provides the basis for a new understanding of some of the psychotic states for which no biological cause can be found. The challenges to modern psychiatry presented by both of these schools of knowledge show us the roots of the idea of spiritual emergency, a concept that we will now examine in greater detail.

THE PROMISE AND PERIL OF SPIRITUAL EMERGENCY

The Chinese pictogram for *crisis* perfectly represents the idea of spiritual emergency. It is composed of two basic signs, or radicals: one of them means "danger" and the other "opportunity." Thus, while passage through this kind of condition is often difficult and frightening, these states have tremendous evolutionary and healing potential. If properly understood and treated as difficult stages in a natural developmental process, spiritual emergencies can result in spontaneous healing of various emotional and psychosomatic disorders, favorable personality changes, solutions to important problems in life, and evolution toward what some call "higher consciousness."

Because of both the attendant danger and the positive potential of these crises, people involved in spiritual emergency need expert guidance from those who have personal and professional experience with nonordinary states of consciousness and know how to work with and support them. In individuals undergoing an evolutionary crisis of this kind, pathological labels and the insensitive use of various repressive measures, including the control of symptoms by medication, can interfere with the positive potential of the process. The ensuing long-term dependence on tranquilizers with their well-known side effects, loss of vitality, and compromised way of life present a sad contrast to those rare situations where a person's transformation crisis has been supported, validated, and allowed to reach completion. Therefore, the importance of understanding spiritual emergency and of developing comprehensive and effective approaches to its treatment and adequate support systems cannot be over-emphasized. (The issue of treatment will be more fully addressed in our essay "Assistance in Spiritual Emergency.")

TRIGGERS OF TRANSFORMATIONAL CRISIS

In some instances, it is possible to identify the situation that seems to have triggered the spiritual emergency. It can be a primarily physical factor, such as a disease, accident, or operation. At other times, extreme physical exertion or prolonged lack of sleep may appear to be the immediate trigger. In women, it can be childbirth, miscarriage, or abortion; we have also seen situations where the onset of the process coincided with an exceptionally powerful sexual experience.

Occasionally, the beginning of a spiritual emergency can follow a powerful emotional experience. This can be loss of an important relationship, such as the death of a child or another close relative, the end of a love affair, or divorce. Similarly, a series of failures, being fired from a job, or property loss can immediately precede the onset of evolutionary crisis. In predisposed individuals, the "last straw" can be an experience with psychedelic drugs or a session of experiential psychotherapy.

However, one of the most important catalysts of spiritual emergency seems to be deep involvement in various forms of meditation and spiritual practice. These methods have been specifically designed to activate spiritual experiences. We have been repeatedly contacted by persons whose unusual experiences occurred during the pursuit of Zen, Vipassana Buddhist meditation, Kundalini yoga, Sufi exercises, or Christian prayer and monastic contemplation. As various Oriental and Western spiritual disciplines are rapidly gaining popularity, more and more people seem to be having transpersonal crises—yet another reason that the correct understanding and treatment of spiritual emergencies is an issue of ever-increasing importance.

INNER MAPS OF SPIRITUAL EMERGENCY

The experiential spectrum of spiritual emergencies is extremely rich: it involves intense emotions, visions and other changes of perception, and unusual thought processes, as well as various physical symptoms ranging from tremors to feelings of suffocation. However, we have observed that the content of these experiences seems to fall into three major categories. The first group involves experiences closely related to an individual's life history, known as the *biographical* category. The second category revolves around issues of dying and being reborn; a close relationship to the trauma of biological birth earns this group the name *perinatal*. The third category is far beyond the limits of ordinary human experience and is closely related to the Jungian collective unconscious; we call these *transpersonal* experiences because they involve images and motifs that seem to have a source outside the individual's personal history.

Biographical aspects of spiritual emergencies involve the reliving and healing of traumatic events in one's life history. The emergence of important childhood memories, such as physical or sexual abuse, loss of a parent or loved one, close encounters with death, illness, or surgery, and other difficult events can sometimes play an important part in crises of transformation. This domain has been thoroughly explored and mapped by biographically oriented therapists, and thus requires no further discussion in these pages.

The next level of experiences in spiritual emergency is the perinatal (from the Greek *peri*, meaning "around," and the Latin *natal*, meaning "pertaining to birth"). This aspect of spiritual emergency centers around themes of dying and being reborn, unfolding in a pattern bearing such a close relationship to the stages of biological birth that it seems to involve a reliving of the memory of one's own delivery.

Because most of us do not consciously remember our own births, we have difficulty believing that the experience of being born has any formative impact on the human being. Recent evidence, however, suggests otherwise. The burgeoning perinatal movement in psychology, finding its origins in the theories of Freud's disciple Otto Rank and gaining impetus from the research of David Chamberlain and others, asserts convincingly that the buried memory of birth trauma has a profound effect on the psyche and can resurface later in life.

Reliving the memory of birth often results in preoccupation with death and death-related imagery, reflecting both that birth is a difficult and life-threatening event and that it is in itself the "death" of the prenatal period of existence, the only kind of life the fetus has yet experienced. People reliving the birth trauma feel that their lives are biologically threatened; this alternates or coincides with experiences of struggling to be born or freeing oneself from some very uncomfortable forms of confinement. Fears of going insane, losing control, and even of imminent death can become so pronounced under these conditions as to resemble psychosis.

These episodes often have profound spiritual overtones, felt as a powerful mystical opening and reconnection with the Divine. They are often interspersed with mythological motifs from the collective unconscious that Jung described as archetypes, suggesting intriguingly that the perinatal level of the mind somehow represents the interface between the individual and the collective unconscious. While the many fascinating themes and facets of this category of spiritual emergency and its relationship to biological birth are beyond the scope of the present work, a more comprehensive and detailed discussion can be found in *The Adventure of Self-Discovery* by Stanislav Grof.

In addition to biographical and perinatal themes, many spiritual emergencies have a significant component of experiences that belong to the third category—episodes that are distinctly spiritual or "transpersonal" in content. The word *transpersonal* refers to transcendence of the ordinary boundaries of personality and includes many experiences that have been called spiritual, mystical, religious, occult, magical, or paranormal. Since these terms are associated with many popular misconceptions, a proper understanding of the transpersonal realm is extremely important for correct evaluation of the problems related to spiritual emergencies.

The best way to begin our discussion of this domain of experience is to define the factors that bind and limit us in everyday life, preventing us from contacting the transpersonal dimension. In ordinary states of consciousness, we experience ourselves as physical beings, material bodies enclosed in our skin. Alan Watts, the famous philosopher who popularized Eastern religious thought for Western audiences, referred to this situation as "identification with the skin-encapsulated ego." We can never experience with the ordinary five senses anything but what is happening "here and now," the events present in our immediate environment. We cannot see events from which we are separated by a mountain, hear conversations in a remote city, or feel the softness of lambskin without touching it.

In nonordinary states of consciousness, these limitations do not seem to apply. When we enter the transpersonal arena, we can experience historically or geographically remote events as vividly as if they were happening here and now. We can participate in sequences that involve our ancestors, animal predecessors, or even people in other centuries and other cultures who have no ancestral relationship to us.

Our personal boundaries may appear to melt and we can become identified with other people, groups of people, or all of humanity. We can actually feel that we have become things that we ordinarily perceive as objects outside of ourselves, such as other people, animals, or trees. Very accurate and realistic experiences of identification with various forms of life and even inorganic processes such as the subatomic events described in quantum physics can occur in transpersonal states.

But the content of transpersonal experiences is not limited to the world of things that exist in our everyday reality. It includes elements that Western culture does not accept as objectively real: we can encounter deities, demons, spirit guides, inhabitants of other universes, or mythological figures, all of whom appear as real to us as the things we encounter in daily life. Thus, in the transpersonal state, we do not differentiate between the world of "consensus reality," or the conventional everyday world, and the mythological realm of archetypal forms.

The above discussion might appear absurd to a skeptical reader educated in the tradition of Western science. Why are such experiences important, and how are they relevant to the problem of spiritual emergency? The fact that transpersonal phenomena *seem* real and convincing does not mean that they should be taken seriously. Our brains have a fantastic capacity to store with photographic detail all that we have heard, read, or seen in books and movies and on television. Why should it not be possible that we simply concoct from this incredibly rich material countless imaginary sequences without deeper meaning and relevance? Is it not a waste of time to give so much attention to these phenomena?

This point of view, however logical it might seem, does not withstand the test of existing evidence. Researchers who have seriously studied transpersonal experiences have come to the conclusion that they are remarkable phenomena that challenge the very basis of the traditional Western worldview. Transpersonal experiences cannot be explained as products of neurophysiological processes within the traditional scientific framework, which holds that consciousness resides solely in the organ within our skulls.

The main reason for this conclusion is the frequent observation that in experiences of this kind, we can, without the mediation of the senses, directly tap sources of information about the universe that lie outside the conventionally defined range of the individual psyche. Experiences involving our ancestors and events from the history of our race, episodes from lives in other cultures, and sequences that have the quality of memories from other lifetimes often involve quite specific and accurate details about the costumes, weapons, rituals, and architecture of social structures and historical periods to which we have never personally been exposed.

The experiences of identification with various animals or our animal ancestors can result in extraordinary insights concerning animal psychology, instincts, habits, and courtship. Fascinating new information can often emerge from experiences involving plants or inorganic processes. Such information is typically far beyond the level of knowledge of the person receiving it.

However, the most convincing evidence for the authenticity of transpersonal phenomena comes from the study of out-of-body experiences, during which one feels that one's consciousness has separated from the body and can travel to and observe events happening in remote locations. The accuracy of observations made in out-of-body states has been repeatedly corroborated by researchers studying near-death experiences, which frequently entail out-of-body phenomena.

What is most astonishing is that even transpersonal experiences involving entities and realms that are not objectively real according to the Western worldview can convey absolutely new information. For example, in nonordinary states, many people have encountered deities and mythological realms specific to cultures about which they have no personal knowledge. Accurate details from such experiences have been verified by research into the corresponding mythology of those societies. (It was such observations, as we noted earlier, that led Jung to the discovery of the collective unconscious.)

While it is beyond the scope of this essay to go into detailed discussions of the evidence and give specific examples, we hope that this brief outline has succeeded in showing that transpersonal experiences, which play a critical role in spiritual emergencies, are extraordinary events that deserve serious study. (Those who are specifically interested in this research can find more information in Stanislav Grof's *Beyond the Brain* and *The Adventure of Self-Discovery*.) It would be a grave mistake to disregard these states of mind as irrelevant or insignificant products of brain pathology.

More important from a practical point of view than the authenticity of information received in transpersonal states is their remarkable therapeutic and transformative potential. Many emotional and psychological difficulties are caused by repressed and forgotten memories of traumatic events from life history. However, other complications seem to arise from frightening or threatening information lying just beneath the threshold of conscious awareness in the perinatal and transpersonal domains. Included here are traumatic memories from birth and what seem to be "past lives," identification with wounded animals, demonic archetypes, and many other phenomena. When, by various techniques, we allow this kind of material to emerge into consciousness to be fully experienced and closely examined, it loses the disturbing power that it can otherwise exert in our lives, and chronic psychological and even physical problems whose origins were previously unknown can be fully healed.

In a similar way, deeply positive and liberating experiences, such as the recovery of happy intrauterine memories or feelings of unity and oneness with nature, other people, and the divine have a remarkably direct healing impact. They often give us a greater sense of well-being, a refreshed perspective on current difficulties, and a greater sense of purpose and direction in life. These extraordinary possibilities impel us to treat spiritual emergencies with great respect and to cooperate fully in realizing their healing and transformative potential.

FORMS OF SPIRITUAL EMERGENCY

The manifestations of evolutionary crises are highly individual, and no two spiritual emergencies are alike. Within the individual human psyche there are no distinct boundaries; all its contents form one indivisible continuum. In addition, the Freudian individual unconscious is not clearly separated from the Jungian collective unconscious. One should not, therefore, expect that different types of spiritual emergency will fall into clean diagnostic pigeonholes that can be easily distinguished from one another.

However, our work with individuals in crises, discussions with colleagues who do similar work, and reading of related literature have convinced us that it is possible and useful to define certain major forms of spiritual emergency, which have specific features differentiating them from others. Naturally, their boundaries are somewhat fuzzy, and combinations and overlaps of various kinds are the rule rather than the exception.

We will first present a list of the most important varieties of "spiritual emergency" and then give a brief description of each. (A more detailed discussion of some of these conditions can be found in the second section of this book, "Varieties of Spiritual Emergency.")

1. The shamanic crisis
2. The awakening of Kundalini

3. Episodes of unitive consciousness ("peak experiences")
4. Psychological renewal through return to the center
5. The crisis of psychic opening
6. Past-life experiences
7. Communications with spirit guides and "channeling"
8. Near-death experiences
9. Experiences of close encounters with UFOs
10. Possession states

The Shamanic Crisis

Shamanism is humanity's most ancient religion and healing art. A universal phenomenon, it very likely originated in the Paleolithic era and has survived in most preindustrial cultures to this day. It is thus clearly related to some very basic and primordial aspects of the human psyche.

The career of many shamans—witch doctors or medicine men and women—in different cultures begins with a dramatic involuntary visionary episode that anthropologists call "shamanic illness." During this time, future shamans might lose contact with the environment and have powerful inner experiences that involve journeys into the underworld and attacks by demons who expose them to incredible tortures and ordeals. These often culminate in experiences of death and dismemberment followed by rebirth and ascent to celestial regions.

When these episodes are successfully completed, they can be profoundly healing; not only the emotional but also the physical health of the future shaman is often dramatically improved as a result of such a psychospiritual crisis. This involuntary initiation can also lead to many important insights into the forces of nature and the dynamics of diseases. Following such a crisis, one becomes a shaman and returns to the community as a fully functioning and honored member. (More detailed discussion of this subject can be found in this book in Holger Kalweit's essay "When Insanity Is a Blessing.")

We have seen instances where modern Americans, Europeans, Australians, and Asians have experienced episodes that bore a close resemblance to shamanic crises. Besides the elements of physical and emotional tortures, death, and rebirth, such states involved experiences of connection with animals, plants, and elemental forces of nature. People experiencing such crises can also show spontaneous tendencies to create rituals that are identical to those practiced by shamans of various cultures.

The Awakening of Kundalini

The manifestations of this form of crisis resemble the descriptions of the awakening of the serpent power, or Kundalini, found in historical Indian literature. According to the yogis, Kundalini is a form of creative cosmic energy that resides in a latent form at the base of the human spine. It can become activated by meditation, specific exercises, the intervention of an accomplished spiritual teacher, or sometimes for reasons that are unknown.

The activated Kundalini rises through the channels in the "subtle body," which is described in the yogic literature as a field of non-physical energy surrounding and infusing the physical body. As it ascends, it clears old traumatic imprints and opens the centers of psychic energy, called *chakras*. This process, although highly valued and considered beneficial in the yogic tradition, is not without dangers and requires expert guidance by a guru whose Kundalini is fully awakened and stabilized.

The most dramatic signs of Kundalini awakening are physical and psychological manifestations called *kriyas*. One can experience intense sensations of energy and heat streaming up the spine, associated with violent shaking, spasms, and twisting movements. Powerful waves of seemingly unmotivated emotions, such as anxiety, anger, sadness, or joy and ecstatic rapture, can surface and temporarily dominate the psyche. Visions of brilliant light or various archetypal beings and a variety of internally perceived sounds, as well as experiences of what seem to be memories from past lives, are very common. Involuntary and often uncontrollable behaviors complete the picture: talking in tongues, chanting unknown songs, assuming yogic postures and gestures, and making a variety of animal sounds and movements.

Recently, unmistakable signs of this process have been observed in thousands of Westerners. California psychiatrist and eye doctor Lee Sannella, who first brought the Kundalini syndrome to the attention of Western audiences, single-handedly collected nearly one thousand such cases. He discusses his experiences in his contribution to this book, entitled "Kundalini: Classical and Clinical."

Episodes of Unitive Consciousness ("Peak Experiences")

In the states that belong to this group, one experiences dissolution of personal boundaries and has a sense of becoming one with other people, with nature, or with the entire universe. This process has a very sacred quality and feels like one is merging with creative cosmic energy, or God. The usual categories of time and space seem to be transcended, and one can have a sense of infinity and eternity. The emotions associated with this state range from profound peace and serenity to exuberant joy and ecstatic rapture.

The American psychologist Abraham Maslow, who studied these experiences in many hundreds of people, gave them the name "peak experiences." While writing about them, he expressed sharp criticism toward Western psychiatry for its tendency to confuse such states with mental disease. According to Maslow, they should be considered supernormal, rather than abnormal, phenomena. If they are not interfered with or discouraged, they typically lead to better functioning in the world and to "self-actualization," a capacity to express one's potential more fully. Because of the vast available literature on unitive experiences, we have not included an essay on this subject in the present work. We highly recommend Maslow's work for further study.

Psychological Renewal through Return to the Center

Another important type of transpersonal crisis has been described by the California psychiatrist and Jungian analyst John Weir Perry, who called it the "renewal process." For a superficial observer, the experiences of the people involved in a renewal process are so strange and extravagant that it might seem logical to attribute them to some serious disease process affecting the functioning of the brain.

The psyche of people in this kind of crisis appears to be a colossal battlefield where a cosmic combat is being played out between the forces of Good and Evil, or Light and Darkness. They are preoccupied with the theme of death—ritual killing, sacrifice, martyrdom, and afterlife. The problem of opposites fascinates them, particularly issues related to the differences between sexes.

They experience themselves as the center of fantastic events that have cosmic relevance and are important for the future of the world.

Their visionary states tend to take them farther and farther back—through their own history and the history of humanity, all the way to the creation of the world and the original ideal state of paradise. In this process, they seem to strive for perfection, trying to correct things that went wrong in the past.

After a period of turmoil and confusion, the experiences become more and more pleasant and start moving toward a resolution. The process often culminates in the experience of "sacred marriage"; this either happens with an imaginary archetypal partner, or is projected onto an idealized person from one's life. It usually reflects that the masculine and the feminine aspects of the personality are reaching a new balance.

At this time, one can have experiences involving what Jungian psychology sees as symbols representing the Self—the transpersonal center that reflects our deepest and true nature and is comparable to the Hindu concept of Atma-Brahma, the divine within. In visionary states, it appears in the form of a source of light of supernatural beauty, precious stones, pearls, radiant jewels, and other similar symbolic variations.

There is usually a stage in which these glorious experiences are interpreted as a personal apotheosis, a procedure that raises one to a highly exalted human status or to a state above the human condition altogether—a great leader, a world savior, or even the Lord of the Universe. This is often associated with a profound sense of spiritual rebirth that replaces the earlier preoccupation with death.

At the time of completion and integration, one usually envisions an ideal future—a new world governed by love and justice, where all ills and evils have been overcome. As the intensity of the process subsides, the person realizes that the entire drama was a psychological transformation that was by and large limited to the inner world of the main protagonist.

According to Perry, the renewal process moves one in the direction of what is called in Jungian psychology "individuation," a fuller expression of one's deeper potential. The positive outcome of these episodes and their rich connections with archetypal symbols from ancient history make it very unlikely that the renewal process is a chaotic product of a dysfunctional brain. More information on this type of spiritual emergency can be found in Perry's contribution to this book, entitled "Spiritual Emergence and Renewal."

The Crisis of Psychic Opening

An increase in intuitive abilities and the occurrence of psychic or "paranormal" phenomena are very common during spiritual emergencies of all kinds. However, in some instances the influx of information from nonordinary sources, such as precognition, telepathy, or clairvoyance, becomes so overwhelming and confusing that it dominates the picture and constitutes a major problem.

Among the most dramatic manifestations of psychic opening are frequent out-of-body experiences; when they occur, one's consciousness seems to detach from the body and travel around with independence and freedom. It is possible to observe oneself from a distance, witness what is happening in other areas close by, or perceive accurately events in locations that are miles away. Out-of-body travel occurs frequently in near-death situations, where the accuracy of this "remote viewing" has been established by systematic studies.

A person experiencing dramatic psychic opening might also be so much in touch with the inner processes of others that he or she appears to have telepathic abilities. Indiscriminate verbalization of accurate insights about the contents of other people's minds can alienate others so severely that they may react by unnecessarily hospitalizing the person who is exhibiting this ability. Correct precognition of future situations and clairvoyant perception of remote events, particularly if they occur repeatedly in impressive clusters, can disturb the person experiencing them, as well as those around him or her, since they seriously undermine our ordinary notions of reality.

In experiences that can be called "mediumistic," one has a sense of losing one's own identity and taking on the identity of another person. This can involve assuming another's body image, posture, gestures, facial expression, feelings, and even thought processes. Accomplished shamans, psychics, and spiritual healers can use such experiences in a controlled and productive way. However, during crises of psychic opening, their sudden and unpredictable occurrence and the loss of one's own identity that accompanies them can be very frightening.

At times, the life of someone in crisis seems to be full of uncanny coincidences that link the world of inner realities, such as dreams and visionary states, with happenings in everyday life. This phenomenon was first recognized and described by Jung, who gave it the name "synchronicity." It is important to know that such extraordinary meaningful coincidences represent authentic phenomena; they should not be ignored and dismissed as delusions, as often occurs in contemporary psychiatry. Extraordinary synchronicities accompany many forms of spiritual emergency, but are particularly common in crises of psychic opening.

A dramatic personal study of this variety of spiritual emergency is provided in Anne Armstrong's essay "The Challenges of Psychic Opening" in this book.

Past-Life Experiences

Among the most dramatic and colorful transpersonal episodes occurring in nonordinary states of consciousness are experiences of sequences taking place in other historical periods and other countries. They are usually associated with powerful emotions and physical sensations and often portray the persons, circumstances, and historical settings in which they take place in minute detail. Their most remarkable aspect is a convincing sense of personally remembering and reliving something that one had experienced previously.

This is clearly the same type of experience that inspired the Indian belief in reincarnation and the law of karma. According to this belief, each of us has an entire chain of lifetimes; our present life is shaped by merits and debits of the preceding ones and, in turn, forges our destiny in future incarnations. Various forms of this concept are of critical importance for all the great religions of India and spiritual systems in other parts of Asia influenced by Buddhism. However, similar ideas have also existed quite independently in many other cultures and historical periods. While we do not know whether the model of "past lives" accurately reveals the source of these experiences, their healing potential impels us to take these episodes seriously, apart from whatever we may believe about their origins.

When the content of a karmic experience fully emerges into consciousness, it can suddenly provide an "explanation" for many otherwise incomprehensible aspects of one's daily life. Strange difficulties in relationships with certain people, unsubstantiated fears, and peculiar idiosyncrasies and attractions as well as obscure emotional and psychosomatic symptoms now seem to make sense as "karmic carry-overs" from a "previous lifetime." These very often disappear when the karmic pattern in question is fully and consciously experienced.

Past-life experiences can present problems in several different ways. Before their content emerges fully into consciousness and reveals itself, one can be haunted in everyday life by strong emotions, physical feelings, and visions without knowing where these are coming from or what they mean. Since they are experienced out of context, they naturally appear incomprehensible and completely irrational.

Another kind of complication occurs when a particularly strong karmic experience starts emerging into consciousness in the middle of everyday activities and interferes with normal functioning. One might feel compelled to act out some of the elements of the karmic pattern before it is fully experienced and understood or "completed." For instance, persons in one's present life often seem to have played an important role in "previous incarnations" in the emerging past-life experience; thus one may seek confrontations with one's family or friends based on what one experiences as interactions with them in a "past life." This kind of activity can create serious and long-lasting difficulties and complications in one's relationships with other people, who have no basis for understanding this behavior.

And even after the past-life experience is completed and its content and implications are fully known, there might remain one more challenge. One has to reconcile one's experience with the traditional beliefs and values of Western civilization, which has no explanation for this kind of phenomenon. This might be an easy task for someone who does not have a strong commitment to the conventional worldview. The experiences are so convincing that one simply accepts their message and might even feel pleasantly excited about it. However, those with much investment in rationality and the traditional scientific perspective can be catapulted into a long period of confusion when confronted with disquieting but highly convincing personal experiences that seem to invalidate their belief system.

Because of the wealth of literature on past-life experiences, we have chosen not to include an essay on this subject in the present volume. Roger Woolger's book *Other Lives, Other Selves* can provide much valuable information about these experiences and effective work with them.

Communications with Spirit Guides and Channeling

Occasionally, one can encounter in a transpersonal experience a "being" who seems to show interest in a personal relationship and assumes the position of a teacher, guide, protector, or simply a convenient source of information. Such beings are usually perceived as discarnate humans, suprahuman entities, or deities existing on higher planes of consciousness and endowed with extraordinary wisdom.

Sometimes they take on the form of a person; at other times they appear as radiant sources of light or simply let their presence be sensed. Their messages are usually received in the form of direct thought transfer or through other extrasensory means. Occasionally, communication can take the form of verbal messages.

A particularly interesting phenomenon in this category is "channeling," which has in recent years received unusual attention from the public and mass media. In channeling, a person transmits messages from a source purportedly external to his or her consciousness through speaking in a trance, using automatic writing, or recording telepathically received thoughts. Channeling has played an important role in the history of humanity. Among the channeled spiritual teachings are many scriptures of enormous cultural influence, such as the ancient Indian Vedas, the Koran, and the Book of Mormon.

The main reason experiences of this kind can trigger a serious crisis is the reliable nature and quality of information that can be received from a really good source, whatever that source may actually be. On occasion, channeling can bring consistently accurate data about subjects to which the recipient was never exposed. This phenomenon is then experienced as undeniable proof of the existence of spiritual realities and can lead to serious philosophical confusion for someone who had at the outset a conventional scientific worldview.

Another source of problems can be the fact that spirit guides are usually perceived as beings on a high level of consciousness development, with superior intelligence and extraordinary moral integrity. This can easily lead to ego inflation in the channeler, who might see the fact of having been chosen for a special mission as a proof of his or her own superiority. Jon Klimo's book *Channeling* is an excellent source of information on this subject.

Near-Death Experiences

World mythology, folklore, and spiritual literature abound with vivid accounts of the experiences associated with death and dying. Special sacred texts have been dedicated solely to descriptions and discussions of the posthumous journey, such as the Tibetan *Book of the Dead*, the Egyptian *Book of the Dead*, and their European counterpart, *Ars Moriendi*, or the *Art of Dying*.

In the past, this "funeral mythology" was discounted by Western science as a product of the fantasy and imagination of uneducated people. This situation changed dramatically after the publication of Raymond Moody's best-seller *Life After Life*, which brought scientific confirmation of the fact that dying can be a fantastic transpersonal adventure. Moody's report was based on reports of 150 people who had experienced a close confrontation with death—and in many cases were pronounced medically dead—but regained consciousness to tell their stories.

Moody reports that people having near-death experiences frequently witness a review of their entire lives in the form of a colorful, incredibly condensed replay occurring within seconds of clock time. Consciousness can detach from the body and float freely above the scene, observing it with curiosity and detached amusement, or travel to distant locations.

Many people describe passing through a dark tunnel or funnel that brings them to a light of supernatural brilliance and beauty, a divine being that radiates infinite, all-embracing love, forgiveness, and acceptance. In a personal exchange, perceived as an audience with God, they receive a lesson about existence and its universal laws and have an opportunity to evaluate their past by these new standards. Then they choose to return to ordinary reality and live their lives in a new way congruent with the principles they have learned.

In only one of the cases reported by Moody was the attending physician at all familiar with the characteristics of near-death experiences. This is astonishing considering that medicine is a profession that deals with death and dying on a daily basis. Since the publication of *Life After Life*, many additional studies confirming Moody's findings have been published in popular books and have received widespread media attention.

Near-death experiences frequently lead to spiritual emergencies, because they fundamentally challenge the beliefs about reality held by many people who undergo them. These totally unexpected events take people by surprise: a car accident in the middle of rush-hour traffic or a heart attack during jogging can catapult someone into a fantastic visionary adventure that tears ordinary reality asunder. The specific complications emerging from these experiences are addressed in Bruce Greyson and Barbara Harris's contribution to this book, entitled "Counseling the Near-Death Experiencer."

As noted above, many emerge from these experiences with a

more spiritual outlook, values, and goals based on the revelations they have reached in the near-death state, a kind of life transformation common to all successfully completed spiritual emergencies. Because of the recent dissemination of new information by Moody and others, people who have serious brushes with death in the future will likely be more prepared for this awe-inspiring experience.

Experiences of Close Encounters with UFOs

The experiences of encounters with and abduction by what appear to be extraterrestrial spacecrafts or beings can often precipitate serious emotional and intellectual crises that have much in common with spiritual emergencies. Jung, who dedicated a special study to the problem of "flying saucers," suggested that these phenomena might be archetypal visions originating in the collective unconscious of humanity, rather than extraterrestrial visits from distant civilizations. He illustrated his thesis by careful analysis of legends about flying discs that have existed throughout history and reports about actual apparitions that have occasionally caused crises and mass panic.

Descriptions of UFO sightings typically refer to lights that have an uncanny, supernatural quality. These lights resemble those mentioned in many reports of visionary states. It has been pointed out that the beings encountered have important parallels in world mythology and religion, which have their roots in the collective unconscious.

Reports of abductions often include procedures such as physical examinations and scientific experiments, which are experienced as unimaginable tortures. This brings them close to shamanic crises and to ordeals of initiates in rites of passage conducted by aboriginal cultures. This aspect of the UFO phenomenon is discussed in Keith Thompson's essay "The UFO Encounter Experience as a Crisis of Transformation" in Part Two.

The alien spacecrafts and cosmic flights described by those who were allegedly invited for a ride have their parallels in spiritual literature, such as the chariot of the Vedic god Indra or the flaming machine in Ezekiel's biblical version. The fabulous landscapes and cities visited during these journeys resemble the visionary experiences of paradise, celestial realms, and cities of light.

There is an additional reason that the UFO experience might precipitate a spiritual crisis; we have discussed a similar problem in relation to spirit guides and channeling. The alien visitors are usually seen as representatives of civilizations that are incomparably more advanced than ours, not only technologically but intellectually, morally, and spiritually. Such contact often has very powerful mystical undertones and is associated with insights of cosmic relevance.

It is easy for the recipients of such special attention to interpret this as an indication of their own uniqueness. They might feel that they have attracted the interest of superior beings from an advanced civilization because they themselves are in some way exceptional and particularly suited for a special purpose. In Jungian terminology, such a situation, in which the individual claims the luster of the archetypal world for his or her own person, is referred to as "ego inflation."

As we have seen, there are good reasons that experiences of "close encounters" can lead to transpersonal crises. People who have been exposed to the strange world of UFOs might need help from someone who has knowledge of archetypal psychology, as well as of the specific characteristics of this phenomenon, in order to be able to assimilate the experience.

Possession States

People in this type of transpersonal crisis have a distinct feeling that their psyche and body have been invaded and are being controlled by an entity or energy with personal characteristics, which they perceive as coming from outside their own personality and as hostile and disturbing. It can appear to be a confused discarnate entity, a demonic being, or an evil person invading them by means of black magic and hexing procedures.

There are many different types and degrees of such conditions. In some instances, the true nature of the disorder remains hidden. The problem manifests itself as serious psychopathology, such as antisocial or even criminal behavior, suicidal depression, murderous aggression or self-destructive behavior, promiscuous and deviant sexual impulses, or excessive use of alcohol and drugs. It is not until such a person starts experiential psychotherapy that "possession" is identified as a condition underlying these problems.

In the middle of an experiential session, the face of a possessed person can become cramped and take the form of a "mask of evil," and the eyes can assume a wild expression. The hands and body might develop strange contortions, and the voice may become altered and take on an otherworldly quality. When this situation is allowed to develop, the session can bear a striking resemblance to exorcisms in the Catholic church, or exorcist rituals in various aboriginal cultures. The resolution often comes after dramatic episodes of choking, projectile vomiting, and frantic physical activity, or even temporary loss of control. Sequences of this kind can be unusually healing and transformative and often result in a deep spiritual conversion of the person involved.

In other instances, the possessed person is aware of the presence of the entity and might spend much effort trying to fight it and control its actions. In the extreme version, this problem can quite spontaneously occur in the middle of everyday life in the form described earlier for experiential sessions. Under such circumstances, one can feel extremely frightened and desperately alone; relatives, friends, and often therapists tend to withdraw, because they respond with a strange mixture of metaphysical fear and moral rejection of the possessed individual. They often label the person as evil and refuse further contact.

This condition clearly belongs in the category of spiritual emergency, in spite of the fact that it is associated with many objectionable forms of behavior and involves negative energies. The demonic archetype is by its very nature transpersonal since it represents the negative mirror image of the divine. It also often appears to be a "gateway phenomenon," comparable to the terrifying guardians of the Oriental temples, since it hides access to a profound spiritual experience, which often follows after a possession state has been successfully resolved. With the help of somebody who is not afraid of its uncanny nature and is able to encourage its full conscious manifestation, its energy can become dissipated, and remarkable healing occurs.

The works of Wilson van Dusen provide good further information on possession states perceived as an invasion of evil spirits.

As we have seen, spiritual emergency takes many forms. Our attempts at understanding and classifying transformational crises represent the cutting edge of an endeavor that is still in its infancy; our efforts are therefore preliminary and tentative. We hope, nonetheless, that our undertakings will be of help to those in spiritual crisis and will inspire further research in these directions.

As is the case with incidents of those phenomena we call possession, channeling, UFO encounters, and past-life memories, many of these experiences challenge the Western scientific worldview so fundamentally that we can only speculate about their actual sources. We

have observed in countless cases that these conditions do not necessarily precipitate a plunge into insanity. When we treat such crises
with respect and support, they can result in remarkable healing, a
more positive and spiritual outlook, and a higher level of functioning
in everyday life. For this reason, we must take spiritual emergencies
seriously no matter how bizarre their manifestations may seem when
viewed from the perspective of our traditional belief systems.

Roberto Assagioli

SELF-REALIZATION AND PSYCHOLOGICAL DISTURBANCES

So the lively force of his mind
Has broken down all barriers,
And he has passed far beyond,
The fiery walls of the world,
And in mind and spirit
Has traversed the boundless universe.

LUCRETIUS, *De rerum natura*

*I*n more popular versions of the history of psychiatry and psychology, Carl Gustav Jung seems to tower as a lonely giant and early pioneer. It might appear that he single-handedly challenged the dominance of the medical model in these disciplines and emphasized the importance of spirituality. However, at the same time that Jung questioned the limited and biologically based thinking of Freudian analysis, another psychiatrist working quietly in Italy was arriving at conclusions that had much in common with the Jungian approach— Roberto Assagioli, M.D. Assagioli's work had not been widely publicized until the 1960s, a time of great renaissance of interest in consciousness and spirituality. It is of particular interest that Assagioli paid special attention to the relation between spirituality and mental disorders.

Assagioli was a psychiatrist and psychotherapist who developed an original transpersonal system of therapy called "psychosynthesis." Trained as a Freudian, he was one of the pioneers of psychoanalysis in Italy. However, as early as 1911 he voiced serious objections to Freud's teachings and discussed their limitations and shortcomings. Here he portrayed psychoanalysis as an approach to human problems that was not incorrect, but rather partial and incomplete. He was particularly critical of Freud's neglect and misrepresentation of the spiritual dimension in human life.

In the following years, Assagioli formulated the principles of psychosynthesis, his own theory and practice of therapy and self-exploration. Its basic assumption was that an individual is in a constant process of personal growth, realizing his or her hidden potential. In contrast to Freud, who focused on the base instincts in human nature, Assagioli emphasized the positive, creative, and joyful elements and the importance of will.

Assagioli's map of the human personality bears some similarity to the psychological system of Jung, since it explicitly acknowledges and honors spirituality and includes the concept of the collective unconscious. It has several main constituents that are in mutual interplay.

The lower unconscious directs the basic psychological activities, such as primitive instinctual urges and emotional complexes. The middle unconscious is a realm where experiences are assimilated before reaching consciousness; it corresponds roughly to Freud's preconscious. The superconscious domain is the seat of higher feelings and capacities, such as intuition and inspiration. The field of consciousness contains feelings, thoughts, and impulses that are available for analysis. Assagioli distinguished the conscious self, defined as the point of pure awareness, from the higher self, which exists apart from the consciousness of mind and body. All these components are then contained in the collective unconscious that we all share.

An important element in Assagioli's psychosynthesis is the concept of subpersonalities. According to him, the human personality is not a unified and fully integrated whole, but consists of many dynamic substructures that have a relatively separate existence and alternate in their governing influence on the psyche, depending on circumstances. The most common and obvious subpersonalities reflect the roles that we have played in the past or are currently playing in our lives, such as that of child, friend, lover, parent, teacher, doctor, or officer. Others can be fantasized heroes, mythological figures, or even animals. An important task of psychosynthesis is to identify and integrate subpersonalities into a well-functioning dynamic whole.

The therapeutic process of psychosynthesis involves four consecutive stages. At first, the client learns about various elements of his or her personality that were previously hidden and accepts them on a conscious level. The next step is freeing oneself from their psychological influence and developing the ability to control them; this is what Assagioli calls "disidentification." After the client has gradually discovered his or her unifying psychological center, it is possible to achieve psychosynthesis, characterized by a culmination of the self-realization process and integration of various selves around the new center.

Assagioli was born in Venice in 1888 and lived and worked in Florence. His remarkable vitality, joy in life, optimism, and humor accompanied him until his last days. Despite his formidable age and a progressive hearing loss, he continued to be active as a psychiatrist and in a variety of other professional activities until his death in 1974. He was chairman of the Psychosynthesis Research Foundation in New York and president of the Istituto di Psicosintesi in Italy. His publications consist of more than three hundred papers and several books, including Psychosynthesis *and* The Act of Will.

His contribution to this anthology is truly a classic in the field. It is a clear and concise statement about the importance of spiritual development and a discussion of the problems and complications associated with this process. There are very few other passages in the psychiatric literature that emphasize so clearly the need to distinguish between common psychopathology and the crises preceding, accompanying, and following spiritual opening.

Spiritual development is a long and arduous journey, an adventure through strange lands full of surprises, joy and beauty, difficulties, and even dangers. It involves the awakening of potentialities hitherto dormant, the raising of consciousness to new realms, a drastic transmutation of the "normal" elements of the personality, and a functioning along a new inner dimension.

I am using the term "spiritual" in its broad connotation, and always in reference to empirically observed human experience. In this sense, "spiritual" refers not only to experiences traditionally considered religious but to *all* the states of awareness, all the human functions and activities which have as their common denominator the possession of *values* higher than average—values such as the ethical, the aesthetic, the heroic, the humanitarian, and the altruistic.

In psychosynthesis we understand such experiences of higher values as deriving from the superconscious levels of the human being. The superconscious can be thought of as the higher counterpart of the lower unconscious so well mapped by Freud and his successors. Acting as the higher unifying center for the superconscious and for the life of the individual as a whole is the Transpersonal or Higher Self. Thus spiritual experiences can be limited to superconscious realms or can include the awareness of the Self. This awareness gradually develops into Self-realization—the identification of the "I" with the Transpersonal Self. In the following discussion I shall consider the various stages of spiritual development including the achievement of Self-realization.

We should not be surprised to find that so fundamental a transformation is marked by several critical stages, which may be accompanied by various mental, emotional, and even physical disturbances. To the objective, clinical observation of the therapist, these may appear to be the same as those due to more usual causes. But in reality they have quite another meaning and function, and need to be dealt with in a very different way.

The incidence of disturbances having a spiritual origin is rapidly increasing nowadays, in step with the growing number of people who, consciously or unconsciously, are groping their way towards a fuller life. Furthermore, the greater development and complexity of the personality of modern man and his increasingly critical mind have rendered spiritual development a richer, more rewarding, but also a more difficult and complicated process. In the past a moral conversion, a simple whole-hearted devotion to a teacher or savior, a loving surrender to God, were often sufficient to open the gates leading to a higher level of consciousness and a sense of inner union and fulfillment. Now, however, the more varied and complex aspects of modern man's personality are involved and need to be transmuted and harmonized with each other: his fundamental drives, his emotions and feelings, his creative imagination, his inquiring mind, his assertive will, and also his interpersonal and social relations.

For these reasons it is useful to have a general outline of the disturbances which can arise at the various stages of spiritual development and some indications about how best to deal with them. We can recognize in this process four critical stages, or phases:

- Crises preceding the spiritual awakening
- Crises caused by the spiritual awakening
- Reactions following the spiritual awakening
- Phases of the process of transmutation

I have used the symbolic expression "awakening" because it clearly suggests the becoming aware of a new area of experience, the opening of the hitherto closed eyes to an inner reality previously unknown.

CRISES PRECEDING THE SPIRITUAL AWAKENING

In order to best understand the experiences that often precede the awakening, we must review some of the psychological characteristics of the "normal" human being.

One may say of him that he "lets himself live" rather than that he lives. He takes life as it comes and does not question its meaning, its worth, or its purpose; he devotes himself to the satisfaction of his personal desires; he seeks enjoyment of the senses, emotional pleasures, material security, or achievement of personal ambition. If he is more mature, he subordinates his personal satisfactions to the fulfillment of the various family and social duties assigned to him, but without seeking to understand on what bases those duties rest or from what source they spring. Possibly he regards himself as "religious" and as a believer in God, but usually his religion is outward and conventional, and when he has conformed to the injunctions of his church and shared in its rites he feels that he has done all that is required of him. In short, *his operational belief is that the only reality is that of the physical world which he can see and touch* and therefore he is strongly attached to earthly goods. Thus, for all practical purposes, he considers this life an end in itself. His belief in a future "heaven," if he conceives of one, is altogether theoretical and academic—as is proved by the fact that he takes the greatest pains to postpone as long as possible his departure for its joys.

But it may happen that this "normal man" becomes both surprised and disturbed by a change—sudden or slow—in his inner life. This may take place after a series of disappointments; not infrequently after some emotional shock, such as the loss of a loved relative or a very dear friend. But sometimes it occurs without any apparent cause, and in the full enjoyment of health and prosperity. The change begins often with a growing sense of dissatisfaction, of lack, of "something missing." But this "something missing" is nothing material and definite; it is something vague and elusive, that he is unable to describe.

To this is added, by degrees, a sense of the unreality and emptiness of ordinary life. Personal affairs, which formerly absorbed so much of his attention and interest, seem to retreat, psychologically, into the background; they lose their importance and value. New problems arise. The individual begins to inquire into the origin and the purpose of life; to ask what is the reason for so many things he formerly took for granted; to question, for instance, the meaning of his own sufferings and those of others, and what justification there may be for so many inequalities in the destinies of men.

When a man has reached this point, he is apt to misunderstand and misinterpret his condition. Many who do not comprehend the significance of these new states of mind look upon them as abnormal fancies and vagaries. Alarmed at the possibility of mental unbalance, they strive to combat them in various ways, making frantic efforts to reattach themselves to the "reality" of ordinary life that seems to be slipping from them. Often they throw themselves with increased ardor into a whirl of external activities, seeking ever new occupations, new stimuli, and new sensations. By these and other means they may succeed for a time in alleviating their disturbed condition, but they are unable to get rid of it permanently. It continues to ferment in the depths of their being, undermining the foundations of their ordinary existence, whence it is liable to break forth again, perhaps after a long time, with renewed intensity. The state of uneasiness and agitation becomes more and more painful, and the sense of inward emptiness more intolerable. The individual feels distracted; most of what constituted his life now seems to him to have vanished like a dream, while no new light has yet appeared. Indeed, he is as yet ignorant of the existence of such a light, or else he cannot believe that it will ever illuminate him.

It frequently happens that this state of inner turmoil is accompanied by a moral crisis. His value-consciousness awakens or becomes more sensitive; a new sense of responsibility appears, and the individual can be oppressed by a heavy sense of guilt. He judges himself with severity and becomes a prey to profound discouragement, even to the point of contemplating suicide. To the man himself it seems as if physical annihilation were the only logical conclusion to his increasing sense of impotence and hopelessness, of breakdown and disintegration.[1]

The foregoing is, of course, a generalized description of such experiences. In practice, individuals differ widely in their inner experiences and reactions. There are many who never reach this acute stage, while others arrive at it almost in one bound. Some are more harassed by intellectual doubts and metaphysical problems; in others the emotional depression or the moral crisis is the most pronounced feature.

It is important to recognize that these various manifestations of the crisis bear a close resemblance to some of the symptoms regarded as characteristic of neurotic and borderline psychotic states. In some cases the stress and strain of the crisis also produce physical symptoms, such as nervous tension, insomnia, and other psychosomatic disturbances.

To deal correctly with the situation, it is therefore essential to determine the basic source of the difficulties. This is generally not hard to do. The symptoms observed isolatedly may be identical; but a careful examination of their causes, a consideration of the individual's

All notes and references are located at the back of the book.

personality in its entirety, and—most important of all—the recognition of his actual, existential situation reveal the different nature and level of the underlying conflicts. In ordinary cases, these conflicts occur among the "normal" drives, between these drives and the conscious "I," or between the individual and the outer world (particularly people closely related to him, such as parents, mate, or children). In the cases which we are considering here, however, the conflicts are between some aspect of the personality and the progressive, emerging tendencies and aspirations of a moral, religious, humanitarian, or spiritual character. And it is not difficult to ascertain the presence of these tendencies once their reality and validity are recognized rather than being explained away as mere fantasies or sublimations. In a general way, the *emergence* of spiritual tendencies can be considered as the result of turning points in the development, in the *growth* of the individual.

There is this possible complication: sometimes these new emerging tendencies revive or exacerbate old or latent conflicts between personality elements. Such conflicts, which by themselves would be regressive, are in fact progressive when they occur within this larger perspective. They are progressive because they facilitate the achievement of a new personal integration, a more inclusive one, at a higher level—one for which the crisis itself paved the way. So these crises are positive, natural, and often necessary preparations for the progress of the individual. They bring to the surface elements of the personality that need to be looked at and changed in the interest of the person's further growth.

CRISES CAUSED BY THE SPIRITUAL AWAKENING

The opening of the channel between the conscious and the superconscious levels, between the "I" and the Self, and the flood of light, energy, and joy which follows, often produce a wonderful release. The preceding conflicts and sufferings, with the psychological and physical symptoms which they generated, vanish sometimes with amazing suddenness, thus confirming the fact that they were not due to any physical cause but were the direct outcome of the inner strife. In such cases the spiritual awakening amounts to a real resolution.

But in other cases, not infrequent, the personality is unable to rightly assimilate the inflow of light and energy. This happens, for instance, when the intellect is not well coordinated and developed; when the emotions and the imagination are uncontrolled; when the nervous system is too sensitive; or when the inrush of spiritual energy is overwhelming in its suddenness and intensity.[2]

An inability of the mind to stand the illumination, or a tendency to self-centeredness or conceit, may cause the experience to be wrongly interpreted, and there results, so to speak, a "confusion of levels." The distinction between absolute and relative truths, between the Self and the "I" is blurred, and the inflowing spiritual energies may have the unfortunate effect of feeding and inflating the personal ego.

The author encountered a striking instance of such a harmful effect in the Psychiatric Hospital at Ancona, Italy. One of the inmates, a simple little man, formerly a photographer, quietly and persistently declared that he was God. Around this central idea he had constructed an assortment of fantastic delusions about heavenly hosts at his command; at the same time he was as peaceful, kind, and obliging a person as one could imagine, always ready to be of service to the doctors and patients. He was so reliable and competent that he had been entrusted with the preparation of medicines and even the keys to the pharmacy. His only lapse in behavior in this capacity was an occasional appropriation of sugar in order to give pleasure to some of the other inmates.

Therapists with materialistic views would be likely to regard this patient as simply affected by paranoid delusions; but this mere diagnostic label offers little or no help in understanding the true nature and causes of such disturbances. It seems worthwhile, therefore, to explore the possibility of a more profound interpretation of this man's illusory conviction.

The inner experience of the spiritual Self, and its intimate association with the personal self, gives a sense of internal expansion, of universality, and the conviction of participating in some way in the divine nature. In the religious traditions and spiritual doctrines of every epoch one finds numerous attestations on this subject—some of them expressed in daring terms. In the Bible there is the explicit sentence, "I have said, Ye are gods; and all of you are children of the most High." St. Augustine declares: "When the soul loves something it becomes like unto it; if it should love terrestrial things it becomes terrestrial, but if it should love God does it not become God?" The most extreme expression of the identity of the human spirit in its pure and real essence with the Supreme Spirit is contained in the central teaching of the Vedanta philosophy: *Tat Tvam Asi* (Thou Art That) and *Aham evam param Brahman* (In truth I am the Supreme Brahman).

In whatever way one may conceive the relationship between the individual self, or "I," and the Universal Self, be they regarded as similar or dissimilar, distinct or united, it is most important to recognize clearly, and to retain ever present in theory and in practice, the difference that exists between the Self in its essential nature—that which has been called the "Fount," the "Center," the "deeper Being," the "Apex" of ourselves—and the little self, or "I," usually identified with the ordinary personality, of which we are normally conscious.[3] The disregard of this vital distinction leads to absurd and dangerous consequences.

The distinction gives the key to an understanding of the mental state of the patient referred to, and of other extreme forms of self-exaltation and self-glorification. The fatal error of all who fall victim to these illusions is to attribute to their *personal* self, or "I," the qualities and powers of the Transpersonal or Higher Self. In philosophical terms, it is a case of confusion between a relative and an absolute truth, between the empirical and the transcendent levels of reality. Instances of such confusion are not uncommon among people who become dazzled by contact with truths too great or energies too powerful for their mental capacities to grasp and their personality to assimilate. The reader will doubtless be able to record instances of similar self-deception which are found in a number of fanatical followers of various cults.

Clearly, in such a situation, it is a waste of time at best to argue with the person or ridicule his aberration; it will merely arouse his opposition and resentment. The better way is to sympathize, and, while admitting the ultimate truth of his belief, point out the nature of his error and help him learn how to make the necessary distinction of levels.

There are also cases in which the sudden influx of energies produces an emotional upheaval which expresses itself in uncontrolled, unbalanced, and disordered behavior. Shouting and crying, singing and outbursts of various kinds characterize this form of response. If the individual is active and impulsive he may be easily impelled by the excitement of the inner awakening to play the role of prophet or savior; he may found a new sect and start a campaign of spectacular proselytism.

In some sensitive individuals there is an awakening of para-psychological perceptions. They have visions, which they believe to be of exalted beings; they may hear voices, or begin to write automatically, accepting the messages at their face value and obeying them unreservedly. The quality of such messages is extremely varied. Some of them contain fine teachings, others are quite poor or meaningless. One should always examine them with much discrimination and sound judgment, and without being influenced by their uncommon origin or by any claim of their alleged transmitter. No validity should be attributed to messages containing definite orders and commanding blind obedience, and to those tending to exalt the personality of the recipient.

REACTIONS TO THE SPIRITUAL AWAKENING

As has been said, a harmonious inner awakening is characterized by a sense of joy and mental illumination that brings with it an insight into the meaning and purpose of life; it dispels many doubts, offers the solution of many problems, and gives an inner source of security. At the same time there wells up a realization that life is one, and an outpouring of love flows through the awakening individual towards his fellow beings and the whole of creation. The former personality, with its sharp edges and disagreeable traits, seems to have receded into the background and a new loving and lovable individual smiles at us and the whole world, eager to be kind, to serve, and to share his newly acquired spiritual riches, the abundance of which seems to him almost too much to contain.

Such a state of exalted joy may last for varying periods, but it is bound to cease. The inflow of light and love is rhythmical, as is everything in the universe. After a while it diminishes or ceases, and the flood is followed by the ebb. The personality was infused and transformed, but this transformation is seldom either permanent or complete. More often a large portion of the personality elements involved revert to their earlier state.

This process becomes clearer if we look at the nature of a peak experience in terms of energies and levels of organization.[4] Because of their synthesizing nature, the superconscious energies act on the personality elements in ways that tend to bring them to their next higher level of organization. When this higher level is reached, synergic energy is released and this energy in turn produces the ecstasy, elation, and joy characteristic of such experiences. Depending on the amount of superconscious energy radiated by the Self, on the responsiveness of the personality at the time, and on many other factors, this higher level of organization may or may not be stable. In the majority of cases, it is maintained only as long as the Self keeps radiating its energy. But once this energy is withdrawn—as it eventually is because of the cyclic nature of the activity of the Self—there is a more or less pronounced trend in the personality to revert toward its previous level of organization. For purposes of clarity, we can consider three different possible outcomes which typify the results of this process:

1. The energy of the Self is strong enough to achieve this higher personality integration and, also, to transform or break down the patterns and tendencies inherent in the personality that would tend to have it revert to the previous state. The new integration is then permanent. This outcome is relatively rare and is exemplified by those instances in which an individual's life is suddenly and permanently uplifted and transformed as a direct and immediate result of a spiritual awakening.

2. The energy transmitted by the Self is less intense and/or the personality is less responsive, so that although a higher level of organization is reached, only some of the regressive tendencies and patterns in the personality are fully transformed, while most of them are only *neutralized* temporarily by the presence of the higher energies. As a consequence, the higher integration achieved by the personality is sustained only as long as the energy of the Self is being actively transmitted. Once this energy is withdrawn, the personality reverts toward its previous state. But what remains—and this is often the most useful part of the experience—is an ideal model and a sense of direction which one can use to complete the transformation through his own purposeful methods.

3. The energy transmitted by the Self is not sufficient to bring about the higher level of organization. The energy is then absorbed by the hidden blocks and patterns that prevent the higher integration. It has the effect of energizing them and thus bringing them to light, where they can be recognized

and dealt with. In such cases, the experience is usually of a painful quality and its transpersonal origin often goes unrecognized. But in reality it is just as valuable, because it can show the individual the next steps he needs to make to achieve the same goals and states of being as in the other cases.

Of course, it is important to remember that a person's experience does not usually fall neatly into one of these three clear-cut categories. Most spiritual experiences contain a combination in various proportions of permanent changes, temporary changes, the recognition of obstacles that need to be overcome, and the lived realization of what it is like to exist at this higher level of integration. It is this awareness that then becomes an ideal model, a luminous beacon toward which one can navigate and which one can eventually achieve by his own means.[5]

But experiencing the withdrawal of the transpersonal energies and the loss of one's exalted state of being is necessarily painful, and is apt in some cases to produce strong reactions and serious troubles. The personality reawakens and asserts itself with renewed force. All the rocks and rubbish, which had been covered and concealed at high tide, emerge again. Sometimes it happens that lower propensities and drives, hitherto lying dormant in the unconscious, are vitalized by the inflow of higher energies, or bitterly rebel against the new aspirations and purposes that are constituting a challenge and a threat to their uncontrolled expression. The person, whose moral conscience has now become more refined and exacting, whose thirst for perfection has become more intense, judges with greater severity and condemns his personality with a new vehemence; he is apt to harbor the mistaken belief of having fallen lower than he was before.

At times the reaction of the personality becomes intensified to the extent of causing the individual to actually deny the value and even the reality of his recent experience. Doubts and criticism enter his mind, and he is tempted to regard the whole thing as an illusion, a fantasy, or an emotional intoxication. He becomes bitter and sarcastic, ridicules himself and others, and even turns his back on his higher ideals and aspirations. Yet, try as he may, he *cannot* return to his old state; he has seen the vision, and its beauty and power to attract remain with him in spite of his efforts to suppress it. He cannot accept everyday life as before, or be satisfied with it. A "divine homesickness" haunts him and leaves him no peace. In extreme cases, the reaction can be so intense as to become pathological, producing a state of depression and even despair, with suicidal impulses. This state bears a close resemblance to psychotic depression—once called "melancholia"—characterized by an acute sense of unworthiness, a systematic self-depreciation and self-accusation, which may become so vivid as to produce the delusion that one is in hell, irretrievably damned. There is also an acute and painful sense of intellectual incompetence; a paralysis of the will power accompanied by indecision and inability to act. But in the case of those who have had an inner awakening or a measure of spiritual realization, the disturbances should not be considered as a mere pathological condition; they have different, far deeper causes, as has been indicated by both Plato and St. John of the Cross with similar analogies.

Plato, in the famous allegory contained in the Seventh Book of his *Republic*, compares unenlightened men to prisoners in a dark cave or den, and says:

> At first, when any of them is liberated and compelled suddenly to stand up and turn his neck around and walk toward the light, he will suffer sharp pains; the glare will distress him, and he will be unable to see the realities of which, in his former state, he had seen the shadows.

St. John of the Cross uses words curiously similar in speaking of the experience which he called "the dark night of the soul":

> The self is in the dark because it is blinded by a light greater than it can bear. . . . As eyes weakened and clouded suffer pain when the clear light beats upon them, so the soul, by reason of its impurity, suffers exceedingly when the Divine Light really shines upon it. And when the rays of this pure Light shine upon the soul in order to expel impurities, the soul perceives itself to be so unclean and miserable that it seems as if God had set Himself against it and itself were set against God.

St. John's words about the "light" which "shines upon the soul in order to expel impurities" deal with the essential nature of the process. Even though from the limited point of view of the personality it may seem a setback, or an undesirable phase—"as if God had set Himself against it and itself were set against God"—from the much broader perspective of the Transpersonal Self this phase, often rightly called "purgation," is in fact one of the most useful and rewarding stages of growth. The light of the Self shines on the "impurities" and brings them to the consciousness of the individual to facilitate his process of working them out. Although this process can be, at times, a laborious one, it is a basic aspect of a reliable and permanent channel of contact between the individual and his transpersonal or superconscious nature.

The proper way to deal with someone beset by this type of crisis consists in conveying to the person a true understanding of the crisis' nature. It is as though he had made a superb flight to the sunlit mountain top, realized its glory and the beauty of the panorama spread below, but had been brought back, reluctantly, with the rueful recognition that the steep path to the heights must be climbed step by step. The recognition that this descent—or "fall"—is a natural happening affords emotional and mental relief, and encourages the individual to undertake the arduous task of confronting the path to Self-realization. Ultimately, the crisis is overcome with the realization that the true and deepest value of the experience is that it offers, as I have said, a "tangible vision" of a better state of being, and thus a roadmap, an ideal model toward which one can proceed and which can then become a permanent reality.

THE PROCESS OF TRANSMUTATION

This stage follows the recognition that the necessary conditions to be fulfilled for the high achievement of Self-realization are a thorough regeneration and transmutation of the personality. It is a long and many-sided process which includes several phases: the active removal of the obstacles to the inflow and operation of superconscious energies; the development of the higher functions which have lain dormant or undeveloped; and periods in which one can let the Higher Self work, being receptive to its guidance.

It is a most eventful and rewarding period, full of changes, or alternations between light and darkness, between joy and suffering. It is a period of transition, a passing out of the old condition without having yet firmly reached the new; an intermediate stage in which, as it has been aptly said, one is like a caterpillar undergoing the process of transformation into the winged butterfly. But the individual generally does not have the protection of a cocoon in which to undergo the process of transformation in seclusion and peace. He must—and this is particularly so nowadays—remain where he is in life and continue to perform his family, professional, and social tasks as well as he can.

His problem is similar to that which confronts engineers in reconstructing a railway station without interrupting the traffic.

Despite the challenges of the task, as he does his work he is conscious of gradual, increasing progress. His life becomes infused with a sense of meaning and purpose, ordinary tasks are vitalized and elevated by his growing awareness of their place in a larger scheme of things. As time goes on, he achieves fuller and clearer recognitions of the nature of reality, of man, and of his own higher nature. He begins to develop a more coherent conceptual framework which allows him to better understand what he observes and experiences, and which serves him not only as a means of guidance to further knowledge but also as a source of serenity and order in the midst of life's changing circumstances. As a result, he experiences a growing mastery of tasks which formerly seemed beyond him. Operating, as he increasingly does, from a higher unifying center of personality, he harmonizes his diverse personality elements into a progressive unity, and this more complete integration brings him greater effectiveness and more joy.

Such are the results, over a long period of time, which one generally observes to arise from the process of transmutation of the personality under the impulse of superconscious energies. But the process does not always proceed with absolute smoothness. This is not surprising, given the complex task of remaking the personality in the midst of the circumstances of daily life. As a general rule, some difficulties are almost always experienced, and one can observe temporary stages which manifest conditions the reverse of what I have just described. This often occurs immediately after the flood-tide of exaltation has passed, and the individual settles down to his dual task of self-transformation while meeting life's many demands. Learning the skill of using one's energies in this fashion generally takes some time, and it may be a while before the two tasks are implemented in a balanced manner, and ultimately recognized as one. As a consequence, it is not surprising to find stages in which the individual may become so engrossed in his task of self-transformation that his ability to cope successfully with the problems and activities of normal life may be impaired. Observed from the outside and gauged in terms of ordinary, task-oriented efficiency, he may seem temporarily to have become less capable than before. During this transitory stage, he may not be spared unfair judgment on the part of well-meaning but unenlightened friends or therapists, and he may become the target of pungent and sarcastic remarks about his "fine" spiritual ideals and aspirations making him weak and ineffective in practical life. This sort of criticism is experienced as very painful, and its influence may arouse doubts and discouragement.

Such a trial, when it occurs, constitutes one of the tests that may have to be faced on the path of Self-realization. Its value lies in the fact that it teaches a lesson in overcoming personal sensitivity, and is an occasion for the development of inner independence and self-reliance, without resentment. It should be accepted cheerfully, or at least serenely, and used as an opportunity for developing inner strength. If, on the other hand, the people in such an individual's environment are enlightened and understanding, they can help a great deal and spare him much unnecessary friction and suffering.

This stage passes, with time, as the individual learns to master his dual task and unify it. But when the complexities of the task are not recognized and accepted, the natural stresses of growth that are involved in the process can be exacerbated, last for long periods, or recur with an unnecessary frequency. This is especially so when the individual becomes too engrossed in the process of self-transformation, excluding the outer world with a single-minded and excessive introversion. Periods of healthy introversion are natural in human growth. But if they are carried to extremes or prolonged into a general attitude of removal from the life of the world, the individual may experience many difficulties not only with impatient and critical friends, coworkers, and family members, but also within, as natural introversion becomes self-obsession.

Similar difficulties may arise if the individual does not deal with the negative aspects of himself revealed in the process of spiritual awakening. Rather than transmuting these, he may flee from them into inner fantasies of achieved perfection or imaginary escapes. But the suppressed knowledge of actual imperfections haunts him, and those around him challenge his fantasies. Under such dual stress it is not unlikely for the person to succumb to a variety of psychological troubles, such as insomnia, emotional depression, exhaustion, aridity, mental agitation, and restlessness. These in turn can easily produce all kinds of physical symptoms and disorders.

Many of these troubles can be greatly reduced or altogether eliminated by pursuing one's growth process with energy, dedication, and zeal, but without becoming *identified* with it. This cultivation of a disidentified commitment allows a person the flexibility needed for the optimal pursuit of the task. The individual can then *accept* the necessary stresses of the new and complex process; he can refuse to fall into a self-pity born of frustrated perfectionism; he can learn to view himself with humor and be willing to experiment and risk changes; he can cultivate a cheerful patience; and he can turn with self-acceptance of his present limitations to competent people—whether professional therapists, counselors, or wise friends—for help and guidance.

Another set of difficulties can be caused by an excessive personal effort to hasten higher realizations through the forceful inhibition and repression of the aggressive and sexual drives—an attempt which only serves to produce intensification of the conflicts and their effects. Such an attitude often is the outcome of too rigid and dualistic moral and religious conceptions. These lead to condemnation of the natural drives as "bad" or "sinful." Today a large number of people have *consciously* abandoned such attitudes but still may be *unconsciously* conditioned by them to some extent. They may manifest either ambivalence or oscillation between two extreme attitudes—one of rigid suppression, and the other of uncontrolled expression of all drives. The latter, while cathartic, is not an acceptable solution either from the ethical standpoint or the psychological. It inevitably produces new conflicts—among the various basic drives or between these drives and the boundaries imposed by social conventions, and by the demands of interpersonal relations.

The solution lies, rather, along the lines of a gradual reorientation and harmonious integration of all personality drives, first through their proper recognition, acceptance, and coordination, and then through the transformation and sublimation of the excessive or unused quota of energy.[6] The achievement of this integration can be greatly facilitated by activating the superconscious functions and by deliberately reaching toward the Transpersonal Self. These larger and higher interests *act as a magnet which draws up the "libido" or psychic energy* invested in the "lower" drives.

A final kind of difficulty which deserves mention may confront the individual during periods in which the flow of superconscious energies is easy and abundant. If not wisely controlled, this energy flow may either be scattered in feverish excitement and activity or, on the contrary, it may be kept too much in abeyance, unexpressed, so that it accumulates and its high pressure can cause physical problems. The appropriate solution is to direct the inflowing energies purposefully, constructively, and harmoniously for the work of inner regeneration, creative expression, and fruitful service.

THE ROLE OF THE GUIDE

These are times in which more and more people are experiencing spiritual awakening. Because of this, therapists, counselors, and others in the helping professions, as well as informed lay persons, may be called upon to act as resources and guides to people undergoing a spiritual awakening. It may be useful therefore to consider the role of the individual who may be close to someone else going through the process and some of its problems.

First, it is important to remain aware of the central fact that while the problems which may accompany the various phases of Self-realization can be outwardly very similar to, and sometimes appear identical with, those of normal life, their causes and significance are very different, and the way to deal with them must be correspondingly different. In other words, the existential situation in the two instances not only is not the same, but it is, in a sense, opposite.

The psychological difficulties of the average person have generally a *regressive* character. These individuals have not been able to accomplish some of the necessary inner and outer adjustments that constitute the normal development of the personality. In response to difficult situations, they have reverted to modes of behavior acquired in childhood or they have never really grown beyond certain childhood patterns whether they are recognized as such or are rationalized.

On the other hand, the difficulties produced by the stress and strife in the various stages toward Self-realization have, as I said earlier, a specifically *progressive* character.[7] They are due to the stimulation produced by the superconscious energies, by the "pull from above," by the call of the Self, and are specifically determined by the ensuing conflict between these energies and the "middle" and "lower" aspects of the personality. This crisis has been described in striking terms by Jung:

> To be "normal" is a splendid ideal for the unsuccessful, for all those who have not yet found an adaptation. But for people who have far more ability than the average, for whom it was never hard to gain successes and to accomplish their share of the world's work—for them restriction to the normal signifies the bed of Procrustes, unbearable boredom, infernal sterility and hopelessness. As a consequence there are as many people who become neurotic because they are only nor-

mal, as there are people who are neurotic because they cannot become normal.

It is obvious that the way to help the two diverse kinds of individuals must be altogether different.

What is appropriate for the first group is likely to be not only unsatisfactory, but even harmful for the second. The lot of the latter is doubly hard if they are being guided by someone who neither understands nor appreciates the superconscious functions, who ignores or denies the reality of the Self and the possibility of Self-realization. He or she may either ridicule the person's uncertain higher aspirations as mere fancies, or interpret them in a materialistic way, or persuade the person to harden the shell of the personality against the insistent knocking of the Transpersonal Self. This course can aggravate the condition, intensify the struggle, and retard the solution.

On the other hand, a guide who is spiritually inclined, or has at least an understanding of and a sympathetic attitude towards the higher achievements and realities, can be of great help to the individual when, as is often the case, the latter is still in the first stage, that of dissatisfaction, restlessness, and unconscious groping. If he has lost interest in life, if everyday existence holds no attraction for him, if he is looking for relief in wrong directions, wandering up and down blind alleys, and he has not yet had a glimpse of the higher reality—then the revelation of the real cause of his trouble and the indication of the unhoped-for solution, of the happy outcome of the crisis, can greatly help to bring about the inner awakening which in itself constitutes the principal part of the resolution.

The second stage, that of emotional excitement or elation—when the individual may be carried away by an excessive enthusiasm and cherishes the illusion of having arrived at a permanent attainment, calls for a gentle warning that his blessed state is, of necessity, but temporary; and he should be given an indication of the vicissitude on the way ahead of him. This will prepare him for the onset of the inevitable reaction in the third stage, which often involves, as we have seen, a painful reaction and sometimes a deep depression, as the person "comes down" from his high experience. If he has been forewarned, this will enable him to avoid much suffering, doubt, and discouragement. When he has not had the benefit of a warning of this sort, the guide can give much help by assuring him that his present condition is *temporary* and not in any sense permanent or hopeless as he seems compelled to believe. The guide should insistently declare that the rewarding outcome of the crisis justifies the anguish—however intense—he is experiencing. Much relief and encouragement can be afforded him by quoting examples of those who have been in a similar plight and have come out of it.

In the fourth stage, during the process of transmutation—which is the longest and most complicated—the work of the guide is correspondingly more complex. Some important aspects of this work are:

- To enlighten the individual as to *what is really going on* within him, and help him to find the *right attitude* to take.
- To teach him how, *by the skillful use of the will, to wisely control and master the drives* emerging from the unconscious, without repressing them through fear or condemnation.
- To teach him the techniques of the *transmutation and sublimation* of sexual and aggressive energies. These techniques constitute the most apt and constructive solution of many psychological conflicts.
- To help him in the proper *recognition and assimilation* of the energies inflowing from the Self and from superconscious levels.
- To help him *express and utilize those energies in altruistic love and service.* This is particularly valuable for counteracting the tendency to excessive introversion and self-centeredness that often exists in this and other stages of self-development.
- To guide him through the various phases of the *reconstruction of his personality around a higher inner center,* that is, in the achievement of his spiritual psychosynthesis.[8]

Throughout this article I have stressed the more difficult and painful side of spiritual development, but it should not be inferred that those who are on the path of Self-realization are more likely to be affected by psychological disturbances than other men and women. The stage of most intense suffering often does not occur. In many individuals such development is accomplished in a gradual and harmonious way so that inner difficulties are overcome and the different stages passed through without causing severe reactions of any kind.

On the other hand, the emotional disorders or neurotic symptoms of the average man or woman are often more serious, intense, and difficult for them to bear and for therapists to deal with than those connected with Self-realization. It is often difficult to deal with them satisfactorily because—the higher psychological levels and functions of these individuals being not yet activated—there is little to which one can appeal to show the value of making the necessary sacrifices or accepting the discipline required in order to bring about the needed adjustments.

The physical, emotional, and mental problems arising on the way of Self-realization, however serious they may appear, are merely *temporary* reactions, by-products, so to speak, of an organic process of inner growth and regeneration. Therefore they either disappear spontaneously when the crisis which has produced them is over, or they yield easily to proper treatment. Furthermore, the sufferings caused by periods of depression, by the ebbing of the inner life, are abundantly compensated for by periods of renewed inflow of superconscious energies, and by the anticipation of the release and enhancement of the whole personality to be produced by Self-realization. This vision is a most powerful inspiration, an unfailing comfort, and a constant source of strength and courage. Therefore, as we have said, it is most valuable to make a special point of recalling that vision as vividly and as frequently as possible. One of the greatest services we can render to those struggling along the way is to help them keep the vision of the goal ever present before their eyes.

Thus one can anticipate, and have an increasing foretaste of, the state of consciousness of the Self-realized individual. It is a state of consciousness characterized by joy, serenity, inner security, a sense of calm power, clear understanding, and radiant love. In its highest aspects it is the realization of essential Being, of communion and identification with the Universal Life.

R. D. Laing

TRANSCENDENTAL EXPERIENCE IN RELATION TO RELIGION AND PSYCHOSIS

The illumination grew brighter and brighter, the roaring louder, I experienced a rocking sensation and then felt myself slipping out of my body, entirely enveloped in a halo of light . . . I felt the point of consciousness that was myself growing wider, surrounded by waves of light . . . I was now all consciousness, without any outline, without any idea of corporeal appendage, without any feeling or sensation coming from the senses, immersed in a sea of light . . . I was no longer myself, or to be more accurate, no longer as I knew myself to be, a small point of awareness confined in a body, but instead was a vast circle of consciousness in which the body was but a point, bathed in light and in a state of exaltation and happiness impossible to describe.

MEDITATION EXPERIENCE DESCRIBED BY GOPI KRISHNA,
Kundalini: The Evolutionary Energy in Man

The idea that psychoses are mental diseases that can be adequately understood in medical terms and should be treated by biological means, although widespread and highly influential, is not unanimously accepted. Many clinicians and theoreticians have offered important explanations of the psychotic process that are purely psychological in nature and have developed nonmedical treatment strategies.

Others have suggested that the dominant role played by the medical model in the approach to psychoses cannot be scientifically justified, since no specific biological causes have been found for the majority of the conditions psychiatrists are treating. The current situation thus does not reflect the "state of the art," but a variety of factors of a historical, political, legal, and economic nature. Thomas Szasz, one of the most outspoken representatives of this view, has gone so far as to speak and write about the "myth of mental illness."

In his unique approach to psychosis, the Scottish psychiatrist R. D. Laing combines a penetrating critique of Western society with an innovative psychological understanding and treatment of this condition. Probably the most radical and controversial figure in the field of psychiatry, he is the author of a series of books that challenge the very roots of modern psychiatric thinking. Laing is usually seen as a representative of "antipsychiatry," a movement initiated by the South African physician and psychotherapist David Cooper, although he himself refuses that label.

According to Laing, psychoses cannot be understood in terms of abnormal biological processes inside the human body, but are products of disturbed patterns of human communication. They reflect problems in important relationships with individuals, small groups such as the family, and society as a whole.

Laing's ideas represent a radical and revolutionary departure from mainstream thinking. The "sane" are not really sane, and the psychotics are not as mad as they appear to be. Modern society is *founded on denial of the self and of experience; it is dangerously insane, and the psychotics, finding its values and norms unbearable, are not able to adjust to them.*

Psychotics are individuals whose total life experience is divided, because they have an unsatisfactory connection with the world and human society, as well as a disruptive relation with the self. Their withdrawal into the world of fantasies provided by their unconscious is an escape from the reality they find unacceptable. This results in an incomplete existence characterized by fear, despair, aloneness, and a sense of isolation.

Such people feel unreal and disconnected from the common-sense world, as well as from their bodies—to such an extent that their identity and autonomy are always in question. Their fear of losing themselves is so consuming and overwhelming that it results in preoccupation with self-preservation rather than self-satisfaction. Laing calls this "ontological insecurity."

According to Laing, psychiatrists do not pay proper attention to the inner experiences of psychotics, because they see them as pathological and incomprehensible. However, careful observation and study show that these experiences have profound meaning and that the psychotic process can be healing. Laing believes that psychotics have in many respects more to teach psychiatrists than psychiatrists do their patients. The "psychiatric ceremony" of examination, diagnosis, and treatment invalidates the clients as human beings and interferes with the healing potential of their process.

Laing's strategy of psychotherapy replacing biological treatment emphasizes the importance of human interaction and relationship, both on a one-to-one basis and on the larger scale of an entire therapeutic team. The experiences emerging from the unconscious are seen as valid, important, and meaningful. Accepting and respecting them facilitates communication and is conducive to healing. According to Laing, special places should be provided where people receive the support and sympathetic understanding that facilitate the healing process.

R. D. Laing was born in 1927 in Glasgow, Scotland, and was educated at the University of Glasgow, where he received his medical degree. His introduction into the world of mental patients occurred when he served for two years as a psychiatrist in the British army. From 1956 to 1962, he conducted clinical research at the Tavistock Institute of Human Relations in London.

Between 1962 and 1965, he was director of the Langham Clinic in London; it was at this time that he founded the Kingsley Hall Clinic, where he conducted a unique experiment in the treatment of psychotic patients without suppressive medication. He continued these activities based on his therapeutic philosophy in the Philadelphia Association, an organization dedicated to the problems of psychosis and focusing on therapy, as well as to the education of professionals and the public by lectures and publications. It deserves special note that in 1973, Laing spent a year in Ceylon studying Theravada Buddhism and Vipassana meditation. In the last decade, his professional time has been divided between writing, private practice, consulting work, and lecturing.

Laing is the author of many articles in professional journals and of the books The Divided Self, The Self and Others, The Politics of Experience, The Bird of Paradise, Reason and Violence, Knots, The Facts of Life, The Voice of Experience, The Politics of the Family, Do You Love Me?, Sanity, Madness and the Family, *and the autobiographical* Wisdom, Madness, and Folly.

In the following paper, Laing goes beyond acknowledging the psychological importance of the unconscious content of psychotic experiences. He explicitly recognizes and emphasizes the value of the transcendental aspect of such experiences and the utmost importance of the spiritual dimension in human life. His discussion of the historical importance of visionary experiences and of the urgent need to draw a clear distinction between pathology and mysticism is of great relevance for the problem of spiritual emergency.

We must remember that we are living in an age in which the ground is shifting and the foundations are shaking. I cannot answer for other times and places. Perhaps it has always been so. We know it is true today.

In these circumstances, we have all reason to be insecure. When the ultimate basis of our world is in question, we run to different holes in the ground; we scurry into roles, statuses, identities, interpersonal relations. We attempt to live in castles that can only be in the air, because there is no firm ground in the social cosmos on which to build. Priest and physician are both witness to this state of affairs. Each sometimes sees the same fragment of the whole situation differently; often our concern is with different presentations of the original catastrophe.

In this paper I wish to relate the transcendental experiences that *sometimes* break through in psychosis to those experiences of the divine that are the Living Fount of all religion.

Elsewhere I have outlined the way in which some psychiatrists are beginning to dissolve their clinical-medical categories of understanding madness. I believe that if we can begin to understand sanity and madness in existential social terms, we, as priests and physicians, will be enabled to see more clearly the extent to which we confront common problems and share common dilemmas.

The main clinical terms for madness, where no organic lesion has so far been found, are schizophrenia, manic-depressive psychosis, and involutional depression. From a social point of view, they characterize different forms of behavior, regarded in our society as deviant. People behave in such ways because their experience of themselves is different. It is on the existential meaning of such unusual experience that I wish to focus.

Experience is mad when it steps beyond the horizons of our common, that is, our communal sense.

What regions of experience does this lead to? It entails a loss of the usual foundations of the "sense" of the world that we share with one another. Old purposes no longer seem viable. Old meanings are senseless; the distinctions between imagination, dream, external perceptions often seem no longer to apply in the old way. External events may seem magically conjured up. Dreams may seem direct communications from others: imagination may seem to be objective reality.

But most radically of all, the very ontological foundations are shaken. The being of phenomena shifts, and the phenomenon of being may no longer present itself to us as before. The person is plunged into a void of nonbeing in which he founders. There are no supports, nothing to cling to, except perhaps some fragments from the wreck, a few memories, names, sounds, one or two objects, that retain a link with a world long lost. This void may not be empty. It may be peopled by visions and voices, ghosts, strange shapes, and apparitions. No one who has not experienced how insubstantial the pageant of external reality can be, how it may fade, can fully realize the sublime and grotesque presences that can replace it, or exist alongside it.

When a person goes mad, a profound transposition of his position in relation to all domains of being occurs. His center of experience moves from ego to Self. Mundane time becomes merely

anecdotal, only the Eternal matters. The madman is, however, confused. He muddles ego with self, inner with outer, natural and supernatural. Nevertheless, he often can be to us, even through his
profound wretchedness and disintegration, the hierophant of the sacred. An exile from the scene of being as we know it, he is an alien, a
stranger, signaling to us from the void in which he is foundering.
This void may be peopled by presences that we do not even dream of.
They used to be called demons and spirits, that were known and
named. He has lost his sense of self, his feelings, his place in the
world as we know it. He tells us he is dead. But we are distracted
from our cozy security by this mad ghost that haunts us with his
visions and voices that seem so senseless and of which we feel impelled to rid him, cleanse him, cure him.

Madness need not be all break*down*. It is also break*through*. It is
potentially liberation and renewal, as well as enslavement and existential death.

There are now a growing number of accounts by people who
have been through the experience of madness. (See, for example, the
anthology *The Inner World of Mental Illness: A Series of First-Person
Accounts of What It Was Like,* ed. Bert Kaplan [New York: Harper
and Row, 1964].) I want to quote at some length from one of the
earlier contemporary accounts, as recorded by Karl Jaspers in his
General Psychopathology (Manchester University Press, 1962):

> I believe I caused the illness myself. In my attempt to penetrate
> the other world I met its natural guardians, the embodiment of my
> own weaknesses and faults. I first thought these demons were lowly
> inhabitants of the other world who could play me like a ball because I
> went into these regions unprepared and lost my way. Later I thought
> they were split-off parts of my own mind (passions) which existed
> near me in free space and thrived on my feelings. I believed everyone
> else had these too but did not perceive them, thanks to the protective
> and successful deceit of the feeling of personal existence. I thought the
> latter was an artifact of memory, thought-complexes, etc., a doll that
> was nice enough to look at from outside but nothing real inside it.
>
> In my case the personal self had grown porous because of my
> dimmed consciousness. Through it I wanted to bring myself closer to
> the higher sources of life. I should have prepared myself for this over a
> long period by invoking in me a higher, impersonal self, since "nectar"
> is not for mortal lips. It acted destructively on the animal-human self,
> split it up into its parts. These gradually disintegrated, the doll was
> really broken and the body damaged. I had forced untimely access

to the "source of life," the curse of the "gods" descended on me. I recognized too late that murky elements had taken a hand. I got to know them after they had already too much power. There was no way back. I now had the world of spirits I had wanted to see. The demons came up from the abyss, as guardian Cerberi, denying admission to the unauthorized. I decided to take up the life-and-death struggle. This meant for me in the end a decision to die, since I had to put aside everything that maintained the enemy, but this was also everything that maintained life. I wanted to enter death without going mad and stood before the Sphinx: either thou into the abyss or I!

Then came illumination. I fasted and so penetrated into the true nature of my seducers. They were pimps and deceivers of my dear personal self which seemed as much a thing of naught as they. A larger and more comprehensive self emerged and I could abandon the previous personality with its entire entourage. I saw this earlier personality could never enter transcendental realms. I felt as a result a terrible pain, like an annihilating blow, but I was rescued, the demons shriveled, vanished, and perished. A new life began for me and from now on I felt different from other people. A self that consisted of conventional lies, shams, self-deceptions, memory-images, a self just like that of other people, grew in me again but behind and above it stood a greater and more comprehensive self which impressed me with something of what is eternal, unchanging, immortal, and inviolable and which ever since that time has been my protector and refuge. I believe it would be good for many if they were acquainted with such a higher self and that there are people who have attained this goal in fact by kinder means.

Jaspers comments: "Such self-interpretations are obviously made under the influence of delusion-like tendencies and deep psychic forces. They originate from profound experiences and the wealth of such schizophrenic experience calls on the observer as well as on the reflective patient not to take all this merely as a chaotic jumble of contents. Mind and spirit are present in the morbid psychic life as well as in the healthy. But interpretations of this sort must be divested of any causal importance. All they can do is to throw light on content and bring it into some sort of context."

I would rather say that this patient has described with a lucidity I could not improve upon, a Quest, with its pitfalls and dangers, which he eventually appears to have transcended. Even Jaspers still speaks of this experience as morbid, and discounts the patient's own construction. Both the experience and construction seem to me valid in their own terms.

I should make it clear that I am speaking of certain *transcendental experiences* that seem to me to be the original wellspring of all religions. Some psychotic people have transcendental experiences. Often (to the best of their recollection) they have never had such experiences before, and frequently they will never have them again. I am not saying, however, that psychotic experience necessarily contains this element more manifestly than sane experience.

The person who is transported into such domains is likely to act curiously. In other places, I have described in some detail the circumstances that seem to occasion this transportation, at least in certain instances, and the gross mystification that the language and thinking of the medical clinic perpetrates when it is brought to bear on the phenomena of madness, both as a social fact and as an existential experience.

The schizophrenic may indeed be mad. He is mad. He is not ill.

I have been told by people who have been through the mad experience how what was then revealed to them was veritable manna from Heaven. The person's whole life may be changed, but it is difficult not to doubt the validity of such vision. Also, not everyone comes back to us again.

Are these experiences simply the effulgence of a pathological process, or of a particular alienation? I do not think they are.

When all has been said against the different schools of psychoanalysis and depth psychology, one of their great merits is that they recognize explicitly the crucial relevance of each person's experience to his or her outward behavior, especially the so-called "unconscious."

There is a view, still current, that there is some correlation between being sane and being unconscious, or at least not too conscious of the "unconscious," and that some forms of psychosis are the behavioral disruption caused by being overwhelmed by the "unconscious."

What both Freud and Jung called "the unconscious" is simply what we, in our historically conditioned estrangement, are unconscious of. It is not necessarily or essentially unconscious.

I am not merely spinning senseless paradoxes when I say that we, the sane ones, are out of our minds. The mind is what the ego is unconscious of. *We* are unconscious of our minds. Our minds are not unconscious. Our minds are conscious of us. Ask yourself who and what it is that dreams our dreams. Our unconscious minds? The Dreamer who dreams our dreams knows far more of us than we know of it. It is only from a remarkable position of alienation that the source of life, the Fountain of Life, is experienced as the It. The mind of which we are unaware is aware of us. It is we who are out of our minds. We need not be unaware of the inner world.

We do not realize its existence most of the time.

But many people enter it—unfortunately without guides, confusing outer with inner realities, and inner with outer—and generally lose their capacity to function competently in ordinary relations.

This need not be so. The process of entering into *the other* world from this world, and returning to *this* world from the other world, is as "natural" as death and childbirth or being born. But in our present world, that is both so terrified and so unconscious of the other world, it is not surprising that, when "reality," the fabric of this world, bursts, and a person enters the other world, he is completely lost and terrified, and meets only incomprehension in others.

In certain cases, a man blind from birth may have an operation performed which gives him his sight. The result: frequently misery, confusion, disorientation. The light that illumines the madman is an unearthly light, but I do not believe it is a projection, an emanation from his mundane ego. He is irradiated by a light that is more than he. It may burn him out.

This "other" world is not essentially a battlefield wherein psychological forces, derived or diverted, displaced or sublimated from their original object-cathexes, are engaged in an illusionary fight—although such forces may obscure these realities, just as they may obscure so-called external realities. When Ivan, in *The Brothers Karamazov*, says, "If God does not exist, everything is permissible," he is *not* saying: "If my superego, in projected form, can be abolished, I can do anything with a good conscience." He *is* saying: "If there is *only* my conscience, then there is no ultimate validity for my will."

The proper task of the physician (psychotherapist, analyst) should be, in select instances, to educt the person from this world and induct him to the other. To guide him in it: and to lead him back again. ·

One enters the other world by breaking a shell: or through a door: through a partition: the curtains part or rise: a veil is lifted. It is not the same as a dream. It is "real" in a different way from dream, imagination, perception, or fantasy. Seven veils: seven seals, seven heavens.

The "ego" is the instrument for living in *this* world. If "the ego" is broken up, or destroyed (by the insurmountable contradictions of certain life situations, by toxins, chemical changes, etc.), then the person may be exposed to this other world.

The world that one enters, one's capacity to experience it, seems to be partly conditional on the state of one's "ego."

Our time has been distinguished, more than by anything else, by a mastery, a control, of the external world, and by an almost total forgetfulness of the internal world. If one estimates human evolution from the point of view of knowledge of the external world, then we are in many respects progressing.

If our estimate is from the point of view of the internal world, and of oneness of internal and external, then the judgment must be very different.

Phenomenologically the terms "internal" and "external" have little validity. But in this whole realm one is reduced to mere verbal expedients—words are simply the finger pointing to the moon. One of the difficulties of talking in the present day of these matters is that the very existence of inner realities is now called into question.

By "inner" I mean all those realities that have usually no "external," "objective" presence—the realities of imagination, dreams, fantasies, trances, the realities of contemplative and meditative states: realities that modern man, for the most part, has not the slightest direct awareness of.

Nowhere in the Bible, for example, is there any argument about the *existence* of gods, demons, angels. People did not first "believe in" God: they experienced His Presence, as was true of other spiritual agencies. The question was not whether God existed, but whether this particular God was the greatest God of all, or the only god; and what was the relation of the various spiritual agencies to each other. Today, there is a public debate, not as to the trustworthiness of God, the particular place in the spiritual hierarchy of different spirits, etc., but whether God or such spirits *even exist*, or ever have existed.

Sanity today appears to rest very largely on a capacity to adapt to the external world—the interpersonal world, and the realm of human collectivities.

As this external human world is almost completely and totally estranged from the inner, any personal direct awareness of the inner world already entails grave risks.

But since society, without knowing it, is *starving* for the inner, the demands on people to evoke its presence in a "safe" way, in a way that need not be taken seriously, is tremendous—while the ambivalence is equally intense. Small wonder that the list of artists in, say, the last 150 years, who have become shipwrecked on these reefs is so long—Hölderlin, John Clare, Rimbaud, Van Gogh, Nietzsche, Antonin Artaud, Strindberg, Munch, Bartók, Schumann, Büchner, Ezra Pound . . .

Those who survived have had exceptional qualities—a capacity for secrecy, slyness, cunning—a thoroughly realistic appraisal of the risks they run, not only from the spiritual realms that they frequent, but from the hatred of their fellows for anyone engaged in this pursuit.

Let us *cure* them. The poet who mistakes a real woman for his Muse and acts accordingly . . . The young man who sets off in a yacht in search of God . . .

The outer divorced from any illumination from the inner is in a state of darkness. We are in an age of darkness. The state of outer darkness is a state of sin—i.e., alienation or estrangement from the Inner Light. Certain actions lead to greater estrangement; certain others help one not to be so far removed. The former are bad; the latter are good.

The ways of losing one's way are legion. Madness is certainly not the least unambiguous. The countermadness of Kraepelinian psychiatry is the exact counterpart of "official" psychosis. Literally, and absolutely seriously, it is as *mad*, if by madness we mean any radical estrangement from the subjective or objective truth. Remember Kierkegaard's objective madness.

As we experience the world, so we act. We conduct ourselves in the light of our view of what is the case and what is not the case. That is, each person is a more or less naive ontologist. Each person has views of what is, and what is not.

There is no doubt, it seems to me, that there have been profound changes in the experience of man in the last thousand years. In some ways this is more evident than changes in the patterns of his behavior. There is everything to suggest that man experienced God. Faith was never a matter of believing He existed, but of trusting in the Presence that was experienced and known to exist as a self-validating datum. It seems likely that far more people in our time neither experience the Presence of God, nor the Presence of His absence, but the absence of His Presence.

We require a history of phenomena—not simply more phenomena of history.

As it is, the secular psychotherapist is often in the role of the blind leading the half-blind.

The fountain has not played itself out, the Flame still shines, the River still flows, the Spring still bubbles forth, the Light has not faded. But between *us* and It, there is a veil which is more like fifty feet of solid concrete. *Deus absconditus.* Or we have absconded.

Already everything in our time is directed to categorizing and segregating this reality from objective facts. This is precisely the concrete wall. Intellectually, emotionally, interpersonally, organizationally, intuitively, theoretically, we have to blast our way through the solid wall, even if at the risk of chaos, madness, and death. For from *this* side of the wall, this is the risk. There are no assurances, no guarantees.

Many people are prepared to have faith in the sense of scientifically indefensible belief in an untested hypothesis. Few have trust enough to test it. Many people make-believe what they experience. Few are made to believe by their experience. Paul of Tarsus was picked up by the scruff of the neck, thrown to the ground, and blinded for three days. This direct experience was self-validating.

We live in a secular world. To adapt to this world the child abdicates its ecstacy. (*L'enfant abdique son extase.*—Mallarmé.) Having lost our experience of the Spirit, we are expected to have faith. But this faith comes to be a belief in a reality which is not evident. There is a prophecy in Amos that there will be a time when there will be a famine in the land, "not a famine for bread, nor a thirst for water, but of *hearing* the words of the Lord." That time has now come to pass. It is the present age.

From the alienated starting point of our pseudosanity, everything is equivocal. Our sanity is not "true" sanity. Their madness is not "true" madness. The madness of our patients is an artifact of the destruction wreaked on them by us, and by them on themselves. Let no one suppose that we meet any more "true" madness than that we are truly sane. The madness that we encounter in "patients" is a gross travesty, a mockery, a grotesque caricature of what the natural healing of that estranged integration we call sanity might be. True sanity entails in one way or another the dissolution of the normal ego, that false self competently adjusted to our alienated social reality: the emergence of the "inner" archetypal mediators of divine power, and through this death a rebirth, and the eventual reestablishment of a new kind of ego-functioning, the ego now being the servant of the Divine, no longer its betrayer.

Part Two

VARIETIES OF SPIRITUAL EMERGENCY

John Weir Perry

SPIRITUAL EMERGENCE AND RENEWAL

For when it is quite, quite nothing, then it is everything.
When I am trodden quite out, quite, quite out,
every vestige gone, then I am here
risen, and setting my foot on another world
risen, accomplishing a resurrection
risen, not born again, but risen, body the same as before,
new beyond knowledge of newness, alive beyond life,
proud beyond inkling or furthest conception of pride,
living where life was never yet dreamed of, nor hinted at,
here, in the other world, still terrestrial
myself, the same as before, yet unaccountably new.

D. H. LAWRENCE, "New Heaven and Earth,"
Selected Poems

John Weir Perry, M.D., is a California psychiatrist and Jungian analyst specializing in psychotherapy with psychotic patients. He received his medical degree from Harvard Medical School in 1941 and went on to serve in China with medical teams of the Friends Ambulance Unit during World War II.

This stay in a culture so radically different from his own had a profound impact on him. It showed him the relativity of cultural perspectives and inspired him to search for universal elements in the human psyche. His understanding of Oriental philosophy and culture also helped him to accept the radically new ideas in psychology and psychiatry formulated by Jung and his followers, since Jung himself was profoundly impressed and influenced by Eastern spiritual psychologies.

In 1947, Perry was awarded a Rockefeller Foundation fellowship to prepare for research in psychology and religion and spent the next two years at the C. G. Jung Institute in Zurich, Switzerland. After returning to the United States, he taught at the University of California and at the C. G. Jung Institute of Northern California in San Francisco and also saw patients in private practice. The findings of his systematic and intensive psychotherapeutic research with schizophrenic inpatients inspired a program sponsored by the National Institute of Mental Health in Bethesda, Maryland.

John Perry is a true pioneer in the psychotherapy of psychotic patients. In addition to his revolutionary contributions to the theoretical understanding of psychoses, he also made a giant step in the practical approach to these disorders by cofounding Diabasis, a residential treatment facility where young patients in acute first episodes were encouraged to work through their psychotic experiences without the mitigating effect of tranquilizers. Perry's observations and discoveries are described in his books The Self in Psychotic Process, Lord of the Four Quarters, The Far Side of Madness, Roots of Renewal in Myth and Madness, and The Heart of History.

Perry's paper "Spiritual Emergence and Renewal" summarizes his understanding of the psychotic process and its healing and transformative potential. It also describes his practical clinical experiences with Diabasis.

I am continually puzzled by the extreme turbulence that accompanies profound change in the psyche. When a true spiritual awakening and transformation is under way, one encounters images of death and of the destruction of the world itself. The psyche does not express itself gently, but one would like to think that this movement of the spirit would come about in a more orderly manner through exposure to workshops, exercises, and other instructional techniques. The hope of those of us in the field of psychotherapy is that such techniques might bring about change in a more gentle fashion; but as Jung has observed, there are often periods of very uncomfortable de-adaptation and episodes of altered states of consciousness, called transitory psychosis, which are mild and short.

THE NATURE OF SPIRIT

Why the need for all this upheaval? There are good reasons that rest upon a second query: What is spirit and what is its nature?

People often define the word *spiritual* loosely to signify anything uplifting; at the other extreme it is considered lofty, seraphic, rarefied, high above nature, in some other realm, hence supernatural. In descriptions of cultures, the word often designates any aspect that is not material, economic, or political.

When we look at the actual phenomenology of spirit, we get a different impression. The ancient words for it imply breath or air, particularly air in motion, and thus wind—in Hebrew, *ruach*; in Latin, *animus*; in the Far East, *prana* or *ch'i*. The word itself conveys the meaning of breath, derived from the Latin *spiritus*. All these clearly denote a dynamism that is invisible as air but capable of being powerful as wind. It "bloweth where it listeth," the Bible says, suggesting a will of its own. In short, spirit is a strongly moving dynamism that is free of material structure.

These descriptions lead us to think of spirit as pure energy, but on closer look we find more than that—it is typically experienced as having a voice, when persons are moved by the spirit. It seems then to have the property of intention, to be freighted with information, and this aspect could be defined as "informed energy" or energy with the quality of mind.

Spirit cannot be separated from its plural form, "spirits." In old traditional societies, these are invisible dynamisms that live in the natural world, especially in biological life, but also in mountains, streams, springs, and in a belief system called animism. To clairvoyants, these spirits appear to have a voice and to take on a personified visibility. They also require a great deal of attention from the human community in the form of offerings and sacrifices. When one lives in such a society (as I have in China), one is constantly aware of this other dimension of existence, an existence that we have long since relegated to oblivion.

Less unusual in sophisticated cultures are experiences with spirits that belong in the realm of the afterlife, with the deceased. Death is viewed as a liberation of the spirit from the body by a transformation process called transfiguration. In China, Heaven has been revered as a presence that rules over the affairs of the world, composed of a conglomerate of ancestral spirits (royal ones) and possessed of intention and will. In ancient traditions all over the world, spirits are highly valued ancestral beings that make themselves heard, give advice and counsel, and even make demands. When visiting black communities in Africa I was amazed at the constant attention given to these spirits as a matter-of-fact part of daily life.

From this cursory glance at the range of manifestations of spirit and spirits we may see that spirit can be either free of bodily structure or engaged in a struggle to be liberated from it. I find this helpful in understanding how spirit operates in psychological experiences. For here again we find spirit constantly striving for release from its entrapment in routine or conventional mental structures. Spiritual work is the attempt to liberate this dynamic energy, which must break free of its suffocation in old forms: emotional patterns such as the complexes engendered in the family system; assumptions about the nature of the world and human life; values that need revision as conditions change; and cultural forms derived from family, subculture, or dominant cultural conditioning that must change with the times. Again, there are ancient traditions expressing this work of liberating spirit, such as the emotionally painful labors of the Nature Philosophers who were dedicated to freeing *nous* from *physis*—spirit from imprisonment in matter—in the natural world and in the body.

During a person's developmental process, if this work of releasing spirit becomes imperative but is not undertaken voluntarily with knowledge of the goal and with considerable effort, then the psyche is apt to take over and overwhelm the conscious personality with its own powerful processes. I have observed these processes in many cases and I have recognized a specific sequence that I have formulated and called the "renewal process" (Perry 1953, 1974, 1976).

THEMES OF DEATH AND WORLD DESTRUCTION

Two components of this sequence highlight its disintegrative and re-integrative aspects—emotional experiences and images of death and of world destruction.

Whenever a profound experience of change is about to take place, its harbinger is the motif of death. This is not particularly mysterious, since it is the limited view and appraisal of oneself that must be outgrown or transformed, and to accomplish transformation the self-image must dissolve. In severe visionary states, one may feel one has crossed over into the realm of death and is living among the spirits of the deceased. One is forced to let go of old expectations of oneself and to let oneself be tossed about by the winds of change.

Far less familiar is the companion piece to this death motif—the image of world destruction. Like the self-image, the world image is a compacted form of the very complex pattern of how one sees the world and how one lives in it. We learn most about this from cultural anthropologists, who find that, in times of acute and rapid culture change, visionaries undergo the shattering experience of seeing the world dissolve into a chaos and time whirl back to its beginnings. This dissolution of the world image clearly represents the death of the old culture to pave the way for renovation. Thus, in an individual's life, when a transformation of one's inner culture is under way, dissolution of the world image is the harbinger of change. Expressions of cultural reform are explicit.

These and other archetypal images have the function of implementing the processes of the spirit, of liberating and transforming its energies, which will then slip out of the old structures and into new ones geared to the future. All this happens in the interest of development, of cultivating a more capacious consciousness, open to new dimensions of experience.

Not only are these two motifs, self-image and world image, companion pieces in the process, but they also share the same representative image: the mandala. The entire process of renewal is evidently the work of this powerful image symbolizing the psyche's governing center.

The energy that had been bound up in the structures of the old self-image and world image, in the issues of who one is and what sort of world one lives in, is immense. In dreams or visions, nuclear explosion is a frequent expression of this enormous charge of psychic energy that is loose during the renewal process and raises havoc for a period of time. Though one's own nature is struggling to break through, one may feel that who one is and what one values is up for grabs. Indeed, values and the emotional issues of life seem to be clashing opposites.

This energy does not remain long in suspense, but quickly seeks its reincarnation into new structures, expressed in the form of images and experiences of rebirth and world regeneration. A new sense of oneself appears along with fresh interests and motivations. The new birth activates one's memory of the actual events of one's first birth, thus linking these phenomena with those studied by Stanislav Grof (1976, 1985). In addition, there is an inner reenactment of emotional experiences of early years.

The cataclysm of this kind of crisis of spiritual processes reminds me of the Biblical warning, "It is a fearful thing to fall into the hands of the living God." For during the period of time between the initial visions of death and world destruction and their resolution in renewal, one is apt to be in the grip of fear, and dismayed to find oneself isolated since communication of one's experiences is not often empathetically received. At the very time when one needs loving acceptance one finds oneself either alone or surrounded by professionals who want to suppress the process and make one conform to the ways of the former self and former world.

This fear (and an accompanying rage) produce biochemical effects in the brain and the rest of the body that medical doctors prefer to see as the primary cause of psychological disorder. This biased and mechanistic diagnosis does not hold up, however, since it is now well known that if a person undergoing this turmoil is given love, understanding, and encouragement, the spiritual crisis soon resolves itself without the need for interruption by suppressive medication. The most fragmented "thought disorder" can become quite coherent and orderly within a short time if someone is present to respond to it with compassion. Such a relationship is far better than a tranquilizer in most instances. A haven where there is attentiveness to inner experiences and where, removed from the context of daily life, one can examine one's whole existence is also advantageous.

I have described the more extreme forms of visionary states because the psychic process is so clearly shown that one can understand it. The more usual experience, however, while showing the same psychic contents and processes, may be far less disruptive. Severity ranges from the horrendous to the mild, depending perhaps on how vigorous the resources of a person's consciousness are and how rich in its repertory one's unconscious psyche might be. But the process of renewal needs a partner.

What is the ultimate goal of spiritual emergence and the renewal process? It has the same goal as that of the mystic way or of meditation; in Buddhist practice it is called wisdom and compassion or love.

THE RENEWAL PROCESS

What is the psyche's way of effecting the renewal process? In this discussion, I will continue to describe the more extreme manifestations because they can be most clearly observed.

The moment of slipping over the edge into the onslaught of confusion and welter of visionary images is like the experience of dying and entering the afterlife. Leading up to this crucial point there usually has been a gradual shift of attention from involvement with conventional reality to concerns with the more intense reality of the inner life. At this point energy in the conscious field drops dramatically; at the same time, the archetypal level of the deep psyche with its profusion of mythic imagery is intensely activated. This surcharge of energy produces what Roland Fischer calls the "high arousal state." Such a psychological term is adequate as a dispassionately objective description of these events, but subjectively one must think in the language of overwhelming cataracts of mythic ideation and symbolic forms. During this process, every manifestation conjures up a multiplicity of meanings.

The focus of this activation and energy is the archetype of the center, which Jung has described as the Self, represented by quadrated circles and mandalas. The course of the process and the accompanying imagery point to this center (as that which is being renewed), and all the parts and phases of the renewal are represented as taking place within this center as their vessel of transformation.

I have previously described the components and phases of the renewal process and their myth and ritual parallels in antiquity (Perry 1966, 1976). The process has a venerable history of five thousand years, and has always taken the form of a ritual drama that unfolds within a work center established within the Self. Following the experience of death and afterlife, there occurs a regression of time back to beginnings—in the case of the individual's past, back to the mother, as her infant, or to one's birth or even to the intrauterine state—in the larger dimension of the world's past, back to the creation or even to the state of chaos before it. The self-image and the world image reflect and parallel each other throughout this sequence.

However, all does not move smoothly in this reenactment of the beginnings. Opposites become vividly constellated. Forces that strive to destroy all existence enter a cosmic conflict with the benign forces of preservation and world regeneration. At the same time, opposites on every level tussle for ascendancy. One pair that is quite distressing is the contrasexual component that arouses feelings of being changed into the other sex (not to be construed as homosexual panic).

These are the heavy, frightening, even nightmarish elements in the progress of renewal; there are other lighter elements, such as the inflated image of oneself in an apotheosis of hero or heroine, saint, savior, messiah, or king. Here one has the experience of being brought into a *hieros gamos,* a sacred or heavenly marriage with some mythic or divine figure, with all the accompanying exhilaration of erotic emotion. In this messianic role, one also believes oneself especially elected to bring about reforms of religion or society on a world scale, thus effecting a significant aspect of world regeneration. The self-image is renewed in a rebirth or sometimes a new birth brought about by a fruitful event of the sacred marriage.

Through this interplay of opposites one may discern clashing, reversing one into the other, and union. In the profusion of drawings and paintings that have emerged to express these inner events, each element in the process tends to be staged within the mandala form (representing the archetypal center, the Self), well known as a container of opposites.

But, one might object, is not the Self transcendent and eternal? How can it be going through death and disintegration? Is it not the ego that is supposed to go through a sacrificial death? We look to myth and ritual for the answer.

In Christian tradition, Jesus was the incarnation of the eternal godhead and the representation of the Self; his death and transfiguration symbolized the renewal process in that faith. Baptism, for example, was originally an initiation into the spiritual kingdom of which he was king. Three millennia earlier, the ceremonial of the sacral kingship of the ancient Near East developed. Royal functionaries, as delegates of the deity and personifications of the center, submitted themselves to an annual death-and-renewal ritual in the great communal festivals of the New Year. It is here that we find the close parallels to the renewal process in individuals today. One might think of the dying gods—Baal in the Near East, Adonis in the Mediterranean cultures, or Freyr in the Nordic—as vegetation and fertility spirits, but each of these names is translated as *Lord* in the royal connotation, implying the role of the center (Self).

Recent emphasis on ego-cide or ego death is apt to miss the essential point, for these terms imply a consciously willed event. The truly transformative death comes usually unbidden if not unwelcome, happening to us and in spite of us. It is an autonomous and archetypal process, a movement of the spirit in the realm of myth and ritual.

The nature of the archetypal center (Self) is to undergo cyclic rounds of birth, death, and resurrection. People of ancient or archaic cultures understood this. Yet it has become alien to us moderns who are enamored of linear progress (if there is any such thing) or of an abiding presence that somehow manages to avoid the cyclic world of nature.

Any contradiction in this can be resolved if we refine our understanding of a difference between the archetypal center itself and the image that represents it. The image does not signify its picturing, but rather the form and quality that it takes in our actual experience. For example, when my analytic exploration of depth was going on, this center was first depicted in dreams in the form of nonordinary, mandala-shaped churches in the context of my spiritual upbringing. Later dreams announced a shake-up in this cultural set: A scene revealed Westminster Abbey becoming a delicate, exquisite, but empty shell of stone, while a guide pointed to the mysteriously shaped and colored mountains of China as the area where the numinous, living spirit now resides (such mountains mark the center and four cardinal points of the Chinese world). My worldview is now more Taoist than Christian.

The archetypal center abides, but the image representing it is what needs cyclic renewal, with all that it implies about the outlook, lifestyle, and value system by which one lives.

We are capable of apprehending the center only through its embodiment in images, and these are periodically transformed in the psyche's development; no form that it takes is static. The individuating psyche abhors stasis as nature abhors a vacuum; in it, the spirit shuns imprisonment in nongrowing forms or structures. The Taoists understood very well that opposites are not real entities in themselves but like the Yin and Yang are in perpetual flux revolving around one another in their alternations of ascendancy and yielding, while the Tao abides without name or definition.

From time to time, then, a form of the Self is designated by a certain symbolic or mythic image, which captures the dynamic essence of that phase of a person's life, until it has done its work and its hour has come to be dissolved. The ego does sense that something is dying, and changes only secondarily to the demise of the image of the Self, the center. What happens to the ego reflects the dynamisms in the archetypal psyche. Of the two levels of the self-image, the archetypal one effects in-depth transformations, while the personal one in the conscious personality reflects these more superficial changes. Then the reorganization of the self occurs on both these levels.

The renewal process begins with a predominance of images and feelings of prestige and power, many of which compensate for a debased self-image, a low opinion of oneself; these images reflect the idiom of the family subculture in which the person was raised. But the direction of the process is toward the stirring of motivations and capacities that lead to lovingness and compassion. This is the prime fruit of the work of the spirit, its chief and crowning goal, and may be experienced both as warmth and intimacy in relationships and as a direct sense of the oneness of all beings—not just as a belief or view of how things are, but as the actual realization of it. The outcome of the process has evolutionary implications; among the myth and ritual parallels in history, one can trace the rise of this human-hearted capacity into a cultural awareness and expression that displaces a previous predilection for dominance and violence. This occurred in those several parts of the world where cultures survived through a sufficient number of centuries in order to attain their fulfilled maturity.

HANDLING THE PROCESS

Because the renewal process causes considerable disruption of the ordinary conscious mind by robbing its energy, favorable conditions are required in which to handle this transition during its progress of several weeks.

The psyche seeks its own privacy by withdrawal. Psychiatrists generally disapprove, yet ritual procedures included establishing sacred enclosures for renewal processes to allow a clear differentiation between sacred and secular; what transpired in such a sanctuary had different rules. Perhaps the term "retreat" is more fitting than "withdrawal." One good reason for such safe asylum is that the activity of the mundane world is positively painful to people in this state of high arousal. Such activity can also be confusing since one is dwelling at this time in a mythic world totally alien to the mundane. This experience was overt and conscious to people in the ancient cultures of five thousand years ago, but today it is deeply unconscious and misunderstood.

The confusing discrepancy between the ordinary and the non-ordinary worlds also causes distress to the people surrounding a person in this state. A mutually frightening gulf requires comfortable bridging. A homelike atmosphere is desirable, and in such a sanctuary the most important element is a staff that can empathize with the state of mind in which the client is caught.

Diabasis, our resident facility in San Francisco in the 1970s, was set up to receive people with the most disturbed forms of visionary experiences, the first episode of acute psychosis. All staff members were required to agree on a nonsickness view of this dramatic turmoil, now called nonlabeling. Though the process does need a name, it was important to avoid names with damaging implications. The staff consisted of people who knew the difference between a meaningful inner process and pathology, not through hearsay or because of a liberal intellectual view, but as a result of actual experience. Otherwise, in a moment of crisis, the truth of this knowing or not knowing would come out all too clearly.

Since the process involves a renewing of the Self and the self-image, it was necessary that the staff respond to the newly emerging person with genuine caring, with a loving appreciation of the qualities coming to light. Sensitive discrimination between what is a person's essence and what is the dross derived from the accidents of upbringing was important.

Because the process tends to move a person from motivations of power and prestige to motivations of love and relatedness, this newly emerging capacity must be met with responses in kind. A facility based on the principles of law and order, so prevalent in the hierarchically organized hospital wards, is self-defeating, or may I say, Self-defeating. It is too closely a reenactment of the schizogenic family setting, the initial faulty starting point.

Thus, the selection of Diabasis staff personnel departed from the usual criteria of assessment and was based on personal qualities, not professional qualifications (the categorical prerequisites of education and training). The attributes sought were sensitive receptiveness, a respect for another person's quite different mental state, and especially an understanding of the necessity for the subtle quality of nonintrusive allowing, as well as the experience of "being there" in some form or another, if only through therapy. Emotional vitality and warmth were also necessary in a staff member capable of empathy and honest interactions.

Such a staff forms a community, real, open, close to one another, and devoted to the client. Members are capable of declaring honest feelings and experiences of whatever kind, and of straightforward expression toward each other and toward the clients. If this is the atmosphere the client enters, one has only to witness the effect to realize how vital such a sanctuary is. Utmost confusion is resolved into clarity within a few days. The intent is not merely to be humane and "nice" to clients—it is all geared to the earnest business of discovering Selfhood.

At Diabasis, a significant part of this policy was a declaration that there were no experts—everyone was open to learning and discovering. We provided our gifts and accumulations of experience of various kinds. We had no bosses, no government from the top. The whole staff made policy and decisions. Individuals used their skills in a spirit of effective division of labor; this included administrators and psychiatrists. The entire project was viewed as a creation of the staff by their own vision and effort, belonging to them.

The advantages were evident: the sense of responsibility for the entire house rested in each member so that at crucial moments each staff member felt entitled to act with freedom of judgment. Each represented Diabasis and its way; the whole was represented in the parts; our little microcosm reflected the nature of the macrocosm!

This rationale of handling spiritual emergencies, no matter how disturbed the person, is that in the high-arousal state when the archetypal unconscious is energized and activated, the psyche autonomously does its own work in its own fashion. What it needs for this is not "treatment" but rather a coming into close and deep relationship with another individual who empathizes and encourages but does not interfere. A therapeutic environment is far more effective than medication. It offers the opportunity for the individual to concentrate on the inner work, to sustain the effort, and to move forward in the process. Without such an environment there is a tendency for the process to get stuck, going round and round the same contents without movement.

The archetypal Self or center tends to become activated in intense relationship and to need an emotional framework (a partner) in order to progress along the path of the renewal process. The expression of this process in art pours out and expects a response. In the "rage room," the impulse to lash out and destroy is given safe space and is conveyed to the other in relationship. The past with all its hurts and fears and angers is intensely reenacted in the sessions between the two persons, often from birth to the present, and profound healing can take place.

Holger Kalweit

WHEN INSANITY IS A BLESSING: THE MESSAGE OF SHAMANISM

My body was quivering. While I remained in this state, I began tossing. A chant was coming out of me without my being able to do anything to stop it. Many things appeared to me presently: huge birds and animals. . . . These were visible only to me, not to others in my house. Such visions happen when a man is about to become a shaman; they occur of their own accord. The songs force themselves out complete without any attempt to compose them . . .

ACCOUNT OF ISAAC TENS, A GITSKAN INDIAN,
FROM *The Shaman's Doorway* BY STEPHEN LARSEN

The concept of spiritual emergency, which differentiates transformational crises from psychiatric disorders, is supported independently by evidence from many different fields. Particularly important are the data related to the shamanic traditions found in the historical and anthropological literature. Shamanism is the world's oldest religion and humanity's most ancient healing art; its origins very likely reach back tens of thousands of years to the Paleolithic era.

Shaman is a term used by anthropologists for a special kind of medicine man or woman or witch doctor, who regularly enters nonordinary states of consciousness to heal, obtain information by extrasensory means, or conduct rituals to influence weather or game animals. Shamanism is nearly universal; its practice covers the time span from the Stone Age until the present, and its various forms can be found in Africa, Europe, North and South America, Asia, Australia, and Polynesia. The fact that shamanic cultures attribute great value to nonordinary states of consciousness is extremely important to the concept of spiritual emergency.

The career of many shamans begins with a dramatic episode of an altered state of consciousness that traditional Western psychiatry sees as a manifestation of serious mental disease. It includes visionary experiences of descent into the underworld, attacks from demons, and inhuman tortures and ordeals, followed by a sequence of dying and being reborn and subsequent ascent into celestial realms. During this time, the future shaman can experience a wide spectrum of extreme emotions and behave in most unusual ways.

These symptoms suggest a grave psychiatric disorder when judged by Western medical standards. Yet, if this crisis is successfully overcome and completed, it results in personal healing, superior social functioning, and the development of shamanic abilities. The individual is then accepted by the tribe as an extremely important and useful member of the group. However, it is important to emphasize that strange experiences in themselves are not enough to qualify one as a shaman. Being a shaman requires a successful completion of the episode and a return to full functioning in everyday life. Shamanic cultures make a clear distinction between people who are shamans and those who are sick or crazy.

After having completed the initiatory crisis, a shaman is typically able to enter nonordinary states of consciousness on his or her terms and terminate them at will. The shaman performs this task regularly for the purpose of healing others, gaining deeper insight into reality, and receiving artistic inspiration. Like the shamanic crisis, these states have many features that Western psychiatry tends to see as pathological. In addition, many shamans have the means and the skills to induce similar states in their clients and are thus able to achieve dramatic healing of various emotional and psychosomatic conditions.

These observations suggest that the theoretical understanding of psychotic states and the practical approach to them existing at present in Western psychiatry have to be seriously reexamined and reevaluated. The evidence from shamanic cultures certainly supports the central concept of this book: that it is possible to approach some nonordinary states of consciousness in such a way that they have beneficial results for the individual involved and for the community.

We have chosen an excerpt from the writings of Holger Kalweit, whom we believe to be uniquely qualified to discuss the relationship between shamanism and the problem of spiritual emergency. He is a psychologist with many years of clinical practice, a deep interest in anthropology, and extensive experience in field research as an ethnologist in Hawaii, in the rest of the United States, and in the Himalayas. Kalweit combines in a very original way the study of shamanism, the mythology of various peoples, transpersonal psychology, and near-death experiences. In his approach, the cross-culturally obtained data are subjected to systematic interdisciplinary analysis. The result is a new transpersonal orientation that integrates anthropology, ethnology, and psychology.

Kalweit lives in Switzerland and works as a free-lance writer. His book Dreamtime and the Inner Space: The World of the Shaman describes shamans of different cultures as pioneers who have prepared the ground for modern consciousness research by their inner journeys and discoveries in the unknown territories of the human psyche. His book Ancient Healers, Medicine Men, and Shamans specifically explores the healing aspects of shamanism. Another book, Healing of Knowledge, coauthored by Amalie Schenk, discusses the inner way to knowledge and its relationship to the traditional approach to knowledge as practiced by Western science.

Western culture and medicine have declared total war on sickness and death: on death because it signifies the end of our earthly existence, and on sickness because it impairs our enjoyment of life. We look upon sickness as bad, something to get rid of as quickly as possible, to put an end to. We see it as something invading us: a virus, a bacillus or whatever, and so we experience it profoundly as an alien process that incapacitates, paralyzes, and destroys our body internally, as an unnatural state of affairs that should be suppressed by every conceivable means. In short, sickness and death are the gargoyles of our civilization.

Sickness to us is a blemish, a dirty spot on the self-deceiving mirror of our technological megalomania. Suffering and sickness are seen by our culture as something that emerges from a source hostile to the body, and so our fight against sickness, death, suffering, and physical pain is felt by us to be completely natural. Our static view of the world abhors any kind of change, except perhaps economic and technological. In particular we resent any alteration of consciousness and ontological change.

If we were able to understand sickness and suffering as processes of physical and psychic transformation, as do Asian peoples and tribal cultures, we would gain a deeper and less biased view of psychosomatic and psychospiritual processes and begin to realize the many opportunities presented by suffering and the death of the ego. Our long and continuous battle against death and sickness has so deeply taken root in our consciousness that even modern psychology has felt compelled to take up the cudgel against physical weakness and dying. Consequently, psychic and physical suffering have remained unacknowledged as a means of altering consciousness and as forces and mechanisms of transformation and self-healing.

In recent years a general revaluation of consciousness—that essence which pervades all our actions in life—has taken place, accompanied by a more positive attitude towards states of altered consciousness. Science has thus begun to reassess the sacred knowledge of past cultures and traditional societies which do not regard sickness and death as primarily evil and hostile, but acknowledge their positive internal dynamism. For these traditional cultures sickness, suffering, and death are manifestations of the body's inherent wisdom, to which we only have to surrender to reach areas of perception capable of revealing the true basis of our earthly existence.

They look upon life in the Beyond and on death as a way of regenerating and recovering from our earthly existence. They also see sickness as a process that cleanses us of the bad habits we have accumulated by our false attitude to life. To die and to suffer a severe sickness are part of the basic experience of the shaman's path. This does not mean that every shaman has to undergo this kind of initiation—there are several other possibilities—but in the later stages of shamanic development they are a means of further transformation. We therefore have to let go of the prejudices we have held for generations and of our pessimism towards pain and suffering. We must learn to look death in the face and come to understand sickness as something resulting from an inner imbalance. Only then will we discover its true meaning in the context of our existence. Sickness is a call for self-realization, self-development, and in extreme cases—as the following narrative shows—a variety of shamanic initiation.

On his travels through Siberia, the Hungarian explorer Vilmos Diószegi collected many reports about shamanic vocations experienced as a result of sickness. Once he asked Kyzlasov, a former shaman of the Sagay tribe from Kyzlan on the river Yes, how he had acquired his powers. Kyzlasov reacted with a stony silence. But then his wife began to tell her husband's story:

> How did he become a shaman? Sickness seized him when he was twenty-three years old and he became a shaman at the age of thirty. That was how he became a shaman, after the sickness, after the torture. He had been ill for seven years. While he was ailing, he had dreams: He was beaten up several times, sometimes he was taken to strange places. He had been around quite a lot in his dreams and he had seen many things. . . . He who is seized by the shaman sickness and does not begin to exercise shamanism, must suffer badly. He might lose his mind, he may even have to give up his life. Therefore he is advised, "You must take up shamanism so as not to suffer!" Some even say, "I became a shaman only to escape illness."[1]

Sunchugasev, another shaman who was present, added:

> The man chosen for shamandom is first recognized by the black spirits. The spirits of the dead shamans are called black spirits. They make the chosen one ill and then they force him to become a shaman.[2]

Suzukpen, a former important shaman of the Siberian Soyot community near the Suy-Surmak River, narrated the following about his long illness and his calling to shamanism:

It has been a long time. With two of my brothers, the three of us went to hunt squirrels. Late at night we were crossing a mountain, going after the squirrels, when suddenly I saw a black crow right in the middle of the road.

We were advancing in single file. I was the first. I came nearer, but the crow kept crouching in the middle of the road. It stayed right there and waited for me.

When I reached it, I threw some snow toward it from a branch.

It never moved.

Then I hit its beak with my stick.

Kok-kok. The knock resounded loudly.

What was all this? What was going to happen to me? Because the night before—before seeing the crow—I had already felt miserable.

Next day I went back to where I had seen the crow. Not even a trace of it was to be seen, anywhere! Although the others, that is my brothers, had seen it too.

From then on, from the time I hit the beak of that crow, I became very ill. My mind was deranged.

I have been suffering for as long as seven years.[3]

Among the Siberian Soyot most prospective shamans become ill—girls between the ages of ten and twelve and young men at the age of twenty to twenty-five. They suffer from headaches, nausea, and loss of appetite. When a shaman is called to attend them he says that one of the mountain spirits wants to turn the sick one into a shaman. One shaman by the name of Sadaqpan from the Ulug Dag region was ill in bed for a year prior to his initiation. He suffered from a heart condition, frequently screamed out in pain, and behaved like a madman. He was thirty years old at the time. The Soyot call the time during which a spirit torments a future shaman *albys*. This period frequently remains a blank in the shaman's life; he cannot remember what happened. He gabbles confused words, displays very curious habits of eating, and sings continuously.

The son of a shaman called Sandyk from the area near the Sistig-khem told how his father experienced his call to shamanism:

At first, my father was sickly; he had a weak heart and so he suffered from attacks. That is why people thought he might start practicing the shaman's art. A spirit appeared to him, or rather two spirits: Säräl čoydu and Tämir qastaj. The first one was what we call a "great spirit" (Uluy aza). Near the Khamsara lived a famous shaman of the Aq čódu tribe, called Amyj or Taqqa. He was brought to see my father and told him, "On the fifteenth of this month you will become a shaman." Amyj was a great shaman.[4]

Among the Siberian Tofa, too, shamans become sick before their initiation and are tormented by spirits. A shaman called Anjataj suffered for three years from headaches and pains in his arms and legs. In his dreams the spirits asked him to become a shaman. He slept for three days in a row. When he felt better he followed his calling. The shaman Vassily Mikailovic of the Amastayev clan, who was initiated at the age of eighteen, was so dangerously ill that he could not rise from his bed for a whole year. Only when he agreed to the demands of the spirits did his health improve.[5]

Franz Boas has recorded the experiences of a Kwakiutl Indian who became a healer after having always doubted and been critical of shamans. One day he went out hunting with some others, paddling in a canoe along the coast. He saw a wolf on a boulder which jutted out from the rock face. The wolf was rolling around on its back and scratching its mouth with its paws. To everybody's surprise the wolf did not run away as they came closer but appeared to be very trusting. There was a deer bone stuck in its bloodstained mouth; it looked at the hunters as if it expected help from them.

The young hunter soothed the wolf, saying, "You are in trouble, friend. Now I shall be like a great shaman and cure you, friend. I will take out your great trouble and set you right, friend. Now reward me, friend, that I may be able, like you, to get everything easily, all that is taken by you, on account of your fame as a harpooner and your supernatural power. Now reward my kindness to you, friend. Go on! Sit still on the rock and let me get my means of taking out that bone." Later he dreamt about this wolf which appeared to him in the form of a harpooner. It told him where the seals were to be found and assured him that he would always be a successful hunter.

As time passed, he always managed to bring home a good kill. One day other members of his tribe found some crates full of food and clothing that did not seem to belong to anyone. But the contents of these crates had been contaminated with smallpox (perhaps intentionally by white settlers). All his hunting companions died and he was lying among them without hope when two wolves came trotting along and began to lick him. They vomited foam all over his body, which they then licked off again, only to vomit more foam over him. They continued to do this until he felt stronger. Then he recognized the wolf he had once saved.

Restored by the wolves, he continued to roam around with his brother wolves. One day, however, his wolf friend pressed its muzzle against his chest bone and vomited all its magical force into him. He fell into a deep sleep and dreamt that the wolf changed into a human being and told him that he would now be able to heal the sick, to project energy that makes people ill, and to catch souls. When he awoke he was trembling all over. Now he was a shaman. It felt good and he was all the time in a sort of delirium and sang the four sacred songs the wolf had bequeathed to him.[6]

Here is a somewhat similar story about Lebi'd, another Kwakiutl Indian. Lebi'd was ill for a long time, three winters in a row. When he finally died it was bitterly cold outside. The snow and the storm continued unabated so he could not be buried. Again and again the people had to postpone the burial ceremony. Suddenly he was heard singing a song, and the wolves that began to gather around his corpse were howling with him. Then the people knew that Lebi'd had become a shaman.

He followed the wolves into the forest, and although the people looked for him they could not find him. On the second day, a song could be heard from far off. In the meantime his house had been cleaned and all were waiting for his return. They had started a fire in his hearth, and the people beat the drum three times. Then Lebi'd appeared, stark naked. He sang a sacred song:

I was taken away far inland to the edge of the world,
by the magical power of heaven, the treasure, ha, wo, ho.
Only then was I cured by it, when it was really thrown into me,
the past life bringer of Nau'alakŭmē, the treasure, ha, wo, ho.

Lebi'd danced and danced, and when all the people had withdrawn and only the other shamans remained, he began to relate what had happened to him, as is the custom.

When he died, a man had appeared to him and invited him to go with him. He had risen to his feet and had been surprised to see his body lying on the ground. They had run far into the forest and soon entered a house where he was given a new name by a man called Nau'alakŭmē, who had transferred his shamanic power to him by vomiting a quartz crystal over him. Singing his sacred song, he had caused the crystal to enter him (Lebi'd) through the lower part of his chest bone. That is how he had become a shaman. The wolves, meanwhile, had changed into humans. As Nau'alakŭmē sang, he pressed Lebi'd's head, first with his left hand, then with his right, and finally with both. Then he passed his hands all over Lebi'd's body and shook the illness out of him. He did this four times.

All the other creatures present then took off their wolf masks and approached his dead body. As Nau'alakŭmē breathed his breath into him, the wolves licked his body. Before that, they had caused his soul to shrink to the size of a fly. His soul was then reintroduced into his body through his head. Immediately after that, his body came alive again. He started to sing a sacred song and—this time in his physical body—set out with the wolves into the forest where Nau' alakŭmē taught him not only how to cure illnesses, but also to send out sickness against others. He had also prophesied that Lebi'd would always dream about him and that he could come to him for advice whenever he was in need of it.[7]

These examples of how two Kwakiutl Indians experienced their calling feature an encounter with helping spirits in animal form—in both cases wolves, who were actually humans in disguise. The wolf vomits his magic strength into the Indian who—as is often the case in an altered state of consciousness—becomes euphoric. In most cases the experience of being resurrected after terrible torments, sickness, and near-death is accompanied by a feeling of euphoria, because the suffering has annihilated all former characteristics of the personality. The sickness is a cleansing process that washes away all that is bad, pitiful, and weak. It floods the individual like a raging river and cleanses it of all that is limited and dull. In this way the sickness becomes a gateway to life. In all cultures people who have a near-death experience encounter beings that represent the resurrection of life. These beings bestow life; they are bearers of divine power. After the sickness—providing it was sufficiently severe and frightening—a new life, a transformed existence, begins.

Lebi'd's story shows another typical NDE (near-death experience) characteristic. As he "dies" and leaves his body, he is met by a being from the Beyond and taken to a "house"—symbolic of a transcendent state—where not only is he given a new name to confirm his inner transformation, but quartz crystals—symbols of transparence, illumination, and magical power—are placed into his chest. The life-giving spirit splits off these crystals from himself and spits them out, thereby allowing Lebi'd to share the nature and the living strength of the spirit.

What happens next reminds one very strongly of methods of magnetopathic treatment, the laying on of hands by which negative energy—the illness—is stroked away or literally shaken out of the body. This practice is common to psychic healers the world over. The restored Lebi'd is now the possessor of higher knowledge. The wolves and the life-bringer accompany him to his dead body and cause his soul to reenter it. Thereafter the life-bringer is Lebi'd's helping spirit, who will stand by his side whenever he heals anyone. Lebi'd became a shaman with the help of the essence of life itself, supported by wolves representing the forces of the animal realm. He became a Chosen One, capable of seeing life and nature undistorted, because the mask of earthly ignorance and delusion was removed from his eyes.

On the Indonesian Mentawai Islands, the calling to shamanism is also preceded by a sickness—in this case malaria—sent by the heavenly spirits. The person destined to become a shaman dreams that he ascends to heaven or goes into the forest to look for monkeys. If the spirits abduct someone chosen for shamanism to heaven he is given a beautiful new body like that of the spirit beings. After his return to earth, the spirits help him with his healing. In this way a new seer is born, known as a Si-kerei, someone who possesses magical powers: "seeing eyes" and "hearing ears."[8]

At this point we might properly ask whether the sickness is sent by the heavenly spirits themselves or whether it should be seen as a byproduct of a person's spiritual growth, of a process aimed at revealing to the sick initiate the heavenly—respectively, his inner—world. Be that as it may, in many tribal cultures the initial impetus towards transformation comes either from heaven or from the underworld, because that is where you are given a new body—the spirit body of the beings in the Beyond which equips the initiate with their knowledge and powers and enables him to transcend matter, space, and time.

Among the Zulus someone destined to become a shaman (Inyanga) suddenly becomes ill, behaves in a curious manner, and is unable to eat normal food. He will eat only certain things. He continually complains of pain in various parts of his body and has the most incredible dreams—he becomes a "house of dreams." He is quickly moved to tears, weeping at first softly to himself and then loudly for everyone to hear. He may be ill for several years before he sings his first great song. When that happens, the other members of the tribe come running and join in. Now everyone is waiting for him to die, which might happen any day. The whole village finds hardly any sleep at night, because someone about to become an Inyanga causes a great deal of unrest. He hardly sleeps. And if he falls asleep, he soon wakes up and begins to sing even in the middle of the night. He may get it into his head to climb onto a roof and jump around like a frog, shaking himself and singing. His helping spirit keeps whispering into his ear and promises him that he will soon be able to give advice to those that come to him. He can hear the whistling of the spirits and converses with them in the language of the humans. Often, however, he does not immediately realize what they are trying to tell him.

At this point it is still unclear whether he suffers from a sickness that will turn him into an Inyanga, or whether he is just crazy. If the people think that he is destined to become a shaman they say, "Ah, now we can see. It's in his head." The helping spirit (Itongo) is at first perceived rather vaguely by the sick person, who cannot properly understand it. For that reason, the other members of the tribe must help him to disentangle what he has seen and heard. Soon the Itongo will say, "Go to so-and-so and he will give you medicine." After that the initiate improves. When the helping spirit finally promises to stand by him he says to the sick person, "It is not you that will talk to people but we will tell them everything they need to know, whenever they come for advice." If the relatives of the sick man do not want him to become a shaman they summon another recognized healer and ask him to appease the spirit. In that case the spirit may leave the man but in all likelihood he will be plagued by sickness for the rest of his life. Even if he does not become an Inyanga, he still has higher knowledge and the people say of him, "If he had become a seer he would have been a great seer, a first-class seer."[9]

The Mundu mugo, the shaman of the Kenyan Kikuyu, receives his calling and his spiritual support from God (Ngai). It is however assumed that he has an inborn disposition for healing. The impulse for the initiation as a Mundu mugo arises from a sickness characterized by dramatic dreams, hallucinations, inability to concentrate, weak eyesight, and abnormal forms of behavior. At the same time his family is visited by a series of misfortunes and accidents. If another Mundu mugo then describes all these signs as meaningful, the initiation is confirmed and publicly sanctioned.

This is followed by the initiation ceremony. If the novice is poor and cannot afford the expensive festivities involved, a ritual is nevertheless performed to relieve his suffering and to accord him the status of an "unconfirmed" Mundu mugo. If he is rich and can pay for the appropriate festivities, he becomes a fully recognized Mundu mugo. Thereafter he specializes in particular skills such as prophecy, diagnoses of illnesses, knowledge of herbs, restoration of the fertility of women, unmasking of sorcerers, or curing mental illness.[10]

According to Young Sook Kim, the calling of Korean shamanesses expresses itself in various physiological disturbances, conspicuous forms of social behavior, outrageous activities, impoliteness, and a lifestyle that inverts traditional cultural values. For instance, the prospective shamaness may wear winter clothes in summer, bathe in cold water in winter, reveal secrets which are taboo to mention, or begin to tell the fortune of anyone who happens to be passing in the street. This illness is known as Sinbyong, "caught by the spirits" or "the spirits have descended," and may be accompanied by visual and auditory hallucinations. At first the relatives find it difficult to establish whether such a woman is really mentally deranged or whether they are dealing with a vocation for shamanism, because in many cases the initial symptoms are practically indistinguishable. The Koreans believe that the spirits visit especially those whose maum (heart or soul) are "split" and upon whom a tragic fate has been bestowed.[11]

In Korea, shamans (Mu dang), 60,000 of whom are at present organized in a professional association (the number of nonregistered shamans is estimated at over 140,000),[12] are no longer accorded a high social status but find themselves on the lowest rung of the social ladder, together with prostitutes, shoe menders, soothsayers, Buddhist monks, and dancing girls. Many more women than men feel called upon to become a Mu dang, although there are some men or hermaphrodites who feel attracted to shamanism. On the Korean mainland, 90 percent of practicing shamans are women; on Cheju Island, up to 60 percent. The behavior and dress of male shamans is extremely effeminate.

The calling for shamanism occurs in three ways:

1. By birth into or adoption by a Mu dang family
2. By Mu dang apprenticeship
3. By a spontaneous feeling of vocation

The most frequent case, the psychic experience of a calling, begins with a sickness that cannot be cured by customary methods of treatment. The person concerned hears voices, speaks in tongues, can absorb only liquid nourishment, and grows as thin as a skeleton.

Bouts of depression and a manic compulsion to dance until unconscious alternate. The sick person goes on long walks into the mountains or to the sea and has dreams in which helping spirits give instructions and reasons for founding a new cult. The novice shaman is overcome by visions of the native pantheon of Gods or may acquire his objects of power by suddenly falling to the ground. After a tragic event such as the death of a relative, an epidemic, famine, or economic ruin, a person may become a Mu dang apprentice if the Buddhist monasteries, to which the mentally ill go to be cured, are unable to alleviate the symptoms of the sickness. In such cases the spontaneous calling is followed by an apprenticeship, extending over several years, with an older and experienced Mu dang.[13]

We would like to illustrate the genesis of this sickness with reports about the calling of two Korean shamanesses:

> Mrs. Lee Kum Sun's boyfriend died at the age of twenty, which greatly distressed her. Shortly before that, her parents had arranged for her to be married to her present husband but her dead boyfriend kept appearing to her in her dreams. At the age of thirty-two she began to see him in her dreams continually and developed the first signs of her sickness. One day she dreamt that she ran barefoot and completely naked to the foot of a mountain where a white-bearded man appeared to her and promised her health and good fortune. At the age of forty she was initiated by an old shamaness. After that everything went well and her health was restored.

> Mrs. Oh Un-sook disliked her husband from the very beginning. After several years, unusual symptoms developed. She lost her appetite, was unable to eat meat or fish, only drank cold water, and developed headaches. She spent most of her time alone. These symptoms lasted about ten years. When she was forty years old she dreamt of thunder and lightning and of a pillar of light that struck her head three times. Thereupon three old men from heaven appeared to her in a dream. One day she saw a vision of a great general riding on a white horse who approached her. Thereafter she dreamt many times that she went to bed with this general. At the age of forty-seven she was initiated as a shamaness and all her symptoms disappeared.[14]

In one of these two shamanesses the calling was triggered by the tragic loss of a lover, in the other by an unhappy marriage. Psychologists would no doubt say that these are clear examples of a desire to escape an unsatisfactory reality. However, such a conclusion would be somewhat premature. We must not overlook the fact that an unhappy marriage and the death of a lover are traumatic experiences which can provide fertile ground for entering an altered state of consciousness. Traumatic shock can cause the collapse of psychic structures, whereupon a more subtle and paranormal sensitivity begins to grow from the ruins of normal consciousness. Lee Kum Sun met a white-bearded old man—the archetype of wisdom—and Oh Un-sook had a vision of a Korean cultural hero—also a symbol of wisdom and strength. Moreover, Oh Un-sook shares the General's bed—a further pointer to her intimate connection and fusion with the transpersonal.

Oh Un-sook's vision of a pillar of light also reinforces the impression that we might be dealing with an illuminating manifestation which afforded her contact with the Beyond and heavenly beings. These two simple narratives indicate that we may not be confronted by abstruse creations of a deviant mind but rather a high form of intuitive insight.

Eduardo Calderón, a Peruvian healer (*curandero*), began to be plagued by disquieting dreams and visions in his childhood:

> During my youth from more or less the age of seven or eight years I had some rare dreams. I still remember them. I remember dreams in which I flew, that my ego departed from the state in which it was, and I went to strange places in the form of a spiral. Or I flew in a vertiginous manner: sssssssssss, I departed. I tried to retain myself and I could not. Strange dreams, strange. I had these until the age of more or less twelve or thirteen. . . .
>
> I have seen things as if someone opens a door and the door is closed. I have had nightmares, but not ordinary ones. I have seen myself introduced through a hole in the air, and I went through an immense, immense void. I have felt numbness in all my body as if my hands were huge but I could not grasp. I could not hold up my hand.[15]

He began to follow his call to serve mankind at an early age. However, his ambition to study medicine was frustrated by the poverty of his family. So he had no other choice than to earn a living by the use of his artistic talents. At the age of twenty-one he developed a typical shamanic illness that modern medicine was unable to diagnose or treat therapeutically:

> In Lima I was studying fine arts and suddenly I began drinking and spending everything on drink. I came down with a rare sickness. It

happened that on one occasion I saw a cat on my left shoulder. It was enough that with that impression of a cat everything that I did was overturned . . . and I lost the power to hold things in my hand and to stand up. I completely lost all my strength. I could not hold myself up in a standing position and walked like a sleepwalker, according to what they tell me.[16]

Eduardo's family had faith in the health abilities of curanderos and called in a woman healer conversant with the properties of herbs. She gave Eduardo a mixture of juices extracted from plants, whereupon he vomited up a dark brew despite the fact that he had not drunk any other liquid. He immediately improved. On the basis of his experiences during his sickness he decided to become a healer. He supported himself by working as a longshoreman and by producing pottery at home. At the same time he became the apprentice of a local curandero. He also studied with various shamans in Chiclayo, Mocupe, and Ferranafe in northern Peru. For several years he acted as assistant to these curanderos until finally his teacher in Ferranafe pronounced him fully qualified.

He was twenty-eight years old at the time and had served four years as an apprentice shaman. He swore never to misuse his powers and to apply them only for the benefit of mankind. Eduardo considers shamanism to be a simple matter of "seeing," a skill or trade anyone is capable of acquiring providing he regularly trains himself in it. It is however open to question whether such training and practicing alone will ensure success, because Eduardo—as his life history shows—was called to his trade by a higher power. Moreover, we must not exclude the possibility that he inherited certain shamanic propensities because both his grandfathers were shamans.

From a description given by W. Sieroszewski we can gain an idea of the liberating and healing qualities of the shamanic seance when the shaman himself feels stricken and debilitated by illness. The Yakut shaman Tüsput, who was critically ill for more than twenty years, could find relief from his suffering only when he conducted a seance during which he fell into a trance. In the end he fully regained his health by this method. However, if he held no seances over a long period of time he once again began to feel unwell, exhausted, and indecisive.[17] In general, the symptoms of an illness subside when a candidate for shamanism enters a trance. The same phenomenon was observed by L. W. Shternberg in the case of a Siberian Gold shaman that even his colleagues were unable to cure. Only when he learned how to enter a trance state did his illness leave him.[18] Similarly, G. Sancheyev mentions a shaman who at first refused to follow his-calling but was forced by illness to consort with the spirits and hold seances, which in the end led to his recovery.[19]

The story of the Yakut shaman Uno Harva also features a relief from illness once he agreed to take up shamanism:

> I became ill when I was twenty-one years old and began to see with my eyes and hear with my ears things others could neither hear nor see. For nine years I fought against the spirit, without telling anyone what had happened because I feared they might not believe me or make fun of me. In the end I became so ill that I was close to death. So I began to shamanize, and very soon my health improved. Even now I feel unwell and sick whenever I am inactive as a shaman over a longer period of time.[20]

Adrian Boshier describes the illness of Dorcas, the daughter of a Methodist preacher, who is now a recognized Zulu shamaness (sangoma). For three years she was bedridden and during this time could absorb only small quantities of food and drink. At night she left her body and visited distant places; in this way she traveled everywhere. Even the white doctors were at a loss. Then one night her dead grandfather appeared to her in a dream. He said he would enter her body and continue his work on earth in this fashion. Being a devout Christian she did not agree to this. After that, other shamans appeared in her dreams, scolded her, and called upon her to become one of them. These visions became more and more frequent, passing before her inner eye like pictures on a cinema screen.

One night several famous sangomas came to her bedside. Chanting a song, they seriously advised her to submit and make a shamanic headdress for herself. She still failed to understand what was happening and wanted to be cured by ceremonies and rites of the Apostolic church. She was taken to a river to be christened. They guided her into the water, and just as they were about to submerge her she was lifted up by a gigantic snake under her feet—her grandfather! Her mother then took her to an aunt who was herself a shamaness. Soon many other healers and shamans assembled, beating their drums and exhorting her to get up and sing. She then danced and sang hour after hour. That was the beginning of her training, and from then on she followed the instructions of the spirits.[21]

A refusal to follow the call leads to unnecessary suffering. The

South American Guajiro shamaness Graziela, for example, was asked by her helping spirits to travel with them to the other world. But she says:

> I do not like traveling to these distant places. My spirits often invite me go there, but I prefer not to go with them. Sometimes I say to them, "I do not want to go with you." Whenever I turn down such an invitation I develop a fever and become very ill. That is my punishment. Then I must chew manilla to get better again. I receive many invitations.[22]

Every sickness is an attempt at healing and every healing an attempt to escape from the everyday neurosis of ordinary consciousness so as to arrive at a more subtle and, in the last resort, superhuman form of perception. The sicknesses that arise as a result of a calling are surely the highest form of illness—a sacred illness which by its power makes it possible for mystical and metaphysical insights to arise. As we have seen, this frequently happens without regard to the feelings and wishes of the chosen one who, in most cases, is not aware of the fact that his body is undergoing an initiation. To resist such a process of transformation is a natural reaction to that which is unaccustomed, mysterious, and without limit. The initiate struggles against both his pain and suffering as well as the future social functions he will have to perform as a shaman, which all too often will deprive him of the possibility of leading a normal everyday life.

Resistance to psychophysical change and a disintegration of the normal structure of existence has always been part and parcel of the transformative process. Because of this, it forms at least a partial aspect of every rite of transformation. Rejection of the new and unknown is a standard human response. True, existence itself is change, but the leap from three-dimensional to multidimensional perception and experience is the most fundamental change. To reach a translogical form of knowledge or realm of wisdom, celestial beauty, and spiritual essence is one of the most ancient experiential goals of mankind.

The central issue raised by this chapter is therefore: Why do we have to become ill before we can accept a new insight? Why is the entry into a more comprehensive level of experience so frequently marked by sickness or, one might say, a cleansing process? Purification plays a prominent role in the life of all communities that are close to nature. While our culture attaches primary importance to physical cleanliness, other cultures still have knowledge of psychic and spiritual methods of purification which might well be compared to our psychotherapeutic techniques. We see life as a relatively uniform and continuous process marked by merely peripheral changes, whereas so-called primitive cultures tend to see personal development as a series of leaps from one mode of existence to another. This is clearly shown by the traditional rites of passage conducted not only at birth, puberty, and death but especially at the breakthrough from everyday existence to a spiritual dimension, as experienced by religious adepts—the leap from the human to the superhuman.

The important stages in a person's life are connected by periods of inner purification so that the individual, being properly prepared and in a clear state of mind, undistracted by customary thought processes and memories, may progress to a new and unburdened existence. This purification may take many forms: either purely physical such as vomiting, perspiration, fasting, pain, fever, and cleansing of the body with water, or intense psychic isolation during which the memory of the constitution of one's ego is shed; extreme exhaustion which disrupts the regular functioning of the organism and the psyche; and actual sickness which brings internal obstacles and defilements to the surface and, indeed, expels them, thereby producing a heightened sensitivity for the process of being—a sensitivity that ultimately enables the shaman to diagnose and heal the illnesses of others.

Frequently the shaman enters a patient's state so thoroughly that he himself experiences the symptoms and pains of the illness and, in this way, acquires special knowledge as to its cause. There are several reports about shamans who went so far as to take a patient's illness upon themselves in order to destroy it. In the course of their painful existence, many shamans have physically experienced countless illnesses and are therefore conversant with a wide range of physical and psychic reactions.

Modern Western medicine might consider it superfluous, even somewhat obscure or eccentric, for a healer to involve himself so intensely in the process of an illness. Nevertheless, the logic of doing so can hardly be doubted. It is based on the premise that someone who has himself experienced and overcome the pain and suffering of an illness will best be able to diagnose and effectively treat it. Western medicine, of course, rejects the image of the wounded healer, the sick doctor who has cured himself. It places too much stress on the purely technological manipulation of the patient and has therefore become increasingly alienated from the actual experience of the patient's condition.

If we wanted to summarize the effect of a long psychosomatic sickness on a shaman, we would have to say that the essential criterion lies in his talent to enter into an intensified exchange with reality, thereby transcending the material demarcations between objects and people. It lies in the very nature of the shaman to perceive the pulse of the universe in himself and others and, by going along with it, to influence and change it. His approach is based on empathy and unity with actual life-forces and therefore is inimically incompatible with the dichotomies and codified differentiations of a materialist philosophy.

A sickness that is understood as a process of purification, as the onset of enhanced psychic sensitivity giving access to the hidden and highest potentials of human existence, is therefore marked by very different characteristics than those ascribed to pathological conditions by modern medicine and psychology—namely, that suffering has only negative consequences. According to the modern view illness disrupts and endangers life, whereas the shaman experiences his sickness as a call to destroy this life within himself so as to hear, see, and live it more fully and completely in a higher state of awareness.

The symptoms of shamanic sickness are in most cases confused, undefinable, and follow no known pattern. Moreover, physical, psychic, and social reactions are closely interwoven. Particularly noticeable are forms of behavior that reject, and even deride and ridicule, accepted customs and standards. Initiates become holy fools who systematically put the world on its head or indulge in unworthy, shameless, and perverse behavior incompatible with established morality.

The fool exposes the limitations of human criteria, confronts us anew with the undefined nature of our cosmic existence, leads us backstage to make us aware of the artificiality of our cultural values, and then shows us a world without limit, because it is neither categorized nor ordered in accordance with artificial opposites. The sick jester removes these opposites, tears down external and internal barriers, and causes us to tumble head over heels from our tailor-made world of lines and demarcations into a more comprehensive and holistic dimension that has no beginning or end.

We have seen that often not only the shaman himself but his

whole family are visited by misfortune, as for instance in the case of the *kikuyu* or the Korean shamanesses. In Siberia, too, the relatives of a shaman are "sacrificed" as soon as signs of shamanic sickness appear in a member of the clan. The effects of the call to shamanism are wide-ranging, and sacrifices have to be made for that call.

The Koreans talk about a "bridge of people" (*indari*) that comes into being when a member of the family is chosen to be a shaman and another member has to die as a result of this. They refer to this process as "spanning a bridge over a human being" (*indari non-nunda*). A God has "entered into" the shaman and, in return, demands another human life. However, if the clan is willing to submit the member destined to become a shaman to the requisite ceremony of initiation as soon as the first symptoms of obsession or sickness manifest themselves, indari is not inevitable. But most families are unwilling to have a shaman in their circle, so the indari phenomenon occurs quite frequently. According to the investigations made by Cho Hung-Youn, indari occurs on average seven or eight times in every twenty cases of shamanic vocation.[23]

Frequently we find a combination of sickness and out-of-body experiences. The suffering drains the organism of its will to live, whereupon consciousness feels itself freed of the body and sheds it like a lifeless container. The dying are led to far and distant places. "There is not a single place the exact location of which I do not know," says the Zulu shaman James. Again and again we are told, "At night in my sleep I go everywhere." The Peruvian healer Eduardo flies "into the air through a hole," and Dorcas, the Zulu sangoma, leaves her body at night to fly through space.

If the near-death experience deepens, the person concerned establishes contact with supersensible entities. The journeyer enters a world which presents itself to him symbolically in many different ways: as "a house of life," a "wise old man with a white beard," or a spirit animal that transmits a new understanding of life to him. Sometimes the spirits furnish humans with a body in their own image, as is reported by the natives of the Mentawai Islands, or the bringer of life—as in the case of Lebi'd—vomits a crystal into the adept which fills him with supernatural strength.

His journeys to the Beyond often take the shaman to what he calls "the edge of the world," which we can take to mean the limits of human existence. Equipped with qualities normally found only in spirits or spirit animals, and made sacred by his contact with wise men and bringers of life, the shaman now truly has "eyes that see and ears that hear." He now has "a split soul and a split heart" or feels like "a house of dreams." The sacredness of the world has given him power and thereby has chosen him, sometimes against his own will, to act in accordance with his expanded knowledge of being and to introduce this knowledge to our human world. He has been caught by the spirits and must serve the spiritual world.

Lee Sannella

KUNDALINI: CLASSICAL AND CLINICAL

(The Kundalini) creates the universe out of Her own being, and it is She Herself who becomes this universe. She becomes all the elements of the universe and enters into all the different forms that we see around us. She becomes the sun, the moon, the stars and fire to illuminate the cosmos which She creates. She becomes the prana, the vital force, to keep all creatures, including humans and birds, alive; it is She who, to quench our thirst, becomes water. To satisfy our hunger, She becomes food. Whatever we see or don't see, whatever exists, right from the earth to the sky is . . . nothing but Kundalini. It is that supreme energy which moves and animates all creatures, from the elephant to the tiniest ant. She enters each and every creature and thing that She creates, yet never loses Her identity or Her immaculate purity.

SWAMI MUKTANANDA, *Kundalini: The Secret of Life*

P andit Gopi Krishna from Kashmir made the information about Kundalini available to large Western audiences in a general and popular form. The credit for bringing the process of Kundalini awakening to the attention of medical circles and demonstrating its practical clinical significance belongs to the California researcher Lee Sannella, M.D. He amassed ample evidence that many American patients manifest a syndrome that matches the descriptions of Kundalini awakening and signifies a distinct physiological process.

Coming from a nonscientist and representing essentially an Eastern point of view, Gopi Krishna's books made an impression only on the most open-minded researchers, who put his ideas to a solid scientific test. Sannella's work has played a very important role in demonstrating to both lay and professional audiences in the West that the Kundalini phenomenon has indeed penetrated our culture and deserves serious attention.

Sannella is a psychiatrist and ophthalmologist with special expertise in the area of holistic medicine. He also has extensive theoretical and practical knowledge of various spiritual systems. He graduated from Yale University, where in his early years as a student he was involved in scientific research, the results of which were published in the Yale Journal of Biology and Medicine. He had residencies in both psychiatry and ophthalmology and conducted scientific studies in these areas. For two years he was associate examiner for the American Board of Ophthalmology certifying examinations. During his active medical practice, Sannella held many teaching positions, and since his retirement continues to be involved in clinical work. Currently, he follows spiritual practice based on the teachings of master Da Free John.

Over the years, Sannella conducted clinical research in healing, various aspects of nonordinary states of consciousness, and energies of the body. His pioneering book, The Kundalini Experience: Psychosis or Transcendence, suggests that a wide variety of emotional and phys-

ical disturbances seen by traditional science as medical problems and diagnosed as mental or even somatic diseases are actually manifestations of a psychological and spiritual transformation that has all the characteristics of Kundalini awakening.

Sannella has also demonstrated that similar phenomena have been known in many other cultures, ranging from the high cultures of the Orient to native American tribes and the !Kung bushmen of the Kalahari Desert. The Kundalini Clinic, which he founded, is designed to offer counseling and guidance to clients involved in this process. Since Kundalini awakening is becoming one of the most frequently encountered forms of spiritual emergency, Sannella's work is an important contribution to our understanding of transformational crises.

Every spiritual tradition that is concerned with the rebirth process has its own model. Most of these are descriptions that stress the subjective side of the experience, either treating the objective signs as incidental or ignoring them. Thus, these accounts, however valid they may be on their own terms, are not helpful in making objective comparisons of different traditions. When it comes to physiological interpretations, most of these models have little relevance.

An exception is the Kundalini model from yoga. Kundalini is seen as an "energy" that usually resides "asleep" at the base of the spine. When this energy is "awakened" it rises slowly up the spinal canal to the top of the head. This may mark the beginning of a process of enlightenment.

In its rise, Kundalini causes the central nervous system to throw off stress. The stress points will usually cause pain during meditation. When Kundalini encounters these stress points or blocks, it begins to act "on its own volition," engaging in a self-directed, self-limited process of spreading out through the entire physiopsychological system to remove these blocks.

Once a block is removed, Kundalini flows freely through that point and continues its upward journey until the next stress area is encountered. Further, the Kundalini energy diffuses in this journey, so that it may be operating on several levels at once, removing several different blocks. When the course is completed, the energy all becomes focused again at the top of the head.

The difference between this final state and the initial state is not simply that Kundalini is focused in a different place, but that in the meantime it has passed through every part of the organism, removing blocks and awakening consciousness there. Thus, the entire process of Kundalini action can be seen as one of *purification* or balancing.

Just as an electric current produces light when it passes through a thin tungsten filament, but not when it passes through a thick copper wire, because the filament offers appreciable resistance while the wire does not, so also does the Kundalini cause the most sensation when it enters an area of mind or body that is "blocked." But the "heat" generated by the "friction" of Kundalini against this "resistance" soon "burns out" the block, and then the sensation ceases.

Similarly, just as an intense flow of water through a thick rubber hose will cause the hose to whip about violently, while the same flow through a firehose would scarcely be noticed, so also does the flow of Kundalini through obstructed "channels" within the body or mind cause motions of those areas until the obstructions have been "washed out" and the channels "widened." (The terms "channel," "widen," "blocks," and so on must be taken metaphorically. They may not refer to actual physical structures, dimensions, and processes, but be only useful analogies for understanding this model of Kundalini action. The actual process is undoubtedly much more subtle and complex.)

The spontaneous movements, shifting body sensations, and other phenomena reported in our cross-cultural survey, and in our own cases, can easily be interpreted as manifestations of Kundalini action. Furthermore, Itzhak Bentov has recently proposed a physiological model for Kundalini that accounts for much of what we have reported and observed. His study is evaluated in terms of our results later. Because of the objective orientation of his Kundalini model, its universal applicability, and its susceptibility to physiological interpretation, we shall adopt it as the basis for our discussions.

However, there are differences between our own observations and the classical Kundalini concept. Most notably, we observe, and several traditions report, that the energy or sensation rises up the feet and legs, the body, back and spine to the head, but then passes *down* over the face, and through the throat, finally terminating in the abdomen. This is entirely in accord with predictions from Bentov's model, but somewhat at variance with the reports of Muktananda, Gopi Krishna, and classic yoga scriptures.

Therefore we propose the term *physio-Kundalini* to refer to those aspects of Kundalini awakening, both physiological and psychological, which can be accounted for by a purely physiological mechanism. We shall refer to the physio-Kundalini process, the physio-Kundalini cycle, the physio-Kundalini mechanism, and the physio-Kundalini complex. Bentov's model describes such physiological changes that require no supernormal forces.

The slow progression of "energy-sensation" up through the body, then down the throat, accompanied by a variety of movements, sensations, and mental disturbances that terminate when this traveling stimulus reaches its culmination in the abdomen is so characteristic that we shall call it the *physio-Kundalini cycle.*

When the energy encounters a resistance, then overcomes it and purifies the system of that block, we shall say that the location of that block has been "opened." The "throat-opening" is one typical example. This gives us a terminology linked to the Kundalini concept, suited to the level of our observations, and amenable to physiological interpretation. At the same time, it preserves the full integrity of the classical meaning of Kundalini without committing us to a belief that this mythical concept is accurate to anything objectively real.

We now have two models of Kundalini: the classical yogic description and Bentov's physiological model, plus our own clinical observations. Those aspects of the process which *could* have a purely physiological basis, either that which Bentov proposes or some other, we have designated physio-Kundalini. The majority of our clinical observations fall within the physio-Kundalini category, and we have just examined to what extent they might be accounted for by Bentov's model. But the physio-Kundalini process, as we have observed it, differs from the classical yogic description in certain important respects.

Most notable of these is the pathway taken by the Kundalini "energy" or body sensation as it travels through the system. Classically, the energy "awakens" at the base of the spine, travels straight up the spinal canal, and has completed its journey when it reaches the top of the head. Along this route, however, there are said to be several "chakras" or psychic energy centers which the Kundalini must pass through to reach its goal. These chakras contain "impurities" that Kundalini must remove before it can continue its upward course.

On the other hand, in the usual clinical picture, the energy sensation travels up the legs and back to the top of the head, then down the face, through the throat, to a terminal point in the abdomen. What is the relationship between these two descriptions?

We must be aware that yogic descriptions, in addition to being dogmatic, are often very subtle. Western scientists say that the actual location of sensory perception is in the sensory cortex, even though the sensation is *felt* to be in the periphery. Similarly, the yogis might mean that the sensations, blocks, and openings (such as the throat opening) which are *felt* to be in various body parts are in some subtle way *represented* in the spinal chakras.

Still another possibility is suggested by the experience of one of Muktananda's students (in a personal communication), who says he feels energy spreading throughout his body, but especially descending from his forehead over his face to his throat, then to his chest and abdomen, *then* to the base of his spine, and *only then* into and up the center of the spine itself. He says the sensation in the spine is more subtle and difficult to perceive than that of the peripheral areas—perhaps because most of the energy has not yet entered his spine.

The time factor is also different in the classical and clinical pictures. All the characteristic elements of the physio-Kundalini complex are included in the classic description. And yet we find quite "ordinary" people who complete the physio-Kundalini cycle in a matter of months, whereas yogic scriptures assign a *minimum* of three years for culmination of full Kundalini awakening in the case of the *most advanced* initiates. Here we have the suggestion that full Kundalini awakening includes a larger complex of which the physio-Kundalini process is only a part.

It is too early to say exactly what the relationships are, except that perhaps the physio-Kundalini mechanism is a separate entity which may be activated as part of a full Kundalini awakening. Much of the problem stems from the difficulty of comparing different stages when many processes are happening concurrently. Individual differences complicate the picture. But it would be possible to clarify things by remembering the theoretical definition of Kundalini action as a *purificatory* or balancing process.

If the "impurities" or imbalances have any objective reality, it should be possible to demonstrate them with physiological and psychological tests, and to correlate their removal with specific signs and symptoms observed clinically. Since we now know that the process may be triggered and how it may be recognized in its initial stages, long-term case studies, covering the entire course of the process, are a logical next step in these investigations. They would be invaluable in documenting *specific* objective ways in which the Kundalini process is beneficial.

DIAGNOSTIC CONSIDERATIONS

Our results indicate a clear distinction between the physio-Kundalini complex and psychosis, and provide a number of criteria for distinguishing between these two states. We have seen, in some of our cases, that a schizophrenic-like condition can result when the person undergoing the Kundalini experience receives negative feedback, either from social pressure or from the resistances of his own earlier conditioning.

Evidence that these states are distinct and separate comes from two of our cases who became "psychotic" after being confined to a mental institution for inappropriate behavior. Each of them reported that during their stay in their respective mental institutions they were quite sure that they (and several of the other patients) could tell which of their number were "crazy" and which just "far out and turned on."

Possibly this is a situation where "it takes one to know one," and a person whose own Kundalini has been awakened can intuitively sense the "Kundalini state" of another. This is of special interest, as it may point to a use of such people in assisting to decide which way the balance lies between the two processes in any particular patient.

Clinicians usually have a finely tuned sense of what is psychotic. Mainly, it is this sense for the smell of psychosis that tells us if the patient is unbalanced in this way, or is, instead, inundated with more positive psychic forces. Also, there is a feeling for whether the person is dangerous to himself and others. Persons in the early phases of Kundalini awakening, if hostile or angry, are, in our experience, rarely inclined to act out.

Also, those in whom the Kundalini elements predominate are usually much more objective about themselves, and have an interest in sharing what is going on in them. Those on the psychotic side tend to be very oblique, secretive, and totally preoccupied with ruminations about some vague but "significant" subjective aspect of their experience which they can never quite communicate to others.

With our own results and Bentov's model, we have several more distinguishing features. Sensations of heat are common in these "high" states, but are rare in psychosis. Also very typical are feelings of "vibrations" or flutterings, tinglings, and itchings that move in definite patterns over the body, usually in the sequence described earlier. But these patterns may be irregular in atypical cases or in those who have preconceived ideas of how the energies "should" circulate.

With all this, bright lights may be seen internally. There may be pains, especially in the head, which suddenly arise or cease during critical phases in the process. Unusual breathing patterns are common, as well as other spontaneous movements of the body. Noises such as chirping and whistling sounds are heard, but seldom do voices intrude in a negative way as in psychosis. When voices *are* heard, they are perceived to come from within and are not mistaken for outer realities.

RECOMMENDATIONS AND DISCUSSION

Our results support the view that this force is positive and creative. Each one of our own cases is now successful on his or her own terms. They all report that they handle stress more easily, and are more fulfilled than ever before in relationships with others. The classical cases indicate that special powers, as well as deep inner peace, may result from the culmination of the full Kundalini process. But in the initial stages, stress of the experience itself, coupled with a negative attitude from oneself or others, may be overwhelming and cause severe imbalance.

Experience suggests an approach of understanding, strength, and gentle support. The spontaneous trances which disturbed one individual ceased when we encouraged him to enter a trance state voluntarily. By recognizing a distinction between "psychotic" and "psychically active," we had communicated to him an attitude that the trances were valid and meaningful. Because of our own acceptance of the condition, the patient was able to accept it.

The trances themselves ceased to "control" him as soon as he gave up his own resistance to them and the forces behind them. Similarly, another case had severe headaches, but these stopped as soon as she ceased trying to control the process and simply "went with it." The pain, in other words, resulted not from the process itself but from her resistance to it. We suspect that is true of all the negative effects of the physio-Kundalini process.

Symptoms, when caused by this process, will disappear spontaneously in time. Because it is essentially a "purificatory" or balancing process, and each person has only a finite amount of "impurities" of the sort removed by Kundalini, the process is self-limiting. Disturbances seen are therefore not pathological, but rather therapeutic, constituting a removal of potentially pathological elements. The Kundalini force arises spontaneously from deep within the mind, and is apparently self-directing. Tension and imbalance thus result, not from the process itself, but from conscious or subconscious interference with it. Helping the person to understand and accept what is happening to him may be the best that we can do.

Usually the process, left to itself, will find its own natural pace and balance. But if it has already become too rapid and violent, our experience suggests it may be advisable to take steps such as heavier diet, suspension of meditations, and vigorous physical activity to moderate its course.

The people in whom the physio-Kundalini process is most easily activated, and in whom it is most likely to be violent and disturbing, are those with especially sensitive nervous systems—the natural psychics. Many of our cases had some psychic experience prior to their arousal. Natural psychics often find the physio-Kundalini experience so intense that they will not engage in the regular classical meditation methods that usually further the Kundalini process; instead, they either refrain from meditation or adopt some form of their own devising. But much of their anxiety may be due to misunderstanding and ignorance of the physio-Kundalini process. Rather than increasing their fear, we should be giving them the knowledge and confidence to allow the process to progress at the maximum comfortable natural rate.

Much could be accomplished by changing attitudes, first around people experiencing the Kundalini, but ultimately in society as a whole. This is not just for the person's benefit, but for all of us who need models in our own spiritual search. Some other cultures are more advanced than our own in terms of their recognition of the positive value of spiritually or psychically developed people.

The trance state in Bali serves an important adaptive function for the children. In parts of Africa, trance is a social and religious necessity, required for Kundalini arousal.

In South Africa a state which Western psychiatry would probably call acute schizophrenia is a prerequisite for initiation into the priesthood by one Kalahari tribe.

Here, we must speak of the many creative people who are now suffering because of mistakes that we in the [psychiatric] profession have made in the past. We have a special obligation to make every effort to correct those mistakes. At this time in our society it could be that such charismatic and strangely acting people as shamans, trance mediums, and *masts* (the God-intoxicated) might find themselves in custodial care.

Possibly there are many now so situated who could be found and released to more positive uses among us. The problem is to recognize them among the other inmates of our institutions. Here Meher Baba's work with masts would be a useful precedent to study. If it is true that, to a certain extent, "it takes one to know one," a special and invaluable use for people who have already experienced the physio-Kundalini process would be to assist us in such a project.

There are many undergoing this process who at times feel quite insane. When they behave well and keep silent they may avoid being called schizophrenic, or being hospitalized or sedated. Nevertheless, their isolation and sense of separation from others may cause them much suffering. We must reach such people, their families, and society with information to help them recognize their condition as a blessing, not a curse.

Certainly we must no longer subject people, who might be in the midst of this rebirth process, to drugs or shock therapies, approaches which are at opposite poles to creative self-development.

These people, though confused, fearful, and disoriented, are already undergoing a therapy from within, far superior to any that we yet know how to administer from without.

Anne Armstrong

THE CHALLENGES OF PSYCHIC OPENING: A PERSONAL STORY

Our normal waking consciousness, rational consciousness as we call it, is but one special type of consciousness, whilst all about it, parted from it by the filmiest of screens, there lie potential forms of consciousness entirely different. We may go through life without suspecting their existence; but apply the requisite stimulus, and at a touch they are there in all their completeness.

WILLIAM JAMES, *Varieties of Religious Experience*

W hen the crises of spiritual opening occur under favorable circumstances and are allowed to reach a natural completion,
*they can lead to very different results. The outcome depends on the
individual's history, personality, disposition, and life situation. Sometimes, the process initiated by spiritual emergency simply enhances the
quality of existence by healing various emotional, psychological, and
physical problems, or by leading to a better self-image and self-
acceptance. Because of these changes, the capacity to enjoy daily life
increases considerably.*

*However, in many instances the successful resolution of the crisis
is associated with the emergence of some new capacity or talent. Some
people who have overcome and integrated a spiritual crisis suddenly
develop amazing artistic skills that are expressed through painting,
sculpting, writing, dancing, or original craftswork. Under similar circumstances, others can discover surprising abilities to work with people
as counselors or as healers.*

*Among the changes that occur is a distinct enhancement of intui-
tion. Various psychic phenomena are very common concomitants of the
acute phases of the process, and a moderate increase in intuitive functioning belongs to its lasting aftereffects. However, in rare instances a
transformational crisis can result in the development of a genuine
psychic gift. In this case, the intuitive abilities are so consistent and
reliable that they can be used for psychic counseling.*

*We have chosen for our anthology the story of Anne Armstrong, a
well-known American psychic whose talent emerged gradually during
several years of a challenging emotional, physical, and spiritual crisis.
She and her husband, Jim, are close friends of ours, and we have had
repeated opportunities to witness her extraordinary qualities—the unusual reliability and accuracy of her psychic insights, her humility and
modesty, her solid connection with everyday reality, and her high
ethical standards.*

*Anne Armstrong works as a transpersonal counselor and has of-
fered invaluable psychic guidance to thousands of clients from all over*

the world. The Armstrongs lead workshops in various centers in North America and Europe, where they teach participants to recognize and develop their own intuitive skills.

Personal stories are a far more immediate means of communication than secondhand accounts. Anne Armstrong's story is a unique illustration of the need to distinguish dramatic transformative and healing processes with a positive potential from mental disorders that necessitate control with suppressive medication. Her story is a beautiful example of the effective help that a sensitive and knowledgeable spouse can provide in a situation where discriminating professional assistance is not available.

It is perhaps my own experience that has made me so aware of the many people who are engaged in the process of spiritual emergence; or perhaps it is because this is the experience of a larger percentage of the population than thirty or forty years ago. When I started having what I now know to be the initial symptoms of consciousness expansion, there seemed to be no one in the helping professions to turn to for advice. We are all in the process of spiritual unfoldment—that is our reason for being. The process caught my attention when I was about thirteen years old with what was considered to be a nervous breakdown. I would like to share some of this experience because it illustrates one way the spiritual opening can occur.

Jim and I began going together when I was in high school, so I was still living at home. We frequently discussed esoteric subjects, meditation, parapsychology, and spiritual development, but because my family was Catholic there was not much I could do about it until we got married and I had the freedom to pursue a spiritual practice of my choosing. However, soon after we were married I enrolled in the spiritual development classes offered by the Rosicrucian Fellowship of Oceanside, California. I began to immerse myself in esoteric studies and to meditate twice a day. Within a few months I began to have some rather strange experiences, but since I had had some unusual ones when I was younger I did not think too much about it.

The "nervous breakdown" I had at thirteen was accompanied by vision problems and feelings of disorientation. But now I had a slightly different set of symptoms. I felt dizzy and disoriented when I walked around, but when I lay down I felt as though I were separating into two parts. I know now I was having out-of-the-body experiences. There were not any gurus or spiritual teachers in the small Utah village where we lived, no one who could explain or help me to understand my behavior.

Every time I became still or concentrated on anything, the separation would begin. It felt as though every cell in my body was speeding up. Suddenly, all would become quiet and I would find one part of me looking at some other part. It would happen at a lecture or a movie just as easily as it would sitting at home meditating. Once I got out of my body there was absolute stillness—a beautiful feeling, but I could not enjoy it because I was so frightened. I did not know if I was insane or having delusions. If I was out of my body, could I get back in? I did all the logical things; I went to medical doctors, took pills and shots. They told me I was neurotic, which I already knew, but they did not tell me I was having a spiritual emergency, or a spiritual emergence.

At some point I realized that before I started to study, think about, and meditate on the strange and extraordinary ideas that Jim had brought into my life, I had at least been functional. I had been plagued by migraine headaches since I was seven years old; I had asthma, hay fever, and then a nervous breakdown, but at least I could continue to function. So, reasoning that it was the meditation that was causing my current problems, I stopped the esoteric studies and the meditation and took up gardening and did a lot of cooking—anything to get grounded and centered. But many of the symptoms continued. I still felt as if my feet were several inches off the ground; I was nauseous most of the time, and the migraine headaches that I had had for fifteen or sixteen years became more frequent and more intense, until I lived every moment with a headache. The only medication I could take was aspirin, and that did not help much. The headaches became so intense that I thought I was going out of my mind. I was checked for a brain tumor and everything else that could cause such pain, but the doctors could find no cause.

During the next fifteen years my health got steadily worse. A rough inventory showed that I had asthma, hay fever, a goiter, conditions leading toward a hysterectomy, and almost continuous migraine headaches. As far as I knew I had exhausted all resources for getting well. The Mayo Clinic in Rochester, Minnesota, wanted to perform a couple of operations, but offered no explanations for the headaches. I was about ready to give up.

During the fifteen years since those first out-of-the-body episodes, we moved many times; finally, we lived in Sacramento, California. A new family came to live next door, and the wife and I soon found we had a common ailment in migraine headaches. One day she came in all elated—she had no more headaches! Working with a local doctor who used hypnotism, he had regressed her to a time when she had had a traumatic confrontation with her mother, and in a few more sessions her headaches were gone. Naturally, she wanted me to see her doctor and get rid of mine.

This all sounded fine on the surface, but I had read in some of the esoteric literature that you should not turn your control over to anyone, especially not to a hypnotist. To help allay my misgivings, she loaned me a short do-it-yourself book on hypnotism. One rainy Sunday afternoon I asked Jim if he would hypnotize me. He thought the headaches had finally driven me out of my mind. After he took me seriously, I explained what had happened to our neighbor, but that I did not want just anyone to hypnotize me. I trusted him and wanted him to do it. I then went on to say that I even had a book that he could read to tell him how to do it.

After reading a couple of pages in the middle of the book on "techniques," Jim proceeded to give me my first hypnosis session. It ended when I became hysterical because he asked me about some events in my childhood, but he managed somehow to return me to sanity. We tried it again after he read a couple more pages, but we could not get past the hysterical crying. So we concluded that hypnosis did not work either. Little did we know that this was a beginning, not the conclusion to the process. The following week, through a chain of interesting circumstances, we joined a local hypnosis club. In the succeeding weeks we spent all our spare time learning and practicing hypnotic skills. Then one night while I was in an altered state, Jim assured me that some part of my being knew the cause of the headaches and that all we needed was the key. Then, with a small degree of skill and a lot of luck, he regressed me into what appeared to be a past life, which for therapeutic reasons we both treated as if it were real.

It was as if I had awakened in the body of a 230-pound male, 2,000 years ago, on a torture rack in a Roman dungeon. But at the same time I was aware of "Anne." So I was able to experience myself as this huge male and still analyze the situation as twentieth-century "Anne." The man being tortured was an athlete who lived at the time of Caesar, and who had gotten involved in some political intrigue and was about to be killed because he would not divulge certain secrets.

In addition to the practice therapy Jim and I were doing at

home, I was also seeing a hypnotherapist—the hypnosis club instructor—for a couple of private sessions each week. In the succeeding weeks, both Jim and Irene (the hypnotherapist) took me backward to birth in that life and forward to death many times, trying to take the charge off the traumatic events, and to get me to identify the Roman soldier that was directing the torture.

It seemed that the most significant breakthroughs came when Jim and I were working together. For weeks I had very cleverly avoided identifying my torturer. I would describe the fancy Roman uniform from the sandals right up to the chin strap on the helmet and then jump over the face and describe the helmet with its brillant plume, but never look at the face of the Roman officer. Finally, after weeks of therapy, I identified the Roman officer, my torturer and killer, as Jim.

I do not know whether or not this was my "past life," but it was a great therapeutic tool that allowed me to say "I'm being tortured." I had always allowed everyone to run my life and would never speak up but would resent it. I felt that I had no power, that I was always a victim. Jim did not know it because I had never even hinted at my discomfort. But this gave me a vehicle to speak up, to be courageous, to be straightforward and honest for the first time in my life.

Both Jim and Irene continued with the therapy, digging deeper into this apparent past life, looking for answers. Almost immediately after identifying my torturer, and talking about it, the headaches began to become less frequent, until in about six months or less, I was totally free of migraine headaches. A few weeks after the identification of Jim as my torturer, he said to me one night when I was in an altered state, "Haven't you ever had a lifetime when you were happy?" Almost immediately I felt as if I was in the body of a petite Siamese temple dancer, performing in front of a huge golden statue of Buddha. Jim instructed me to stay in my altered state, and get up and perform the rituals that I said I had been taught since I was a small child. I chanted in a voice range that I could not even approach in my normal state; and I performed beautiful temple dances and elaborate hand rituals for the next 45 minutes, to the utter amazement of some part of me who was witnessing the whole scene. This life was also treated as real and was followed from birth to death, while we sought to reap as much wisdom as possible from the experience.

Then one day, after having tea with one of the ladies from the hypnosis class, I became the hypnotic subject and found myself in the paralyzed body of an unscrupulous Egyptian woman. She was tall, dark, and seemed to possess psychic abilities that she used to gain and maintain power. I was reluctant to reexperience this life for fear of becoming contaminated by her wicked ways. But this was the life that my therapist, Irene, chose to use for most of my therapy, probably because of the issues of good, and evil, and guilt, and the psychic abilities exhibited by this Egyptian woman.

The idea that I might be activating certain psychic abilities was never mentioned by Irene, but she very subtly started giving me books to read on the life of Edgar Cayce, the best documented psychic in the world. So the whole thrust of the therapy around this "lifetime" was to convince me that if I had actually been this wicked woman with these strange psychic abilities, I was now a moral, ethical person who would use psychic abilities for constructive purposes.

If one were to look at the psychological significance of these three "lifetimes," one might say that the life of the Roman athlete gave me an opportunity to reclaim my masculine traits of power, courage, loyalty, and strength. The petite Siamese temple dancer let me reclaim my femininity, spirituality, grace, artistic skills, and talents. And the wicked Egyptian woman impressed upon my consciousness what are the improper ways to use psychic abilities. But at the same time she let me sense the power of these abilities if used for the good of consciousness evolution.

The hypnotic induction was probably a way of returning me to the meditative state I had abandoned fifteen years earlier. Through hypnosis I had been tricked into entering a similar state, but by mechanical means. Within a couple of months I found I no longer needed to be hypnotized to do my therapy. I would just lie or sit down, close my eyes, take a couple of deep breaths, and I was ready to go to work. I continued to do intensive therapy with both Jim and Irene for about a year. At the end of that time we all realized that my health was significantly improved. The migraine headaches were gone, the goiter became dormant, I no longer needed a hysterectomy, and spring came and went with virtually no hay fever or asthma. So we knew we were on the right track.

Irene, my hypnotherapist, was aware that for many months I had more or less run my own therapy, asking the questions and getting my own answers. She was also aware that I was starting to exhibit considerable psychic talent. So one day she said, "You have been very effective in getting information helping you to heal yourself; do you think you could get information to heal someone else?" I found the very thought of it frightening. But just as an experiment, she handed me a case folder and asked that I simply hold it—not read it—and see if anything occurred to me. She gave me the client's name but nothing else. I took the folder, closed my eyes, and in a few seconds I had the feeling that there were several compartments in my head. At her suggestion I "went into" each of these compartments and described and acted out what I felt.

While in one compartment I felt and acted like a socialite, without children, and with lots of money, fancy clothes, an expensive car and home. In another compartment I became a dowdy housewife, with several children, a no-go husband, a dumpy home, and hand-me-down clothes. When I moved into the next compartment I felt like a real flirt. My whole attention seemed to be on looking for someone to seduce. The fourth compartment seemed to contain the personality of a frustrated, down-at-the-heels artist, no husband, no job, just problems.

After about 45 minutes of describing and acting out these several personalities, Irene stopped me and explained that this was the behavior of the client. In her daily life and during therapy she exhibited these and other personalities. Her frustrated husband never knew which personality she would be when he came home from work. She had tried repeatedly to seduce previous male therapists, and while working with Irene she had gone in and out of these personalities and a couple of others. Before Irene let me look at the case folder, she asked me whether I could gain any insight into why the client needed to exhibit these several personalities. She took the information I gave her and used it successfully in future therapeutic sessions.

Even though my own therapy was far from complete, Irene asked me to start working behind the scenes in her office on difficult cases. She would then use the information in her therapy with her clients. I did this for almost a year before I gained enough courage to meet clients face-to-face. Even then I always worked with my eyes closed so I would not be influenced by a client's reactions to the information I was sensing. This was the way I got started doing the transpersonal counseling that I have now done for nearly twenty-five years.

Another phase of my therapy, or training, started about a year or so after the first hypnosis session. By that time it was apparent that my awareness had moved beyond our ordinary so-called real world. It had become very obvious that I had access to information not normally available to our familiar brain/mind system. I could sense presences beyond my normal range of sight, and I could ask a question and the answer would instantly become apparent. Then one day during my morning meditation I had the feeling of such a strong presence and I received a definite telepathic communication that I was to set aside two to three hours a day for "instruction." The next day the instruction began. Again I sensed or knew the presence of some form of intelligence beyond my own. It would not be accurate to say that I "saw" anything, except perhaps the way one sees in a dream— that kind of seeing. The telepathic communication was more a sense of "knowing."

The instruction began with breath training—all kinds of exercises—each day becoming more complicated and more exacting. Next came yoga asanas. I had never even heard the word, but I instinctively knew what to do. Whenever possible, Jim did the exercises along with me. I seemed to know ahead of time what I was going to do and I would pass along the instructions. Along with this, I was given instruction on food, sleep habits, thought and emotional behavior, meditation techniques. In short, I was instructed in how to live a more productive life. Since I found nothing in these instructions that conflicted with good common sense and logic, and since my health had improved so much in the previous year, I followed the instructions. It was like having my own private guru. Irene was so fascinated when she heard about this new development that at times she would invite me to come to her office during my daily instruction period. Within a month or so the breathing patterns and yoga asanas became very complicated. Jim bought and borrowed books on yoga and pranayama just to see what instructions were being given. In most cases we could identify the process or positions.

A month or so after the yoga training started, I became very aware of a presence during the instruction. The awareness was so vivid what I could "see" every detail of the face and headdress. About 18 inches above and to the right of my head would appear this beautiful Hindu face, turban and all. He seemed to be the source of the training I was receiving. I also found that any time I needed clarification on almost any subject, I could put out my hands, palms up, and I would feel an energy surge through my body; then this beautiful Hindu would appear, and information would start flowing through my mind.

This went on for many months, and then one day I put out my hands and nothing happened. I was devastated. By the time Jim got home that night I was in a state of depression. My direct pipeline to the "Source" was gone. What had I done wrong? Jim listened to me for a few minutes and then reminded me that for months I had been receiving information from this "guru" and passing it along without taking responsibility for the content. He suggested that I go meditate on this for a while. I did. I meditated for about an hour, really looking at all the things that had happened to me in the last couple of years, all the help I had been given, and what I had done with the information that had been passed along to me. Suddenly, my Hindu friend appeared one more time, smiled as if to say, "You got the message—so long, kid," then waved good-bye and disappeared. But I felt that he had moved to some place inside my being. That may be where he originally came from.

Even though we lived in a very "straight" neighborhood (a psychiatrist on one side and a professor of philosophy on the other), people began to hear about my remarkable recovery and the interesting things we were doing. Soon a small informal group began to gather—the Friday Night Group. There would usually be random discussion until everyone arrived. We would then meditate for ten to fifteen minutes, asking that we be given information that would be useful for our spiritual growth at that time in our lives. When I was centered, and I felt the impetus, I would begin to deliver a spontaneous lecture, seemingly tailored to the needs of the group. Over the next several years, the subjects covered included esoteric teachings, food, psychology, and commentary on economic, political, and social situations, but all slanted toward how to live a more useful, productive life. I do not recall giving any information in those lectures that was obviously untrue or misleading. The esoteric material, although going beyond most texts that I have seen, was in basic agreement with classic esoteric writings, whether Christian mysticism, the Kabbalah, Tantric Buddhism, the esoteric aspects of Islam and Hinduism, or the teachings of the Mexican Yaqui Indian Don Juan.

During the transmission I was totally present, but I did little or no thinking. However, there seemed to be different levels of awareness and transmission. The lowest level occurred when I was shown something and then I would use my own vocabulary, organizational ability, and sentence structure to describe what I saw. The highest level occurred when, although I was perfectly conscious and totally aware, the words simply formed in my larynx without conscious effort. I literally would not know what the next word would be. I can remember many times saying, in effect, "now I'm going to discuss these five points . . . ," when I had no conscious idea what the first one was going to be, much less the other four. Jim would find that if this material was taken from a tape for printing, it would require little or no editing; it would be almost letter perfect. And of course there were all gradations between these two extremes.

I also found that there were all gradations of integrity in this more subtle realm. Once I submitted to a deep trance, and a hell-fire-and-damnation preacher took over for about thirty minutes. When I returned to consciousness and listened to the tape I was shocked by the religious garbage that I had given voice to. I never let that happen again. But I have found that the more I cleared up my own psychological problems, the better the quality of the lecture material became. I also believe it is for this reason that I have not had an unpleasant experience in this area for fifteen or twenty years.

I feel that humanity can obtain a lot of help from this more subtle realm if it will prepare itself to receive that help. But it takes discrimination. Material received from the psychic realm must be judged just as critically as (or more so than) that from more mundane sources. The unscrupulous entities in these etheric realms will take advantage of the personality weaknesses of the budding sensitive. Our mental institutions are full of examples. The less blatant examples are the corner psychics that will solve all your financial, marriage, sex, professional, and spiritual problems for anywhere between $5 and $250.

The intensive training that began a year or so after my first experiment with altered states of consciousness continued for about six years. In addition to the spontaneous lecture work I did with the Friday Night Group, Jim and I made ourselves available several times during the week for additional instruction. All of this training material was taped. Some was edited and printed for use by the Friday Night Group. Some has been put on cassettes, but most of it has only served as guidelines for our spiritual practice and our way of life. So Jim and I know beyond a shadow of a doubt that it is possible to reach beyond the brain/mind system and obtain information useful for one's own development—physical, mental, emotional, and spiritual.

I want to say again that this is an area for discrimination, logical examination, and skepticism. Budding psychics are not messengers from God. They are just members of the human race who for one reason or another have glimpsed a realm beyond the physical reality. Since most people want someone else to solve their problems and tell them how to live their lives, the budding psychic has a fertile field to till. So many people are just waiting to feed their egos and give them all the power they will accept. If one begins to open up psychically, the information received should be used discreetly to improve one's own life. If one becomes a significantly better person as a result of psychic/intuitive abilities, one can then consider sharing with others—if asked to share.

Keith Thompson

THE UFO ENCOUNTER EXPERIENCE AS A CRISIS OF TRANSFORMATION

They didn't touch me, but they held out their hands as if to assist me. There seems to be a platform there . . . and I'm stepping on the platform. The light's above there. And it's bright—bright, and it's got those streaks of light coming out of it. It seems like it's moving me upward! . . . The light is getting brighter and brighter . . . I'm engulfed in light . . . bright white light. I'm just standing there. It doesn't seem to hurt. It's not hot. It's just white light, all around me, and on me . . .

BETTY ANDREASSON DESCRIBING HER 1967
ENCOUNTER WITH UFO OCCUPANTS IN
The Andreasson Affair

While the existence of intelligent life outside our planet remains an open question, vivid and convincing experiences of communication and encounters with extraterrestrial beings are extremely common. They belong to the most interesting and intriguing phenomena in the transpersonal domain. It is becoming increasingly clear that they deserve to be seriously studied, whether or not they reflect objective reality.

The experiences involving encounters with extraterrestrial intelligence share many important characteristics with mystical experiences and can lead to similar confusion and psychospiritual crises. The most interesting and promising avenue of UFO research has moved away from the heated debate as to whether the earth has actually been visited by beings from other worlds, to the study of the UFO experience as a fascinating phenomenon in its own right.

Keith Thompson is an ardent student of the psychological characteristics of these experiences. He has a degree in English literature from Ohio State University and is a highly sensitive and perceptive writer exploring new developments in contemporary philosophy, psychology, psychotherapy, science, and spirituality. His articles regularly appear in the Common Boundary (of which he is a contributing editor), Esquire, New Age, Utne Reader, the San Francisco Chronicle, and the Yoga Journal. He also writes a weekly feature column for the Oakland Tribune, revolving around themes reflecting "the soul of modern science and the emerging science of the soul."

A resident of Mill Valley, California, Thompson has followed with great interest the developments in the field of transpersonal psychology, a discipline that originated in the San Francisco Bay area. He has been intrigued particularly by its broadening interface with revolutionary advances in science. His close connection with the Esalen Institute in Big Sur, California, made it possible for him to acquire knowledge of a variety of psychotherapeutic techniques.

Having completed advanced training in hypnosis and Gestalt

therapy, Thompson has used these two approaches in studying the deeper meaning of nonordinary states of consciousness, an area that for many years has been among his most passionate interests. The experiences of UFO encounters and contacts with extraterrestrial intelligence seem to him particularly challenging and puzzling. Thompson is currently writing a book, Aliens, Angels, and Archetypes, *exploring the mythic dimension of the UFO phenomenon.*

While Thompson's contribution addresses the specific problems of those who have had UFO-related experiences, the themes he develops with regard to such episodes as forms of initiation speak to all who have been touched by spiritual crisis.

Of all the difficult questions asked by people who have been up-close-and-personal with a UFO, perhaps the most perplexing, and the most common, is "Why me?" This question runs throughout Whitley Streiber's best-selling account of his abduction experience, *Communion* (1987), and Budd Hopkins' chronicle of the UFO-abductions phenomenon, *Intruders* (1987).

It is precisely this sense of having been selected for some unknown reason to carry out some unknown purpose or mission that I want to address. Through many long conversations with individuals who have chosen—quite bravely, I feel—to come to terms with their experience, I have found that the question usually manifests itself as "Have I been inducted or initiated? If so, by what or whom? Toward what end?" Lately I have been looking into anthropological data to get a better understanding of the stages, structures, and dynamics of initiation ceremonies, and to see whether it makes sense to speak of parallels between human-scale initiations and human experiences with the unknown Other called UFOs.

Here I am concerned with what people *report* about their *experience*, not about what is ultimately, objectively true. The latter is a different debate, one that would take me in a very different direction.

Adapted from a presentation made in July 1987 at the Eighth Rocky Mountain Conference on UFO Investigations at Laramie, Wyoming. This annual conference is informally known in UFO circles as "the Contactee Conference." The convener, Dr. Leo Sprinkle, seeks to provide a "safe place" where individuals who have had what they consider a "UFO experience" and UFO investigators can come together to explore the experiential dimensions of a baffling phenomenon.

My approach is phenomenological: I take as primary data *that which is reported by the UFO percipient as his or her experience.* I will leave it to others to draw inferences about the nature of the reality that underlies and causes "mere appearances." That debate invariably is populated by assumptions about what can and cannot be real, whereas in my approach I put these assumptions in brackets. This allows for exploration of UFO experiences (or UFOEs) and other extraordinary phenomena, undebauched by metaphysical biases and exclusionary beliefs about what data are important.

The intensity of the existential or transpersonal crisis that may be precipitated by a UFOE does not appear to depend upon whether a percipient feels he or she has interacted with a traditional unidentified flying object, or instead feels he or she has had a powerful "psychic," "imaginal," "archetypal," "near death," "out of body," or "shamanic" experience. The experiential authenticity of a UFOE seems largely to depend upon the extent to which the percipient experiences interaction with otherworldly beings, presences, or objects as significantly substantial and fundamentally real, even as "more real than real." If these conditions are met, neither does the profundity of a UFO-related transpersonal crisis seem to depend on whether the percipient hypothesizes the "UFO beings" to be denizens from "outer space," "parallel universes," "the collective unconscious," "heaven," "hell," or other numinous locales. It is the patterns of these accounts that I take as a starting point in exploring the initiatory nature of UFOEs.

Professor Arnold Van Gennep has defined rites of passage as "rites which accompany every change of place, state, social position, and age." Our movement from womb to tomb is punctuated by a number of critical transitions marked by appropriate rituals meant to make clear the significance of the individual and the group alike to all members of the community. Such ritualized passages include birth, puberty, marriage, and religious confirmation, including induction into mystery schools of various kinds. To which list I add a new category of experience: the UFO/human encounter, an interaction that has many structural and functional likenesses to other initiatory occasions.

Looking at what I consider the central paradox of human-alien interaction—namely, the continuing unsolvability of the UFO phenomenon by conventional means and models, coupled with the continuing manifestation of the phenomenon in increasingly bizarre forms—it is difficult to avoid the impression that the very tension of this paradox has had an initiatory impact. While the debate between true believers on both sides of the UFO question presses on with predictable banality, our personal and collective belief systems have been changing in ways that have been at once imperceptible and momentous.

Without our notice, the human mythological structure has been undergoing a fundamental shift. Public-opinion surveys and other measures of the collective pulse reveal that more people than ever now take for granted that we are not alone in the universe. The very unwillingness of the UFO phenomenon either to go away or to come considerably closer to us in a single step has been conditioning us— initiating us, if you will—to entertain extraordinary possibilities about who we are at our depths, and what the defining conditions of the game we call reality might be.

Van Gennep showed that all rites of transition are marked by three phases: separation, marginality, and aggregation or consummation. Phase one, separation, involves the detachment of individuals and groups from an earlier fixed social position or set of cultural conditions, a detachment or departure from a previous state. For example, the young male who proceeds into a male initiatory ceremony in a traditional culture is forced to leave his self-identification as "boy" at the door of the initiation lodge.

Phase two, marginality, involves entering a state of living in the margins, betwixt and between, not quite here and not quite there. Marginality (also called liminality, from the Latin *limen,* meaning "threshold") is characterized by a profound sense of ambiguity about who one really is. The young male is no longer a boy but has not yet become, through specially designated ritual, a man.

Aggregation, then, is a time of coming back together but in a new way, moving out of the margins into a new state of being. This is the consummation or culmination of the process. Now the male has earned the right to be called, and to consider himself, a man.

Joseph Campbell, easily the world's most creative and insightful mapper of mythological realms, has written a great deal about the many forms the separation phase might take. In his classic work on the universal myth of the hero's journey, *The Hero with a Thousand Faces,* Campbell writes: "A hero ventures forth from the world of common day into a region of supernatural wonder." What a magnificently succinct description of the first moments of a UFO encounter—even though, of course, UFOs are not mentioned once in Campbell's book. He speaks further of this first phase of the journey as the Call to Adventure, signifying

> that destiny has summoned the hero and transferred his spiritual center of gravity from within the pale of his society to a zone unknown. This fateful region of both treasure and danger may be variously represented: as a distant land, a forest, a kingdom underground, beneath the waves, or above the sky, a secret island, lofty mountaintop, or profound dream state; but it is always a place of strangely fluid and polymorphous beings, unimaginable torments, superhuman deeds, and impossible delights. The hero can go forth of his own volition to accomplish the adventure, as did Theseus when he arrived in his father's city, Athens, and heard the horrible history of the Minotaur; or he may be carried or sent abroad by some benign or malignant agent, as was Odysseus, driven about the Mediterranean by the winds of the angered god Poseidon. The adventure may begin as a mere blunder, as did that of the princess in the fairy tale "The Frog Prince"; or still again, one may be only casually strolling, when some passing phenomenon catches the wandering eye and lures one from the frequented paths of man. Examples might be multipled, ad infinitum, from every corner of the world.

I have taken the liberty of quoting this passage at length because I find myself captivated by the many parallels between the hero's call to adventure in mythology and the numerous examples from UFO lore of individuals summoned "from within the pale of society to a zone unknown." Many contactees open with curiosity, even excitement, to the encounter with UFO aliens; abductees are carried away against their will. I have met many people who have been "in touch" with UFO agents through what they consider some kind of blunder, or simply in consequence of going about their lives, minding their own business.

In any case, the hero (or contactee or abductee; for our purposes the terms are interchangeable) is separated or detached from the collective, the mainstream, in a powerful and life-changing way. This brings us to the quite frequent response to the Call to Adventure: the refusal of the call. Because separation from the collective is frequently terrifying, the hero often simply says, "Hell, no, I won't go," or, more accurately, "I *didn't* go."

In terms of the UFO experience, the contactee or abductee concludes (often as a way to preserve his or her sanity) that "it couldn't have been real . . . It didn't happen to me . . . It was only a dream . . . If I just keep the memory to myself, maybe it will just go away . . ." Refusing the call, writes Campbell, represents the hero's hope that his or her present system of ideals, virtues, goals, and advantages might be fixed and made secure through the act of denial. But no such luck is to be had: "One is harrassed, both night and day, by the divine being that is the image of the living self within the locked labyrinth of one's own disordered psyche. The ways to the gates have all been locked: there is no exit."

The world's great religious and philosophic traditions speak in different ways about this crucial moment, which we may describe as "wrestling with one's angel." The being or beings who guard the threshold admit of no detour; the way beyond is the way through. The numinous Other in any and all of its guises frequently demands something that seems to the initiate unacceptable; yet refusal seems impossible in this new and unfamiliar zone. The terror is often over-whelming, as Whitley Streiber writes in describing his UFO abduction:

> "Whitley" ceased to exist. What was left was a body in a state of fear so great that it swept about me like a thick, suffocating curtain, turn-ing paralysis into a condition that seemed close to death. I do not think that my ordinary humanity survived the transition.

How graphic this depiction of being forceably separated from one's deepest sense of oneself by an utterly alien agency, and left hanging in the ambiguous margins of being. Streiber's experience is common to that of many, but not all, UFO abductees.

Might we be justified in suggesting that what is at stake in human-alien encounters is a certain concept of humanity? It seems more than likely that our culture-wide ambivalence toward accepting the UFO phenomenon as real reflects a collective sense that the stakes of the game are high indeed. Meeting the gaze of the Other requires us to face Rainer Maria Rilke's painful recognition: "There is no place at all that is not looking at you: You must change your life."

As a culture—perhaps as a species—we are fatally drawn to, beckoned by, this mysterious unknown; and yet Streiber's fear is not his alone. Acknowledging the long-term existence of what Streiber calls the "visitor phenomenon" invites us to accept, in his words, "that we very well may be something different from what we believe ourselves to be, on this earth for reasons that may not yet be known to us, the understanding of which will be an immense challenge."

For those of us who have not been borrowed and maligned by aliens, the refusal of the call can be far more subtle. Many whose contact with the Other is telepathic, or characterized by visionary phenomena with mythological motifs, may find themselves at first resisting their experience by simply tuning it out. Who among us looks forward to giving up our familiar, safe sense of who we are? All of us are haunted by the presence of our Shadow, of that within and around us which refuses to be easily colonized by the avaricious focal point called ego. Yet once a certain amount of one's life is lived, it becomes harder to ignore the Other's constant coaxing for recognition, for a return to a central and active place in our lives.

The ancients knew the importance of maintaining an intimate conversation with one's double or *daemon,* called *genius* in Latin, "guardian angel" by Christianity, "reflex man" by Scots, *vardogr* by Norwegians, *Doppelgänger* by Germans. The idea was that by taking care to develop one's "genius," this spiritual being would provide help throughout the mortal human's life and into the next. Humans who did not attend to their personal Other became an evil and menacing entity called a "larva," given to hovering over terrified sleepers in their beds at night and driving people to madness.

The hero, then, moves beyond refusing to accept the call because, finally, it is impossible *not* to accept it. We choose to work with the aftermath of UFO experiences, or to walk the spiritual path, or to accept that which presents itself as a personal calling, when we realize that accepting the call is less painful than the feared ramifications of leaving the collective, the herd, or whatever one wants to describe as one's former way of being. Paracelsus wrote that each of us has two bodies, one compounded of the elements, the other of the stars. Accepting the Call to Adventure—whether in the form of "owning" one's UFO encounter or near-death experience or some other confrontation with nonordinary reality—is tantamount to deciding to inhabit one's Star Body.

Which brings us to the second, and in some ways even more difficult, initiatory phase: living in the ambiguous not-quite-here-and-not-quite-there. It is this transition between states of being that I want to focus on, simply because I believe this is a place of enormous fertility and spacious potential, even though most of us tend to experience openness and receptivity as emptiness and loss. In his classic essay "Betwixt and Between: The Liminal Period in Rites of Passage," Victor Turner writes that the major function of the transition between states is to render the subject invisible. For ceremonial purposes, the neophyte—that is, the one undergoing initiation—is considered structurally "dead." That is, classifiable neither in the old nor in a new way. Invisible—not seen.

In his book examining the details of several UFO abductions, *Intruders*, Budd Hopkins includes an extended section of a letter he received from a young Minnesota woman who reported having been abducted by UFO aliens first as a child and then again as an adult. Because this woman is so articulate in describing the existential crisis faced by abductees, I quote at length from her correspondence:

> For most of us it began with the memories. Though some of us recalled parts or all of our experiences, it was more common for us to have to seek them out where they were—buried in a form of amnesia. Often we did this through hypnosis, which was, for many of us, a new experience. And what mixed feelings we had as we faced those memories! Almost without exception we felt terrified as we relived these traumatic events, a sense of being overwhelmed by their impact. But there was also disbelief. *This can't be real. I must be dreaming. This isn't happening.* Thus began the vacillation and self-doubt, the alternating periods of skepticism and belief as we tried to incorporate our memories into our sense of who we are and what we know. We often felt crazy; we continued our search for the "real" explanation. We tried to figure out what was wrong with us that these images were surfacing. *Why is my mind doing this to me?*

This woman shows that she understands quite well the feelings associated with being rendered "invisible" by virtue of reporting an experience at variance with the possibilities allowed by "consensus reality":

> And then there was the problem of talking about our experiences with others. Many of our friends were skeptics, of course, and though it hurt us not to be believed, what could we expect? We were still skeptics ourselves at times, or probably had been in the past. The responses we got from others mirrored our own. The people we talked to believed us and doubted us, they were confused and looked for other explanations, as we had. Many were rigid in their denial of even the slightest possibility of abductions, and whatever words they used, the underlying message was clear. *I know better than you what is real and what isn't.* We felt caught in a vicious circle that seemed to be imposed on us as abductees by a skeptical society:

Why do you believe you were abducted?
You believe it because you're crazy.
How do we know you're crazy?
Because you believe you were abducted.

. . . We learned the hard way, through trial and error, whom we could and could not trust. We learned the subtle difference between secrecy and privacy. But many of us experienced a strong sense of isolation. We felt the pain of being different, as though we were only "passing" as normal. Some of us came to the difficult realization that there was no one with whom we could be our complete selves, and that felt like a pretty lonely place to be.

To summarize: many UFO contactees and abductees, along with those who have a direct, immediate, incontrovertible experience of the Mysterium, the sacred, know what it feels like to be invisible to those who have not been similarly called—or who are still refusing the call. This ambiguity is especially pronounced for those who have returned from the edge of death. Having been declared clinically dead and having floated toward a tunnel peopled by beckoning beings of light, only to return to the living with an inexplicably radiant sense of being and purpose, many near-death initiates report no longer feeling human in exactly the same way. The ambiguity is heightened when family, friends, and various authority figures discount the experience.

When I have talked informally with UFO initiates about these ideas, they invariably recognize the *feelings* of the marginal world. It is as if the neophyte glimpses something so profound that certain "facts of life" prior to the experience are no longer exclusively true. Often he or she is frustrated that others do not see that the rules of the game have changed, or that the old rules were always one of many ways of organizing perception rather than iron-clad "laws of nature."

On the other side of the frustration of life in the margins lies a perception available to those willing to enter it: not being *able* to classify oneself is also *freedom from having to* cling to a single identity. Living betwixt and between, in the realm of uncertainty and not-knowing, can make possible new insights, new ways of "constructing reality." In this sense the UFO experience serves as an agent of cultural deconstruction, prodding us to take apart easy ideas about the supposedly interminable gulf between mind and matter, spirit and body, masculine and feminine, nature and culture, and other familiar dichotomies.

Living in the ambiguities of marginality can be seen in terms of paradise lost, or else as a refreshing freedom from having to keep a particular one-dimensional sense of paradise intact. We can mourn the loss of clear boundaries, of black and white, right and wrong, us and them, or we can willingly enter the marginal, liminal, twilight realms of being, discovering face-to-face our unmet demons and angels—facing them, if we choose, as fiercely as they face us.

In short, the game can be seen as one of choosing to enter paradox and live there, or, as my friend Don Michael puts it, "landing with both feet planted firmly in midair." Much can be said about this place where fuzzy edges present not just a challenge to restore lost order but an opportunity to play in the vast polymorphous perversity of the Creative Matrix; the space where Trickster resides, part Mother Teresa, part Pee-wee Herman; where, as in the Grimm brothers' fairy tale "Iron John," the wet, hairy Wild Man discovered at the bottom of the pond is found also to have a special connection to gold. One characteristically feels a certain emptiness upon realizing how unremittingly our Judeo-Christian heritage has denied the connection between sensuous, life-affirming wildness and the experience of the sacred.

There is also a collective dimension of marginality, as the continuing borderline awareness of UFOs since the late 1940s makes clear. Whether we like it or not, our culture, human culture, is also living in the margins, on the edge, in between. Heidegger has said that we are living in the time between the death of the old gods and the birth of the new, and Jung believed UFOs to be a fundamental symbol of "changes in the constellation of psychic dominants, of the archetypes, or 'gods' as they used to be called, which bring about, or accompany, long-lasting transformations of the collective psyche."

But how are we to ground, to *real*-ize such ideas? By starting where we are—here, spanning the "crack in the cosmic egg." By definition, transitions are fluid, not easily defined in static or structural terms; and so it is with UFO initiations. Many who have had such initiations feel that they have ceased to exist. In truth, they have ceased to exist at the level that they were familiar and comfortable with. Our culture, too, has gone beyond the pale, beyond the comfort and security of Newtonian-Cartesian dualism. "No creature," said the philosopher Coomaraswamy, "can attain a higher level of nature without ceasing to exist."

People who have had a close encounter tell me they have been forced to come to grips with the idea that the world is not as simple as it seemed when they were growing up with mom and dad nearby. They have had to realize that the world is filled with enormous vistas and abysses. How does a UFO experience accomplish this? I do not know for certain, but I suspect it has something to do with having been let in on the secret, the cosmic joke; with having "seen too much," such that going back to a world of naive Newtonian atomistic thinking is no longer an honest option.

It is possible that UFOs, the near-death experience, apparitions of the Virgin Mary, and other modern shamanic visionary encounters are as much of a prod to our next level of consciousness as rapidly blooming sexual urges are a prod to a teen-ager's move from childhood to adolescence. Both represent a death of a previous naive way of being. The privilege of being young—a young person, a young planet, a young soul—is believing we can remain innocent forever. But once the threshold into the marginal, not-here, not-there realm of being has been crossed, we can avoid dying to prior identities only by taking the path of false-being, the life of denial.

It seems perfectly appropriate to me that the UFO has confounded science, academia, and governmental investigating commissions. This very jamming of our cognitive signals might be taken, if we choose to do so, as a wonderful opportunity to *stop* trying to put Humpty Dumpty together again—to begin instead clearing out the noise from the circuitry of communication, the distortions that arise from individualized, limited, ego-oriented consciousness mistaking itself for the whole. Allowing the cosmic egg to stay broken frees us to begin backing out of the garbage of profane culture, out of a way of life based on denial of a symbiotic relationship to Gaia, earth, whose continuous stream of communication we pretend not to hear, owing to the particular altered state of consciousness we call rational intelligence.

What I believe is that there is not much to be had in waiting around for an abstract "solution" to the UFO "problem," as if such a solution might ever be separate or separable from our very effort to know. We have wandered far from our birthright—the felt presence of the *mysterium tremendum*, the mystery of being that makes you shudder—and only we can turn that around. Terence McKenna puts it this way: "Gnosis is privileged knowledge vouchsafed to the courageous." Can we summon the courage to receive true knowledge?

Joseph Campbell speaks of the one who moves from ordinary reality into contact with supernatural wonders—and then back to ordinary reality again—as the Master of Two Worlds. Free to pass back and forth across the divisions between realms, from time to timelessness, from surfaces to the causal deep and back again to surfaces, the Master knows *both* realities and settles exclusively for neither. Says Campbell:

> The disciple has been blessed with a vision transcending the scope of normal human destiny, and amounting to a glimpse of the essential nature of the cosmos. Not his personal fate, but the fate of mankind, of life as a whole, the atom and all the solar systems, has been opened to him; and this in terms befitting his human understanding, that is to say, in terms of an anthropomorphic vision: the Cosmic Man.

Notice Campbell's insistence that the transformative vision is revealed "in terms befitting his human understanding." Among other things, this cautions us about the enormous ego-inflation that often attends a UFO experience, especially when channeling is involved. Precisely because the UFO vision seems absurd to ordinary, noninitiated consciousness, the experience (and the one who had it) will be ridiculed by the collective. With feelings of rejection as insult added to the injury of the reality shattering UFO experience, the UFO initiate is tempted to relieve the feeling of being rendered *less than* ordinary by pretending to be *super*-ordinary, sometimes taking on the role of a cosmic prophet who has glimpsed the new cosmic horizon.

All of us who have had extraordinary experiences should watch out for this tendency. We must bear in mind that being invisible to the culture at large can be as much a blessing as a curse—that being unregarded, ignored, and devalued can be an impetus to take another route: the quiet way. The gentle, steady, behind-the-scenes path. This is the invisible way of empowerment, the slow path of alchemy. Soul work takes time. This means we must intentionally make time, especially in our increasingly hyperactive, extroverted secular culture. The question we must ask, involved as we are in exploring extraordinary phenomena devalued by mainstream consciousness, is whether the burden of being disregarded by noninitiates is truly greater than the burden of trying to convince them that we have had an experience that, at least by implication, makes us somehow "special."

I prefer the first path, for the sense of freedom it gives from having to know what reality is all about. For as much as a UFO experience is a "wrenching" from old moorings, it also provides an opportunity to thrive outside the accepted realms of classification in our culture, to ask questions about things we once took for granted, and to gain perspective on an even larger transition than our personal one: the shift to a new way of being for humanity.

I can say I have been lucky to have met a few UFO initiates who, like those who have entered into the mystery of the sacred along other paths, have become Masters of the Two Worlds precisely because they have transcended the illusion that their experience, whether positive or negative, belongs to them, or even happened to them, *personally*. Whitley Streiber, who took his UFO experience personally indeed, admits at one point in *Communion* that when he asked his UFO captives, "Why me?" he got this answer: "Because the light was on—we saw the light."

In what would surely be a blow to *my* ego, Whitley is told that they stopped by his place not because they intended to anoint him avatar of the New Age, not even to urge him to write a best-selling confessional account of his experiences. They stopped by, rather, because he left the light burning in the living room! Here again, a wonderful opportunity to make the most of one's invisibility, to allow the UFO encounter to release new levels of ego identifications, personal limitations, and fears. "His personal ambitions being totally dissolved," writes Campbell, "he no longer tries to live but willingly relaxes to whatever may come to pass in him; he becomes, that is to say, an anonymity."

How is one to live "anonymously" in the world, with the secret of extraordinary knowledge so close at hand? Listen to the words of the religious scholar Shankaracharya on this very theme:

> Sometimes a fool, sometimes a sage, sometimes possessed of regal splendor; sometimes wandering, sometimes as motionless as a python, sometimes wearing a benignant expression; sometimes honored, sometimes insulted, sometimes unknown—thus lives the man of realization, ever happy with supreme bliss. Just as an actor is always a man, whether he puts on the costume of his role or lays it aside, so is the perfect knower of the Imperishable always the Imperishable, and nothing else.

Part Three

THE STORMY SEARCH FOR THE SELF: PROBLEMS OF THE SPIRITUAL SEEKER

Jack Kornfield

OBSTACLES AND VICISSITUDES IN SPIRITUAL PRACTICE

*Only to the extent that man exposes himself over and over
again to annihilation, can that which is indestructible
arise within him. In this lies the dignity of daring . . .
Only if we venture repeatedly through zones of annihilation can our contact with Divine Being, which is beyond
annihilation, become firm and stable. The more a man
learns wholeheartedly to confront the world which threatens him with isolation, the more are the depths of the
Ground of Being revealed and the possibilities of new life
and Becoming opened.*

KARLFRIED GRAF VON DÜRKHEIM,
The Way of Transformation

It is well known that the spiritual path has a variety of difficulties and pitfalls and that systematic spiritual practice can occasionally lead to serious psychological and even physical complications. Great prophets, sages, saints, and teachers of all religions had at important junctions of their spiritual development dramatic experiences that from a traditional point of view would be seen as psychotic.

The Buddha's visionary adventure with the master of the world's illusion, Kama Mara, and the demonic hosts who tried to prevent him from reaching enlightenment is a dramatic example of such a situation. The New Testament describes a similar episode in the life of Christ, involving his temptation by the devil. The biographies of Christian saints, fathers, and monks abound in vivid episodes of extraordinary visions involving devils as well as celestial beings.

Countless additional examples can be found in the lives of Hindu saints, Tibetan Buddhist masters, Zen teachers, and famous representatives of other religions. The most outstanding modern description of the vicissitudes of the spiritual journey is the autobiography of Swami Muktananda, Play of Consciousness. Irina Tweedie's spiritual diary Daughter of Fire and Carlos Castaneda's series of best-selling books show that the problems and pitfalls of spiritual apprenticeship are highly relevant for contemporary seekers.

In our anthology, the important problem of obstacles and difficulties of the spiritual path is discussed by Jack Kornfield. Kornfield has very special professional and personal qualifications for this task, since his background includes training in traditional Western psychology, as well as many years of spiritual practice as a monk in various Oriental countries.

He has been fascinated by Asian philosophy and culture since his early years. After majoring in Asian studies and the Chinese language at Dartmouth College, he left for Asia, where for more than six years he studied the theory and practice of Buddhism, at first as a layman and later as an ordained monk. He spent this time in Thailand, Burma, and Laos, in intensive Buddhist retreat centers and forest *monasteries, receiving much of this training in the lineage of two of the foremost teachers of Theravada Buddhism, the venerable Aachan Chah and the venerable Mahasi Sayadaw of Burma.*

After his return to the United States, he obtained a doctorate in clinical psychology from the Saybrook Institute and worked as a psychologist and meditation teacher. In following years, he has returned to Asia many times for additional studies with other teachers in various monasteries in India and Sri Lanka. During the Cambodian crisis in 1979, he did voluntary work with inmates of a refugee camp.

He is also the founding faculty member of the Naropa Institute, the first Buddhist university on the American continent, as well as the founder of the Insight Meditation Society in Barre, Massachusetts, and the Spirit Rock Center in Woodacre, California. For many years, he has led intensive Buddhist meditation retreats worldwide and has also been active as an author. Among his books are Guide to Meditation Temples of Thailand, Living Buddhist Masters, Still Forest Pool, *and* Seeking the Heart of Wisdom.

In recent years, Kornfield has established a home base in California, where he lives with his wife, Liana, and daughter, Caroline, whom he jokingly refers to as his most important guru. He has a unique and rare ability to balance and integrate deep spiritual experiences and insights with ordinary everyday existence.

In his contribution to this book, Kornfield addresses the issue of complications of meditation and the spiritual journey in general from the point of view of the Buddhist tradition, particularly the basic teachings of the Theravada school. He discusses the physical difficulties, mental hindrances, energetic states, and a common sequence of altered perceptions that arise in the course of intensive Buddhist practice. Occasionally, he makes brief excursions into Hinduism, Christian mysticism, and the shamanic traditions.

The topic Kornfield explores in his essay is extremely important in view of the increasing popularity of various forms of spiritual practice in the West and the fact that emotional and physical challenges are inherent in spiritual growth. Knowledge of the cartography of these precarious territories provides invaluable help on the spiritual path.

In this presentation I would like to address the kinds of issues and difficulties that arise for a person undertaking a systematic path of spiritual practice. To be involved in such practice is one of the deepest and most exciting, arduous, wonderful, and difficult adventures that we can take as human beings. It is a journey on which one can explore the farthest inner realms of consciousness, awaken to the myriad parts of oneself, and bring mind and heart as far as they can reach into our deep connection with the whole of the universe.

However, it is not necessarily an easy or gentle journey. I heard a story about Chögyam Trungpa Rinpoche, who, while giving a talk in Berkeley once, sat up in front of a large hall filled with people who had all paid fifteen dollars to see him, and said to them, "How many of you are just beginning a spiritual practice?" A number of people raised their hands. He said, "Fine. My suggestion is that you go home. At the back door, they will give you your money back and you can go home now and not get started in this very difficult and terrible process." He continued, "It is a lot more difficult than you know when you begin. Once you start it is very difficult to stop. So my suggestion to you is not to begin. Best not to start at all. But if you do, then it is best to finish."

For it often happens that people, in their spiritual practice or in the course of everyday life, encounter phases of their inner development in which things fall apart.

Of course these "crises" are experienced not just by people undertaking systematic spiritual practice, but also by many persons who in the course of their lives have a natural spiritual awakening. They can be brought on by many things, such as death of an important person, childbirth, a powerful sexual experience, or having a near-death accident and realizing through an out-of-body experience that you are not this physical body. At other times, they can be triggered by the illuminations that come through spending time in the high mountains or through a difficult divorce or some life-threatening illness like cancer.

In all of the great spiritual traditions there is attention given to the problems or pitfalls of spiritual practice. In the Christian tradition one of the great texts available is *The Dark Night of the Soul* by St. John of the Cross, in which he talks about the dark night that one goes through after the initial awakenings into the Light. Evagrius, who writes in Latin as a teacher of monks in early Egypt for Chris-

Revised version of a talk in the monthlong seminar entitled "Jewel in the Lotus: Buddhism and Western Psychology," coordinated by Stanislav and Christina Grof and held at the Esalen Institute in Big Sur, California, November 1986.

tian Desert Fathers, has a whole text on the demons that arise when people go off in the desert to become hermits and undertake a meditation practice. These include the demons of pride, the demons of fear, the demons of thirst, the noonday demon who is the demon of sleep, and so forth.

In Eastern traditions there are similar descriptions of the kinds of pitfalls that arise—the initial difficulties, the pitfalls of attachment, the pitfalls of false enlightenment. In Zen, the visions and the lights that come are called *makyo,* or illusion. They are a kind of superillusion: this in which we already sit and experience is considered a kind of illusion, and *makyo* is an illusion beyond that.

How does one begin to look at the pitfalls and the difficulties? I would like to begin to answer this by briefly presenting some of the basic Buddhist teachings that talk about the early pitfalls and difficulties in practice. This will be an overview, without much detail, since more specific information is available in current Buddhist literature, especially through the writings of Joseph Goldstein, Stephen Levine, and Tibetans like Chögyam Trungpa Rinpoche. Let us look briefly at how to deal with early hindrances and physical pain in the body, and then move into the more extreme, delightful, and terrifying kinds of visions and states and difficulties that occasionally arise for people in more intensive or advanced spiritual practice.

When one begins a spiritual *sadhana,* whether it is Buddhist meditation practice or some other systematic discipline that trains awareness and concentration, it brings one into the present. This is the first element of any spiritual practice, a technique that focuses and steadies the fluctuating, vibrating mind.

To come into the present moment is the first entry into the spiritual realms, because the spiritual realms are not found in the past and the future. The past is just memory, and the future is just imagination. The present moment provides the gateway to enter into all the realms of consciousness that are beyond our normal everyday busyness. To be here requires a steadying of the mind, a concentration, and an attention. It is that old phrase from the Las Vegas casinos: "You must be present to win." You have to be present at the casino, and you have to be present in your meditation practice.

To start, then, one undertakes the discipline, following the breath, doing a visualization, doing a loving-kindness meditation, one of many kinds of practices that focus and develop our attention. This brings us more fully into the present of our body and mind. As we pay attention, what begins to happen? First of all, there are physical difficulties that arise in the body. There are three categories of pain that arise.

There are the physical pains that are a signal that you are sitting in the wrong way, so you have to find a way to sit comfortably. Then there are the physical pains that arise out of an unaccustomed posture. Our posture has to be stretched out and borne with, allowed, until the knees and the body and the back get used to meditating in a way that is still, where we can allow the body energies to open without too much movement. This is a steadying and bringing together of the body and mind.

The third and most interesting kind of pain that arises is the pain of various releases of tension and holding, a surfacing of the deep patterns of blocks and bound energies in our body that accumulate during the reactions of our daily life. Each of us has areas of holding: our jaws, our neck, our face—whatever it is that becomes tight and accumulates tension in stressful situations. Through the stillness of sitting, these patterns of energy or holding come into awareness or consciousness. As they release, they can bring pain and vibration and sometimes also powerful images from the past. These may be images of surgery or accidents, or times that we got angry and squashed it inside, times of past wounds or even past lives. All kinds of past situations will arise and manifest themselves through the opening of the body.

Most people who have sat for even a day are familiar with these various kinds of physical pains. One of the first parts of practice is to learn how to sit comfortably still and be steady with these physical openings. Beyond the initial physical openings there arise hindrances, or the difficult states of mind that come as one starts to concentrate. To collect or steady the mind—which is initially like a wild monkey, or like a fish that is out of water, flopping around on dry land—is a difficult process. You give it a very simple task: "Mind, please follow the breath." Does it listen? For about two seconds. My daughter, who is a year and four months old, behaves better than my mind, generally speaking, and she is in the phase now where she says, "No, no, no" very often. She will even get up in the middle of the night, kind of roll around, half awake, rustle the covers a little bit and say, "No, no, no, no," and then go back to sleep.

The mind is worse than that, if you have noticed. It is untrained for decades, for millions of mind moments, if not many lifetimes. The process of beginning to collect it is an arduous one. It requires a breaking of our habit of being lost in the past and future. It requires a willingness to be present with experiences from which we usually run away. Five of the common difficulties that arise in practice, called by the Buddha the five hindrances, are written about in many books. A good description of them is found in Joseph Goldstein's *The Experience of Insight*. These five hindrances are quite familiar to all those who have been sitting.

The spirit of working with the hindrances is illustrated in the story of G. I. Gurdjieff's disciple. There was an old man in his community who was difficult for everyone to live with. He was obnoxious and noisy and smelly and a troublemaker and argumentative. Finally, after many months of arguing with the other community members, he got discouraged and quiet and left to live alone in Paris. Gurdjieff, when he heard about this, went directly to Paris, found him and convinced him to come back, but only by offering him a great deal of money, a big monthly stipend. Whereas everyone else paid for their practice, this man was getting paid to return. When they saw him return and found out he was actually being paid for it, the community was quite upset. They said: "What are you doing?" Gurdjieff explained: "This man is like yeast for bread. Without him here you would not really understand the meaning of patience, the meaning of loving-kindness or compassion. You would not learn how to deal with your own anger and irritation. So I bring him here and you pay me to teach and I pay him to help."

The practice of working with our blockages and hindrances is to allow them to arise and to observe them with awareness. We use the opportunity to learn directly about anger, fear, and desire, to learn how to relate to them without being so identified, without resisting, without being caught up in them. It takes quite a bit of practice to do so.

In order to work with the hindrances we must identify them clearly. The first is *desire* and *wanting*. The second is its opposite, which is *aversion*—anger and dislike, judgment and fear—all those states that push away experience. The next pair is *sleepiness, dullness,* and *lethargy,* or resistance to experience, and their opposite, which is *agitation* and *restlessness* of mind. The fifth is *doubt,* the part of the mind that says, "I cannot do it. It is too hard, I am too restless, it is the wrong day to meditate. I should wait to meditate. I should wait until evening. Morning is not a good time. Maybe I should do something a little more entertaining like Sufi dancing. This watching the breath is too boring or too dull."

As we begin working with the hindrances, we actually study

them, observing and allowing them to be incorporated into the meditation practice. When desire arises, we begin to examine desiring mind with mindfulness. We note, "Desiring, desiring," and feel its quality. To look at desire is to experience the part of ourselves that is never content, that always says, "If only I had some other seeing, hearing, smelling, tasting, touching, feeling, that would make me happy, some other relationship, some other job, some more comfortable cushion, less noise, cooler temperature, warmer temperature, another meditation shawl, a little more sleep last night, then I could sit well." All these things come as desire. "If only I had something to eat now. I would eat and then I would be satisfied and then I could get enlightened."

Our way of working with desire is not to condemn it but to turn the attention to the state of mind of desire, look at it and experience it, and label it "hunger, wanting." In this way we can learn to be aware of mental states like desire fully without being so caught up by them, and find a way to observe with the full freedom of our attention. This brings real understanding.

Similarly in working with anger, aversion, or fear. We may have to watch fear eighty times before it becomes familiar to us, or even a hundred or two hundred times. But if we sit and every time fear comes, we note, "Fear, fear," and let ourselves be mindful of the trembling and the coolness and the breath stopping and the images and we just stick with it, one day fear will arise and we will say, "Fear, fear, oh, I know you, you are very familiar!" The whole relationship to the fear will have changed, and we will see it as an impersonal state that comes on the radio for a while and passes away, and we will be freer and wiser in our relationship to it.

This may sound easy, to just observe with a balanced and soft attention, but it is not always so. There were some therapists at one long California retreat I taught who were schooled in the primal-scream tradition. Their way of practice was one of release and catharsis, and they usually set a period aside every morning to release and to scream. After sitting for a few days they said, "This is not working, this practice." I asked, "Why not?" They replied, "It is building up our inner energy and our anger and we need a place to express it. Could we use the meditation hall at a certain hour of the day to scream and release? Because otherwise it gets toxic when we hold it in."

The suggestion that we made was that they go back and sit with it anyway, that it probably would not kill them. We asked them to sit and see what happens since they were there to learn something new. They did. And after a few days they came back and said, "Amazing." I said: "What was amazing?" They said: "It changed!" Anger, fear, desire—all of these things can be a source of wisdom when they are observed, because as we observe them, they come according to certain conditions. They come, and when they are here, they affect the body and mind in a certain way. If we are not so caught up in them, we can observe them like we would a storm, and then, after being there for a time, they pass away.

When we become skillful at observing these hindrances and look carefully and closely, we find that no state of mind, no feeling, no emotion actually lasts more than fifteen or thirty seconds before it is replaced by some other one. But we must look really closely to see this. We might be angry, and then, if we really watch it, "angry, angry," then all of a sudden we discover or realize it is no longer anger, it has now turned into resentment. The resentment is there for a little while and then it turns into self-pity. Then we observe the self-pity and it turns into depression, and we observe the depression for a little while and it turns into thinking, and then that turns back into anger. If we look we see that the mind is constantly changing, and it teaches us about impermanence, movement, and no need to identify.

Similarly, when sleepiness and restlessness arise, one observes them with the eye of awareness and the heart of tenderness and of caring. It is important to allow those to arise, to see sleepiness, to discover its nature, or if resistance is a part of it, to just sit and say, "What is going on here that I put myself to sleep about?" See if you can wake yourself up to it.

The same with restlessness. If you are very restless, you note, "Restless, restless," feel it, and if it is very strong, you allow yourself to surrender and say, "All right, I will just die. I will be the first meditator ever to die of restlessness," and let it take you over and see what happens.

Through systematic training with the hindrances, you discover a way of relating to them wisely and with less identification, without being so caught by them. And finally the same for doubt. You can learn to observe it come and go without identification or concern.

For your further information, there is also a series of antidotes for these hindrances. For desire, there is an antidote of reflection on impermanence and on death. For anger, there is an antidote of loving-kindness that can be done, but only at the completion of a certain degree of forgiveness. For sleepiness, the antidote is to arouse energy through posture, visualization, inspiration. For restlessness the antidote is to bring calm or concentration through inner techniques of calming and relaxing. And for doubt the antidote is faith or inspiration through reading or speaking with someone wise or finding some way to inspire oneself.

This is a brief account of the common hindrances you may encounter when you begin practice. If you do not have training and skill to help work with these, they can seem overwhelming and too difficult and you may want to stop. This is why we need a teacher and systematic training to begin to work with our minds: our minds and the forces we encounter there can be very confusing.

In the beginning of Buddhist practice one hears the basic roots of human difficulty expressed as "greed, hatred, and delusion." These are what get us into trouble. We may say, "Oh, just our desire and aversion, our dislikes and ignorance, and a little bit of unclarity of mind. That is not too bad." Once we have sat for a while, what we discover is that greed means confronting attachment in the deepest sense, that our desires are powerful and primal kinds of forces, and that hatred is discovering a rage within us like Attila the Hun and Hitler. All of these are found in each person's mind. Greed is like the hunger for the world, the deepest kind of hunger. Delusion is the darkest kind of confusion and ignorance.

These forces are tremendously powerful. They are the forces that make war in the world. They are the forces that create poverty and starvation in one country and abundance in another. They are the forces that cause the whole cycling of what is called the samsaric world of life and death to take place. So one encounters them when one tries to live in the present moment with concentrated attention.

It is not an easy process to work with them. It is always difficult, but at times it seems overwhelming. Yet here is where we learn. Thomas Merton said at one point, "True prayer and love are learned in the hour when prayer becomes impossible and the heart has turned to stone." Sometimes in facing the most difficult of your hindrances, if you let yourself sit with them, will come a real opening of the heart. A real opening of the heart, the body, and the mind takes place, because we finally stop running away from our boredom or our fear or our anger or our pain.

In addition to the descriptions of the five hindrances, Buddhist teachings also offer the following five systematic ways of working with difficult energies when they arise. For the sake of this essay, I will mention them, but without extensive elaboration.

The first way of working when something difficult arises—like strong desire, fear, or anger—is to just *let it go*. Or if you cannot let it go, *let it be*. To "let be" is a better expression of letting go anyway, because usually when we hear "let go" we think of it as a way to get rid of it, but we cannot really just get rid of it. To do so is adding more anger; it is saying in effect, "I don't like it." But that is like getting rid of your own arm; it is a part of us in some way. So instead of letting go, letting be means to see it as it is—clearly. There is fear, there is anger, there is joy, there is love, there is depression, there is hatred, there is jealousy. There is something else that is yucky. There is judgment about it. Then there is self-pity, then there is delight. They are just different states of mind. It is the mind, the universal mind that has all of these things, and our task is to learn to relate to the mind in a compassionate and wise way.

The second step, if we are unable to let it be, is to *sublimate it*. This means to take the energy of our difficulty and transform it outwardly or inwardly. For example, in working with anger outwardly we might go out and chop the winter's wood as a way to transform and use the energy. Similarly, for inward transformation there are exercises for moving energy within the body, from a place where it is caught to a more useful expression. For example, the energy of lust and of obsessive sexual desire can be moved inwardly up into the heart, where it becomes an energy of desire for connection, but through compassion or caring. The inner transformation is more difficult.

A third way of approaching difficulties is the appropriate use of *suppression*, which is tricky, but can be very useful at certain times. An example given is of a woman who is a surgeon, and this woman is having a fight with her husband, and her beeper goes off; it is time to go directly to the hospital emergency room. At that point, she is needed to do cardiac or thoracic surgery. That is not the time for her to continue processing what is going on with her husband. It is a time to put it aside and do her surgery, and only later on, when the circumstances are suitable, to go home and continue the dialogue that needs resolution.

So there are suitable times in spiritual practice to suppress or put aside very difficult energies and wait for a circumstance that is quiet or supportive. This might be a quiet period or work with a teacher or a therapy session—using whatever can help us to deal with it in a skillful or wise way.

Additional ways of dealing with difficulties are to explore them through imagination or to mindfully act them out. These practices get more difficult and more Tantric as we go down the list, because if they are not done with careful attention, it is possible to create more desire or give more power to the anger. The fourth way, *to act them out in imagination,* requires a full and careful attention to do it properly. Here you allow yourself to envision the action fully with all its consequences. For example, with anger, you would see yourself biting or hitting, or with greed you would visualize yourself fulfilling that desire, whether it is sex, food, love, or whatever. Get abundance of it and imagine what it is like and then see where you are after you have had your fill. By actually allowing and exaggerating these feelings you can then learn what it means to be released from them.

The fifth way is the most Tantric on this list. That is *to act out the mind state.* Of course, in a way that is what we do most of the time anyway. But here it means "Act it out with awareness, with attention, with mindfulness, so pay attention to driving, to paying bills, or to the people around." It is a frequent and a sincere difficulty for people, and it needs to be discussed.

It is addressed primarily through grounding, and through practices that bring our attention more fully into the body and awaken the lower chakras. One has to do more walking and other physical exercises and bring attention into the belly, rather than having it up in the head, eyes, or nose. Otherwise practice becomes heady, visionary, mental, and one-sided. It is extremely important to integrate the "higher" chakras and states into the body and feelings of this physical incarnation.

This *mental/physical imbalance* is a common phenomenon, even for people who are relatively balanced in practice. A very balanced meditator may require just a few days' integration period. But whenever we take a concentrated and intensive inner journey in a retreat, we have to build into the system a reentry process, and a way to integrate the experiences, either as we go along or at the end.

A second kind of difficulty that arises is *an inability to make decisions.* Many people who have done some spiritual practice tend to lose their ability to remember things and develop an increasing inability to make decisions. In the extremes, they can become "spiritual basket cases"—pushovers, weak, and indecisive. The thinking may go: "Oh, well, it is all happening, and we will just wait and see what the Lord provides for us." They are unable to act and live in terms of work, family, and relationships, or answer questions such as "Where should I go?" or "What should I do next?"

This happens for a couple of reasons. One is because there is a disorientation when we spend time in a retreat setting or ashram or even at home doing a lot of meditation, since our attention is not on the world, but on some other set of experiences and references. Secondly and quite significantly, spiritual practice can often genuinely undermine worldly motivation. We set our motivation to look for the discovery of how the consciousness can grow, or how to develop the mind and feelings of universal love. While all these things are your focus, your motivation to get a job is turned down; you have turned down the heat, the interest in worldly things.

There arises an alternate set of values that brings many students into conflict when they reenter the world. We have to see if in fact we want to ordain or renounce the world and live in a monastery. If not, we have to come to terms with the difficult task of what it means to live in the world in a spiritual way. That again is a part of the natural course of spiritual practice and the kind of difficulty that people have to work with in their path and understand in themselves.

The third difficulty arises because *the thought processes will stop* when we get concentrated. And when the thinking process slows down, because it is the basis for comparison used in making decisions, it is even hard to think straight. Without it we feel empty or confused and unable to actually decide anything.

The fourth difficulty is that as we learn to develop an even-handed attention, our minds come to a state that *neither grasps at the pleasant nor resists the unpleasant,* which is the balanced kind of awareness needed for inner exploration. Yet it is different from the kind of attention that is needed to decide career plans or a marriage choice or how to take care of our house or our car. That is a second kind of attention, called "directed or skillful means," a wise reflection or a wise action, often not strengthened (or even weakened at times) by meditation.

The kind of attention that one develops in inner meditation is more of a passive attention where the active component is simply the brightness of your observation or investigation, but does not include the active component of choosing or deciding.

The way to work with these difficulties as they arise is to develop grounding in practice. There are many exercises and ways of meditation that can bring us back and connect us to our bodies and to the earth-plane. This also requires a willingness to look at our attachments and to realize that unless we are going to choose to live as monks or nuns, we have to come back and integrate our lives in the world. It means we must start our thinking mechanism going again, reflect about our life—looking at money, looking at the particular needs of our society and how we are going to live in it. At first, the process of dealing with these things when the mind is quiet may seem actually somewhat painful. There is an actual reentry through a domain of dizziness and the pain of accepting that we are limited beings in a physical reality, which must be faced for the heart to open and the mind to be able to fully come back into the world.

Another difficulty in leaving retreats or after powerful inner practice arises for those who discover that they have used practice as a way of escape, as a way of denial or suppression in their life. Many students have used meditation not only to discover inner realms and find inner balance but also to escape. Because we are afraid of the world, afraid of living fully, afraid of relationships, afraid of work, or afraid of some aspect of what it means to be alive in the physical body, we run to meditation. Whoever has practiced for a while will probably have seen some element of that in his or her own heart and mind.

We must understand that meditation, like any kind of therapy or discipline, can be used in skillful ways, for freedom, for liberation, for opening the heart. It can also be used in defensive ways, in service of the ego and of our fears, by quieting ourselves so we do not have to deal with certain difficulties, by following our breath in a way that we do not even feel certain difficult emotions, by paying attention to the light so that we can avoid certain aspects of our shadow, our dark side.

There is a brilliant exposition of how spiritual practice can be misused to bolster our ego or to create a new improved self-image; it is all clearly spelled out in the book *Cutting Through Spiritual Materialism* by Chögyam Trungpa Rinpoche. In outward ways, through emotions and especially through attachment to new views and ideals, we may unconsciously do an imitation of spirituality, using its forms and meditations and beliefs as a place to hide or seek security from the ever-changing world.

As we mature in our practice, we have to bring to consciousness and face the ways in which we have tried to escape or imitate or hide if we wish to come to a fuller sense of freedom. Those who do not face this after some period of practice may become stuck, chronic meditators who are inwardly depressed, because the real growth process has stopped, yet on the outside they follow the forms and ideals of practice and pretend to be fulfilled in it. These issues need investigation and heartfelt integrity to open us again to the growth of real spiritual opening.

Each person will also bring his or her neurotic style to practice. In Buddhist psychology these are described based on the three root types of greed, aversion, and confusion, while in other systems other neurotic categories are outlined. Again, to avoid this pitfall, we must become aware of our basic neurotic style so that it does not become a trap for us in practice.

Otherwise, greed types will find themselves being greedy for spiritual experiences, spiritual knowledge, spiritual friends, form, and ceremonies, not seeing the neurotic aspect. Similarly, aversion types who ordinarily dislike experience may use practice to condemn and try to escape from the world or as a way to judge many other ways as wrong. Confusion types have a danger of getting stuck in doubt or in its opposite, "blind" faith, which brings relief but does not serve as an illumination for them. We should also understand that each of these traps presents great possibility for inner development, as well as danger. Every neurotic style can be transformed into useful positive qualities through the development of our awareness. Many of the best books on Tantra describe this process.

Still, it is common for us to encounter ways in which meditation is used for escape or misinterpreted to strengthen our fears and isolation. We are taught that there arises through meditation practice the divine qualities of *loving-kindness, equanimity, sympathetic joy, compassion.* Yet these all have near enemies that come in disguise close to them, and so there is a systematic teaching of how to recognize these and not get caught up in them.

The near enemy of loving-kindness is *attachment.* When it arises, it masquerades as loving-kindness, but actually it is a state of being caught in wanting or desiring some events or people rather than loving them. There arises a sense of separation, and thus we feel "I need you" rather than openly loving that person or thing or experiencing it exactly as it is.

Similarly, the near enemy of compassion is *pity,* which says, "Oh, those poor persons over there, they are suffering," as if somehow they are different from ourselves. It separates us, whereas true compassion sees that we all are in the soup together, that we all suffer universally, we are all a part of the heart of the mother of the world and that, like the mother of the world, each of us is endowed with a certain measure of cosmic pain. Each one of us has a certain amount of suffering. That is part of what it means to have a heart, to be alive. And we are called upon, it is said, to meet this in joy instead of self-pity, to learn how to relate to it with opening rather than with fear.

The third near enemy is the near enemy of equanimity, which is called *indifference*. Indifference says: "I don't care; I will stay calm in myself and forget about the rest. It is all 'empty' anyway. If one marriage does not work out, I can marry somebody else. If this job does not work out, I can get another one. I am not attached." You have probably heard that tone or that phrase. It is not equanimity but indifference. Each one of these three near enemies masquerades as love or compassion or equanimity, but each is based on separation, on ignorance, and on fear.

True spiritual practice and true equanimity are not a removal from life, but a balance that relates totally and fully to life. In practice, one opens the body and mind and heart and in a way becomes more transparent, able more fully than ever to receive life with balance. Spiritual opening is not a withdrawal to some imaged realm or safe cave. It is not a pulling away, but a touching of all the experience of life with wisdom and with a heart of kindness, without any separation.

At this point, we have learned to deal with the preliminary difficulties in our practice. We can deal with pain, we know the difference between equanimity and indifference, and we have learned how to work with the hindrances. They have not gone away, mind you; they are there for a very long time. Even when I ask a group of quite advanced students, "What are the difficulties you are working with?" they inevitably answer: "Laziness, fear, greed, anger, delusion, self-judgment"—the same old stuff. The advanced and the beginners, it seems, are the same. When you have gotten better, you learn how to relate to it more wisely, but it is a very long time before it stops arising.

Still, at this point the heart and mind are calmer and better able to relate wisely and mindfully to what arises in the present. Then we may decide to do further practice. To undertake this journey requires a foundation of virtue, an establishment of basic morality, of non-harming. The traditional Buddhist precepts are five: (1) not killing, (2) not stealing, (3) not speaking falsely or with words that are gossip, undermining, or untrue, (4) refraining from sexual misconduct, from sexual activity that causes suffering or harm to another person, and (5) refraining from intoxicants that lead to the point of heedlessness or loss of awareness. We have to see that practice is not separate from our life, and we have to examine our life for the areas of conflict and unconsciousness. A powerful means of establishing our life in ways that are in harmony with the world around us is through the precepts of nonharming other beings. Otherwise our minds will be filled with conflict, guilt, remorse, and complexity. To follow the precepts is a way of stabilizing the heart and not harming ourselves, as well as not harming others. There are many important teachings about how to employ moral training precepts to develop awareness and a loving, reverent relation to life.

Without these precepts as a safeguard one cannot undertake the spiritual journey in a deep way. Some of the pioneers in recent Western spiritual practice, particularly some of those who used psychedelics and other powerful means, had times when they really got in trouble because they did not understand the ground of these precepts, of not harming others or oneself through wrong speech, through wrong action, through misuse of sexuality or intoxicants. These ways of conduct are the basis for quieting the mind, they are the basis for living a life that is in harmony with the plants and the animals and the planet around us. They become the basis for disconnecting ourselves from the most strident powers of greed, hatred, and delusion. Almost all occasions when we would break such a precept arise when the mind has become filled with one of these forces of greed, hatred, and delusion, often beyond our own wishes. The precepts are a source of consciousness whenever this happens. The foundation for safely going further in spiritual practice requires then that we take care of our words, our actions, our sexuality, our use of intoxicants.

A second understanding that is a foundation for further practice is the realization that practice may initially be used to create a sense of well-being and delight, of spiritual ease and pleasure in our life. But there are two levels to spiritual practice. The first level is that in which we quiet ourselves, do some yoga, open the body, do a few breathing exercises, "aum" before dinner, hold hands with people, and follow a simpler, more moral life. All of those things—developing virtue, living a moral life, and quieting and concentrating the mind—lead us to delight and joy. They lead to happiness and harmony in our lives.

The second kind of spiritual practice, the next level, is undertaken by those who are interested in practicing for the sake of liberation, for the sake of the deepest kind of freedom possible for a human being. And this level of practice has nothing whatsoever to do with happiness or comfort in the normal sense.

One begins with virtue and concentration and calming and a softening of the body and an opening of the heart and the development of loving-kindness. But then when we are ready to go deeper, it means to open the whole of the inner world. What this requires of us is a willingness to face pleasure and pain equally, to open, to touch what Zorba called "the whole catastrophe" and to look directly into the light and the shadow of the heart and the mind.

Suppose we wish to do that. We have already learned how to work with the hindrances, we have our virtue and our actions in the world intact as a basis for practice, we have begun to concentrate the mind and not be so caught up in restlessness and fear and desire, we have learned to pay attention and be more fully in the present moment. What happens next?

What often happens next is that concentration will really start to develop, and with further training the mind starts to get steadier on the meditation object—the breath or the visualization or the light or whatever. As this steadiness of mind builds, it becomes the gateway through which most of the spiritual realms start to emerge.

As concentration develops, a great variety of so-called spiritual experiences can begin to happen. Many are, in fact, just side effects of the meditation, and the better we understand them, the less likely we are to get stuck in them or confuse them with the goal. Let us consider what may arise with the development of stronger concentration.

First of all, for many people there will arise *rapture*. Rapture has five traditional levels or grades to it. While rapture arises for many people, it tends to be more common on intensive and long retreats, ten days or longer, although for some people it comes in their daily practice as well. It does not arise for everybody, nor is it necessary to find rapture before wisdom. But at certain points in many people's practice, there arises rapture.

This process often involves trembling and even powerful, spontaneous releases of physical energies in the body, called *kriyas*, that can be scary to people. These can come in many different forms. Sometimes they appear as a single, involuntary movement, or as a release of a knot or tension. At other times, they can take the form of dramatic, complex movements that can last for days. I remember sitting for a one-year retreat as a monk, meditating by sitting and walking alternately each hour for about eighteen hours a day in a

Thai monastery. At one point a very powerful release came and then my arms started to involuntarily flap like I was a chicken or another bird. I tried to stop them and I could barely do it, and if I relaxed at all they would flap. So I went to the teacher. He said: "Are you being aware of it?" I said, "I sure am." He said: "No, are you really being mindful? You do not like it. You want it to go away." I said, "You are right." He said, "Go back and just observe it." For two days I sat there, watching my arms flap.

It is important to understand and respect how deep our patterns of holding are. There are very profound kinds of releases and openings in the body that take place over months and years in spiritual practice. Some of the deepest kinds of bodywork take place as we sit silently and the energy of our body system opens and balances itself.

Many other kinds of raptures can arise, such as pleasant kinds of thrills through the body, vibrations, tingling, or prickles. Sometimes it is as if ants or some other kind of bugs were crawling all over you; at other times you feel very hot, as if your spine were on fire. This can alternate with feelings of cold, beginning as a little bit of chill and turning into very profound, deep states of cold. You might also see various colored lights; initially, these are blues, greens, or purples. Then as concentration gets stronger there arise golden and white kinds of light and finally very powerful white light. It might be like looking right into a headlamp of an oncoming train, or as if the whole sky were illuminated by a brilliant white sun. Or your entire body may dissolve into light. These are some of the grades of rapture that arise, not just for yogis, but for Westerners who do intensive practice. It is not uncommon for people who get skilled in concentration to have these experiences.

There also can arise a whole series of strange altered perceptions. For example, the body may seem very tall or very short. You may feel that you are heavy like a stone or being squashed under a wheel. Or you may feel that you are floating and you have to open your eyes and peek to make sure that you are still actually on the ground. This has happened to me many times.

There are similar experiences when you are doing walking meditation. One can walk and be so concentrated on the steps that it appears that the whole room begins to sway as if you were on a ship in a storm; you put your foot down and you feel like you are drunk or moving. Or there is dissolution and everything starts to sparkle and turns into light.

All these kinds of things can happen. Sometimes it feels like your nose is located outside your body and your breath is four feet away from you, or your head is twisted on backward. There are also physical pains that arise at times, particularly with the opening of different chakras. Just as there are physical sensations, so too there can be powerful inner sounds released—bells, notes, and things like that. There are a hundred kinds of strange altered states.

Similarly on the emotional level. As one goes deeper in practice, there is a release of the strongest kinds of emotions—despair, delight, rapture, very profound grief, and many kinds of fear. Also there can be worry and remorse and guilt from things in the past and anxiety about the future. The primary unconscious emotional storehouse is allowed to release. Initially, there are very great swings in emotions, which require some guidance of a skilled teacher to help one through with a sense of balance. Then there are visions of past lives, great temples, scenes from other cultures, or things that you have never seen, in addition to colors and lights. These states tap into the collective unconscious that has all the visions of humanity within it, and these can arise in meditation.

There are great openings of the senses that can become incredibly refined. You can hear or smell or see in a way that is by far superior to your everyday perception. I remember walking one time with my begging bowl on alms rounds. I generally cannot smell well because of my allergies. That morning it was as if I were the most sensitive dog. As I walked down the streets, every foot or two there was a different smell—something cooking, the shit on the sidewalk, the fertilizer over there, the new paint on part of a building that I went by, or someone lighting a charcoal fire in a little Chinese store. It was an extraordinary experience to go through the world primarily attuned to smell. I hardly saw or heard anything because the smells were so powerful. The same can happen with the ears or the eyes, and beyond this there is a psychic opening where one can even touch visions and smells and things beyond the present moment, visions of past lives and future events, and so forth.

All of this great variety of unusual experiences poses an obstacle course of repeated difficulties and pitfalls for the spiritual journey. The main difficulty with all these altered states is that people either get frightened by these experiences or resist and judge them: "My body is dissolving, I have got prickles, I am burning up, I am too cold, the sounds are too loud, there are too many inner sounds and they are bothering me." There arise aversion, contraction, and fright of these experiences. Each time we resist them, we get trapped by them—and through fear and misunderstanding we can struggle with them for a long time. If we are not afraid of these experiences and enjoy them, then we can get trapped in the opposite response—an equally powerful attachment to them. Because many of the unusual experiences of lights or rapture and other such phenomena are very pleasant and seem even to be important in meditation, we tend to become immediately attached to them, and because they feel wonderful, we try to hold and repeat them. Repeating them is called settling for "the booby prize" in meditation.

You might have such an experience and then in the next meditation try very hard to get it back. You hold your body at what you found was the right angle and repeat your breathing the way you did the last time. You may succeed, but to do so does not allow you to open to the next experience. It stops you completely. In fact, the true path is one of letting go, and the process of awakening includes opening up every realm of the body and mind, and finding freedom.

The Buddha declared that the sole purpose of his teaching was not merit, or good deeds, or rapture, or insight, or bliss, but the Sure Heart's Release, a real liberation of our being in any realm. This and this alone is the purpose of any true teaching.

Naturally, meditation will produce experiences of calm and rapture and ease and other more unusual phenomena. While beneficial in a way, these must actually be considered side effects on the path. These states are called "the corruptions of insight": concentration, light, rapture, delight, visions. They are called that because even though they are positive results of meditation, when they arise, our tendency is to take them as "I" or "mine," to get identified with them and to grasp onto them. We then end up stuck and do not learn what real freedom means.

So there is a necessary realization that must come at this common sticking point in meditation—the realization that true freedom in practice comes only from letting go of *whatever* is present, no matter how beautiful or how painful. It requires that we learn that as we observe with mindful and wise attention, any one of three things will happen to our experience: it will go away, it will stay the same for a while, or it will get worse. And this is not our business! Our job is to experience the phenomenal world in all its infinite richness—see, hear, smell, taste, touch, and think—and to find a freedom and a greatness of heart in the center of all this overwhelming sensory input.

It is a big stage in practice to learn to deal with the new phenomena that arise; at this point it usually takes guidance from a skilled teacher. When we have learned to observe without getting entangled in the corruptions of insight and their stickiness, to flow with all these positive experiences, then there can arise deeper levels of insight, and with them new difficulties.

At this point, it is important to note that not everyone will have these kinds of experiences in their spiritual life, nor are they necessary. They should not become a source of comparison or judgment, but a reminder of one aspect of the spiritual journey, where some people get caught and some people get free. But these intense experiences are only one aspect of the journey, and may be not even the most important one.

There are many different cycles in practice. Some of the things one encounters in the most ordinary daily practice can be as profound and as essential as, maybe even more essential than, these altered states. Still, it is very important for our spiritual practice to know how to deal with the variety of these altered states when they occur.

At this point in continuing practice, or perhaps earlier for some, there can be a whole series of powerful energetic phenomena, sometimes called the awakening of the Kundalini. What this means is simply a profound opening of the energy centers of the body, or the chakras, and a simultaneous opening of the nadis, or the energy channels of the body. While there is a basic pattern to this, it may happen in many different ways.

Sometimes as one sits and gets more concentrated, the body will begin to burn or there will be a feeling of heat in the spine, vibrations and tingling. At times, one can actually feel energy move physically in the body as if fire, pulsations, or vibrations moved spontaneously through blocked energy channels as a way to open and free them. These energetic openings can take hours, or weeks, or months. It is all a part of the process of psychophysical opening and purification.

When the different chakras open, there will be a whole variety of unusual physical phenomena. At the throat there can be tension and coughing: I have seen people who sat and swallowed for days in a row. With the lower chakras, the initial opening can include tension and fear; there can be nausea and the release of vomiting. With the opening of the sexual chakra there can be other experiences, including visions of every kind of sexual encounter one can imagine, and tremendous waves of lust and rapture.

When the heart chakra opens, there is sweetness and love, but usually this is accompanied by a great deal of pain, because most of us have bands of tension and holding over our heart. In many retreats people, especially physicians and nurses, have come to me asking: "Please, could you call an ambulance? I am having a heart attack; I can tell, I know the symptoms. I am a physician. I understand this." Or "It hurts here and it hurts my arm. It is my angina but it is worse now," and so forth. And almost always what it is is the opening of the heart chakra.

I usually say to them, "What better place to die than a retreat? Don't you think so?" We have not lost anybody yet, although some day it may happen. Still, it is important to have one's heart opened. So I say: "Go back and sit. Either your heart will open in your body or out of your body."

There are many kinds of chakra experiences. The energy released can become very powerful, to the point where there is so much energy coursing through the body that one cannot sleep for a number of nights. The entire body will vibrate. There can be weeks where it is filled with fire and where vision is altered, almost as strongly as being on LSD. The eyes can burn and hurt, and many other kinds of symptoms can be involved.

As far as pitfalls and difficulties go, one may well ask what to do when it gets to a degree of excess, to a level of release that is beyond the capacity of the person to work with it skillfully. The answer is to slow the process down and focus on doing basically grounding things. Take showers, do a lot of jogging, walking, or tai chi, dig in the garden, do anything that connects with the earth. Inwardly, bring the attention down through the body, visualize the earth, get some good bodywork or massage, or use whatever movements help to release it. Also, acupuncture can work very well for heavy Kundalini, especially if it is done by someone who knows how to balance the elements in the system of acupuncture. It also helps to change the diet and eat heavy foods, grains and meats, to ground one. Do the kinds of activities that slow and bring one back down.

Sometimes these experiences can get extraordinarily powerful. There was one young karate student who sat for a three-month retreat at our center in Massachusetts. He was one of those overzealous young spiritual men, and at one point while in the retreat he decided to do anything to get enlightened. Contrary to our instructions, he sat without moving from early morning one day through that day and through the next night. The next morning he got up and came into the dining hall after sitting nonstop for about twenty-four hours.

He had sat through sensations of fire and intense pain; if one does that, consciousness becomes at some point almost wrenched away from its identification with the physical body. The pain, the fire, the heat, or whatever gets so powerful that consciousness gets catapulted out of the body. There are many more gentle ways to have out-of-body experiences, but this happened to him very abruptly and he came in filled with enormous energy. And in the middle of the dining hall he completely flipped out; it was a temporary Kundalini psychosis. He started yelling and went through his karate routine, at three times normal speed. You could not get near him. It was very powerful. Around him were all these people who had been sitting in silence for two months. The whole room was filled with his energy, and in the silence one could feel the fear that arose in many people, sensitive from so much meditation and overwhelmed by that kind of energy.

After he started to make sounds, he said, "I look at each of you and I see not only the body, but I see a whole string of past lives for each person that I look at." He was living in a very different realm of consciousness, which he had attained through stressing his body to that limit. But he could not sit still at all, or focus, and he had a strong fear of the agitation and the manic state in which he found himself. It was as if he had gone temporarily crazy.

What did we do with him? We started him jogging, since he was an athlete anyway. We got him to run ten miles a day, in the morning and in the afternoon. We changed his diet; while everyone else was eating vegetarian food, we got him meat loaf and hamburgers. We made him take frequent baths and showers. We had him walk and work and later dig in the garden. In about three days he came down. While his experiences may have been valid psychic and spiritual openings, they were not brought about in a natural and balanced way, so he could not integrate them.

There are states resembling psychosis that can arise at certain points in meditation. We have had many thousands of people at our retreats over the past twelve years. Out of these about half a dozen had psychotic breaks. For the most part they were people who had been previously hospitalized for mental illness. Many people who have been previously hospitalized will come to do meditation practice and find themselves repeating their so-called psychotic experiences. It is almost a necessity in spiritual practice, because whatever it is that we are most afraid of will eventually come up. It is like saying, "Don't think of an elephant."

When we become silent, it is there. For the most part people are able to reexperience these past traumas in the context of the safety and balance of the retreat. The meditation provides enough support that they can remember and touch the places of fear again and see that it is just another part of the mind. But for a few people intensive meditation can reactivate the psychosis, and they are catapulted out of the body and unable to relate in a normal way.

These cases include auditory and visual hallucinations, so strong that the student could not stop long enough to eat or talk to someone. Other cases were marked by obsession, sleeplessness, and various kinds of paranoia and fear. While most students were encouraged to sit and go through their experiences, in these few extreme cases we would try to calm them or ground them and slow the process down. If that did not work, one of our psychiatrist friends would prescribe a dose of a tranquilizer in small amounts, to bring people down. A couple of these people were then hospitalized for a few weeks. Basically we used the medication as a way to bring someone back down to earth, because we did not have the facilities of a halfway house to continue to work with them.

There is an article by the psychiatrist Roger Walsh that describes his treatment of a number of people at various Buddhist and Hindu retreats, including one taught by Ram Dass. The Ram Dass retreat was the first one where Walsh saw someone flip out, and he said: "Good, I'm going to get to see Ram Dass deal with a psychotic person in a spiritual way." As Walsh tells the story, this young man was ranting and raving and Ram Dass was doing whatever he could, chanting and trying to center and calm him down. Then the man got somewhat violent and as they were trying to hold him down, he bit Ram Dass in the stomach. Ram Dass called for the tranquilizer at that point. Enough is enough. While I do not favor the frequent or indiscriminate use of these drugs, there are circumstances where they, too, have their place.

The basic principle here, as with extreme Kundalini phenomena, is grounding. When I worked in a mental hospital, it was clear that the patients could not meditate; many were already too lost in their minds. In fact, the people who most needed meditation were the staff—the doctors, nurses, social workers, many of whom had their own tension and fear in relation to the patients' difficulties. But on the level of those who are patients one does not try to teach meditation, but to get people to stop sitting. The useful meditation is to work in the garden, touch the earth, use the hands, do yoga, come back into the body, do whatever physical activities bring the mind back to earth. In meditation we are not trying to produce an out-of-body experience, but to get people to have a fully in-the-body experience.

There is an explicit text from the Zen tradition that deals with meditation-induced psychosis, found in a book called *The Tiger's Cave.* It tells the story of one of the most famous Japanese Zen masters, named Hakuin, who entered the way of practice and after making strenuous efforts under the guidance of a great Zen master had an enlightenment experience when he was only thirty years old. For months he experienced a profound joy and a sense of being at peace in the stillness of the forest. But soon after this he found he was no longer in harmony. "Activity and stillness. I was not free to take up anything or leave it. I thought: 'Let me boldly plunge into my practice again and throw my life into it.' Teeth clenched, eyes aglare, I sought to free myself from this new flood of thoughts and sleeplessness."

But to no avail. It got worse. His mouth was burning, his legs were freezing, and in his ears was a rushing sound like a stream. Even after being certified for first *satori*, or enlightenment, by a Zen master, nothing he could do would stop it. He describes a profuse sweating and eyes full of tears, and yet after trying to cure it, it just continued. So he went to the best Zen masters and healers of his day for assistance, but no one was able to help him.

Finally someone said: "We have heard of an old Taoist hermit in the mountains who may know of the secrets to cure your meditation." He climbed the mountain to see the Taoist hermit, who would not talk to him at first. So Hakuin sat outside the cave and persevered until the hermit realized he was a sincere monk with a real problem. Finally, the hermit spoke with him and asked about his problem. Hakuin described the difficulties he had been experiencing.

The hermit gave him a series of teachings outlined in this text that deal primarily with the two aspects of grounding and balancing the inner energy. One involves drawing the attention from the top chakra, where it gets lost and leaves the body, down into the belly, using the belly and special breathing to ground the energy in the physical body. Secondly, the hermit gave Hakuin a series of visualizations based on Taoist inner yoga to create a balanced energy source and circulate it throughout the body. Following this routine and some other exercises he received from the hermit, Hakuin not only regained his balance but in fact reached a deeper level of enlightenment and became a great teacher, particularly skillful with people who had difficulty in their meditation practice.

So these difficulties are not happening just in modern days; there are descriptions of yogis encountering them in all ages and major methods of practice. To give a further sense of the deeper levels of difficulties in meditation, I would like to describe a sequence of states one encounters in advanced Buddhist practice. At the point where one has stabilized meditation and through the power of concentration has passed through the various difficulties and hindrances, one reaches the level of what is called "access concentration." Access concentration means that stage where one has access to deeper realms of insight. At this point, one can also direct consciousness into the realms of absorption up to the level of cosmic consciousness. These *dhyanas*, or absorption levels, begin when the mind becomes filled with rapture and light, and most thoughts and outer perceptions stop. One can enter them through focusing on loving-kindness, through concentrating on a color, through a particular mantra or visualization, or through working with the breath. The path and practices that involve entering these states of high concentration are well described in the Buddhist text *The Path of Purification*. In general, these are difficult levels of practice to attain for busy Western minds, although for those with a natural ease in concentration they can be reached in a few weeks of intensive practice. One of the difficulties that come in relation to these states is that though the mind becomes very still and peaceful, there is not much cause for insight to arise. To concentrate so fully brings a temporary halt to fears and worries and suppresses desires and plans, but when we emerge from this state of peace, the difficulties rearise immediately.

Therefore the Buddha recommended establishing a certain degree of concentration and then using it not to find temporary peace but to examine fully the body and mind. One reaches the level of access concentration where there is great stability, where the mind does not wobble and there is very little thought. At this point awareness is quite fully in the present moment, and it can then be directed to the changing sensory experiences, the breath, or the body to reveal the deeper levels of insight. It will reveal a constantly changing experience of the physical body and rapid mental events, arising and interacting in an almost mechanical way. One will notice movements of the body conditioned by mental states and mental states arising conditioned by sensory input. It will all appear as an obviously impermanent and selfless process.

When the observation and insight into changing body and mind become initially stabilized, a great sense of freedom and joy arises, which is described by Daniel Goleman in *The Meditative Mind* (originally published as *The Varieties of Meditative Experience*) as pseudonirvana. Here one encounters joy, balance, strong faith, concentration, and mindfulness. Yet all these states, which are important fruits of the meditation, pose a new danger, called the *corruptions of insight*. On first experiencing them one is delighted and grasps them, trying to keep them and identifying them as the goal of meditation. There is nothing inherently wrong with these states, but they are a sticking point because we grasp them. So a profound realization must now come that the true path to liberation is to let go of *everything*, even the states and fruits of practice—to be open to that which is beyond this very limited body and mind. Then practice goes on to deepen.

We get to the level where the corruptions of insight arise and we abandon them. We say, "I am not going to be attached to the light and the equanimity and the rapture, or the sense of inner power. I am not going to be attached to these things, but I will let them all come and go freely." These dangers were also described by Castaneda's Don Juan as attachment to the clarity and power that arise. There will arise a sense of tremendous well-being or incredible faith or visions into one's own past lives.

All of these need to be abandoned. And when they have been, we go into the next level of the dark night; our letting go allows an opening to a much deeper level and a profound series of new perceptions. What happens at this point is that the level of concentration and attention becomes yet greater and we actually see and feel the entire world begin to dissolve in front of us.

Wherever we focus, our world of seeing, hearing, smelling, tasting, or touching starts to dissolve. We look at someone, we see them arise, we see them pass away. We look away from that image and we just see it dissolve and the next thing appears and we look away and we notice the dissolution of that. Sounds come and we feel them tinkling on the ear and dissolving one moment after another. Sensations, smells, tastes, thoughts, feelings—wherever we turn our attention, there is a sense of dissolution.

For most people, with this dissolution comes spontaneously a great sense of unease and fear, even an experience of terror. Not only is the outer world dissolving when we observe the lights and colors and sense objects arise and dissolve, but the inner world starts to dissolve as well, and we lose our entire sense of reference. We ask:

"Well, who am I in this? Wherever I look, things start to dissolve." At this point, there can also arise very powerful visions. These sometimes involve visions of one's own death, or the death of other people, wars, dying armies, or charnal grounds. Sometimes we look down and pieces of our body start to melt away and decay as if we were a corpse. These are very compelling visions, where we see more and more clearly not only how the world comes into being—that is the part we saw before—but how it inexorably passes away.

There comes with this a sense of terror, a sense of unease, and a very deep realization of suffering. There can be tremendous sympathy for the sorrow of the world. There is not only the suffering of having things be painful in our life or of having pleasant things dissolve so we cannot hold on to them, but the suffering of the end of all that is created or loved by us. It seems that no matter what there is in the world of our senses—family members, loved ones, one's own body—all of it will be lost.

In this realm of terror there will also arise periods of paranoia. Wherever we look, it is fearful. If we walk out of the door, something could come and run us over. If we take a drink of water, there could be microbes in it, and we could die. Everything becomes a source of potential death or destruction at certain phases in this dark night.

There arise periods of claustrophobia and oppression as well. I do not want to give too much detail, because it does not always happen in exactly the same way. I do not want people to think that this is exactly what is going to happen to them. Some people experience one aspect strongly; others skip right over that or go in a different way through their practice. But dissolution of the solidity of the body and world, fear, and a sense of deep suffering are common experiences. They eventually lead to a new level, a very profound letting go.

Out of this arises a deep desire for deliverance. We say: "I want to relate to this world in a different way than I did before. I want to really find a freedom that is not bound up in seeing, hearing, smelling, tasting, and touching, or in this separate sense of self, of body, and of mind."

There may also arise a sense of how hard it is to let go of the self, which is called "the rolling up of the mat." It is a sense that we cannot do it, it is too hard, the world is too difficult, and the tangle of being identified with all these things is too deep. It seems beyond us to find a way out. We wish only to quit and go home.

These powerful stages of fear and dissolution are tricky to work with. This is a very important place to have a teacher; otherwise we get caught in them, or lost or overwhelmed, or we quit. And if we leave at any of these stages—the stage of fear, or the stage of claustrophobia—because they touch a very deep level of the heart and unconscious mind, they become the undercurrents in our unconscious and can last for months or years until we do something to take ourselves back to that level and resolve it.

The same can happen for people on LSD trips when they have a very deep but difficult experience that is incomplete. That flavor stays close to the surface, and they can be depressed or fearful or angry for a very long time. They must usually go back through deep therapy or meditation or psychedelics, back down to that level, and bring it to resolution.

At these stages, it is very important to work with a teacher who understands what it means to go through them. What it means to go through them is that we get to the place where we look them straight in the eye and say: "This too will pass," and we neither resist it nor grasp it. We look at the horrors and the joys with an equal heart and an open mind, and let go of the very deepest of our attachments.

When we finally can do that, there arises the most beautiful and profound equanimity where everything that appears is singing one song, which is the song of emptiness. It says: "It arises by itself, it is ungraspable, none of it is 'I' or 'mine.' It is just a world of phenomena, of consciousness, and of light and dark playing out. In it there is no sense of separation, no sense of self."

There are just moments of seeing, hearing, smelling, tasting, touching, and mental events, all seen very clearly as *anicca*, *dukkha*, and *annata*, as impermanent, as unsatisfactory, as ungraspable. We cannot grasp them and say, "Here is where I will be happy." From this vantage point all the movements of body and mind have an inherent unreality and unsatisfactoriness to them.

This level of equanimity brings a profound kind of rest, where the mind becomes like a crystal goblet or like the sky, in which all things are balanced. One becomes completely transparent, as if every phenomenon just passes through the mind and body and one is simply space. The whole identity shifts and reveals the empty or true nature of mind before we get caught in a body and identified—thinking, "This is who I am"—and then become afraid to lose it, embarrassed about how it looks and having to take care of it, in all the ways that we do.

This long and deep spiritual process of dissolution and opening takes one to what is called in the Christian mystical tradition "divine apathy." It is not a lack of caring, but it is like the eye of God that sees the creation and the destruction and the light and the dark of the world with a heart that embraces it all, because it is all of that. We see that we are nothing and we are everything.

From this place of balance where the characteristics of impermanence, of selflessness, and of unsatisfactoriness become clearer than any of the content of the world, comes finally the possibility of liberation. We get a taste of what it is like to be in the world but not to be caught by a single thing in it. Out of this balance one has access to extraordinary states of mind, where one can enter the void and the whole thing just disappears and then reappears all by itself. The whole universe comes and goes, just like mind and body and sight and sound. There is also a realization of the inherent completion and perfection in all things. Liberation does not mean changing the world, but touching its true nature.

These are experiences that many people have in deep meditation. Through them one comes to discover the art of balance and the greatness that is possible for the human heart. We know what it means to be free of greed, hatred, delusion, fear, and identification. And even if we do not always remain in that state, it is like climbing to the top of a mountain. We have had a taste of what liberation really means, and it informs and affects our whole life thereafter. We cannot ever again believe that we are separate. We cannot ever really be afraid to die, because we have died already. This is called "dying before death"; it brings the most wonderful kind of detachment and equanimity.

Then we come back at the end of it to realize in a most simple way the basic teachings of the dharma. We see them again and again more deeply. We see clearly Buddha's Noble Truths—that there is suffering in life, that the suffering is inherent in it, that the cause of it for us is our grasping or our identification. When we learn to be free in that way, nothing can touch us. We discover that there is a real liberation that is possible for every human being. We come to understand the teachings of the heart and see that it is possible for the heart to open and to contain the entire universe. We realize that the greatness of the heart is such that every single thing in life, the ten thousand joys and the ten thousand sorrows, can all be contained within the wholeness of the heart.

We finally come to see that spiritual practice is really very simple; it is a path of opening and letting go, of being aware and not attaching to a single thing. As my teacher Aachan Chah said, "The whole teaching is simple. When I see someone getting lost in the sidetrack on the right side of the road or going off in a ditch, I yell, 'Go left.' If that same person is going down the road and they are about to get lost in a sidetrack on the left or they fall off in the ditch, I yell, 'Go right.' That is all I do. Wherever you would be attached, let go of that and come back to the center, to see the movement of life from a place that has a sense of grace and balance and openness."

But even after this tremendous and enlightening journey one inevitably comes down. Very often in coming back one reencounters all the difficulties of the journey again, but at least one can bring to them a greater sense of balance and disidentification, an ease and tenderness of one's heart and mind.

To close, there is a story of an old Chinese monk who decided to go off and practice on top of a mountain, to either get enlightened or die. He had sat in a Zen monastery and had many years of peaceful meditation, but he was never enlightened. Finally he went to the master and said, "Please, may I just go to the mountains and finish this practice? That is all I want from life now, to see what this enlightenment is about." The master, knowing he was ripe, gave permission.

On the way up the mountain he met an old man walking down with a big bundle. The old man was really the bodhisattva Manjusri. He is said to appear to people when they are ready for enlightenment. Usually he is depicted carrying a sword that cuts through all illusions. But here he had this bundle.

The old man comes down the mountain and says: "Where are you going, monk?" The monk says: "I am going up to the top of the mountain with my bowl and a few belongings. I am going to sit there and either get enlightened or die. That is all I want. I have been a monk for a long time, and now I must know what this liberation is about."

Since the old man looked very wise, the monk asked: "Tell me, old man, do you know anything of this enlightenment?" At which point the old man simply let go of the bundle and it dropped to the ground. As in all good Zen stories, in that moment our monk was enlightened! "You mean it is that simple, just to let go in this moment and not grasp anything?"

This truth is very hard for us to realize, because our attachment to the process of the body and the mind, the physical and mental events, is so strong. We take it so powerfully to be ourselves that it takes the whole deep process I have described to untangle and undo the knot of self. For most people it takes a really deep, systematic, and disciplined path of practice to break open the source of inner bondage.

And in the process one passes through all the realms of fire and dissolution, the storms and emotions, the whole series of temptations, hindrances, and difficulties. And in the end, we still must return. So the newly enlightened monk now looks back at the old man and asks, "So now what?" In answer, the old man reaches down and picks up the bundle again and walks off toward town.

The story has both sides of practice. It teaches us to let go in a very profound and deep way to relinquish our grasping, our fears, our identification with all things. It helps us to see directly that we are not this body, we are not the feelings, we are not the thoughts; that we just rent this house for a while. And once we have realized that, it teaches us that we must reenter the world with a caring heart, with a universal compassion, and with a great deal of balance and wisdom. We must pick up our bundle and take it back into the realms of form, the realms of humans. But now we can travel as a bodhisattva, as one who has traversed the terrain of life and death and understands it deeply enough to be free in a whole new way. And from this freedom to bring a deep wisdom, and a heart of understanding and compassion, to a world that needs it so much.

Ram Dass

PROMISES AND PITFALLS OF THE SPIRITUAL PATH

Friend, please tell me what I can do about this world
I hold to, and keep spinning out!
I gave up sewn clothes, and wore a robe,
but I noticed one day the cloth was well woven.
So I bought some burlap, but I still
throw it elegantly over my left shoulder.
I pulled back my sexual longings,
and now I discover that I'm angry a lot.
I gave up rage, and now I notice
that I am greedy all day.
I worked hard at dissolving the greed,
and now I am proud of myself.
When the mind wants to break its link with the world
it still holds on to one thing.
Kabir says: Listen my friend,
there are very few that find the path!

KABIR, _The Kabir Book_

I n the first half of this century, the spiritual quest and its challenges were interesting and relevant for a narrow circle of seekers. The mainstream culture was enmeshed in the pursuit of material values and external goals. This situation started to change very rapidly in the 1960s, a period that brought a wave of interest in spirituality and consciousness evolution. Among its most obvious manifestations were a widespread and often irresponsible experimentation with psychedelic substances, a mushrooming of various non-drug-related techniques of deep self-exploration, such as experiential forms of psychotherapy and biofeedback, and a new enthusiasm about ancient and Oriental philosophies and practices.

This time of extraordinary turmoil and rapid change provided many valuable lessons for a deeper understanding of the transcendental impulse and of the promises and pitfalls of the spiritual path. Besides the widely publicized excesses and casualties of this stormy development, there were also many instances of genuine spiritual awakening leading to a serious search and a life of service. In a less dramatic and ostentatious way, this wave of spiritual fermentation has continued to this day.

An increasing number of people seem to be undergoing a process of gradual spiritual emergence, as well as more dramatic forms of transformational crisis. It would be difficult to find a more articulate and knowledgeable person to convey the lessons of this stormy period than psychologist, consciousness researcher, and spiritual seeker Richard Alpert (Ram Dass).

Alpert received his Ph.D. in psychology from Stanford University and has taught at Harvard, Stanford, and the University of California. In the 1960s, he was one of the pioneers of psychedelic research. This work evoked in him deep interest in consciousness evolution and in the great spiritual philosophies of the East. At this time, he published, jointly with Timothy Leary and Ralph Metzner, The Psychedelic Experience: A Manual Based on the Tibetan Book of the Dead.

In 1967, his personal and professional interest in spirituality and consciousness took him on a pilgrimage to India. In a small village in the Himalayas, he found his guru, Neem Karoli Baba, who gave him the name Ram Dass, or "Servant of God." Since that time, Ram Dass has explored a broad spectrum of spiritual practices, including Zen meditation, Sufi techniques, Theravada and Mahayana Buddhism, and various systems of yoga, or ways toward union with God: through devotion (bhakti yoga), service (karma yoga), psychological self-experiment (raja yoga), and activation of inner energy (Kundalini yoga).

Ram Dass has made great contributions to the integration of Eastern philosophy and Western thought. By reporting with unusual honesty and an extraordinary sense of humor all the successes and mistakes of his personal quest, he has become an important model and teacher. He has generously made this information available through public talks, lectures at professional conferences, audio- and video-tapes, and a series of books.

Ram Dass is the author of many articles and the books Be Here Now, The Only Dance There Is, Grist for the Mill, Journey of Awakening, *and* Miracles of Love. *He coauthored (with Paul Gorman) a unique companion book for people assisting others in crisis, entitled* How Can I Help? *It is written from a spiritual perspective and offers many useful guidelines for professionals, volunteers, friends, and family. Many of its insights are applicable to work with spiritual emergencies.*

For many years, Ram Dass has dedicated his life to service, which he considers his primary yoga, or vehicle for spiritual liberation. In 1973 he founded the Hanuman Foundation, an organization for enhancement of spiritual awareness in the West and for manifesting compassion in action. Among the projects initiated by this foundation are the Prison/Ashram Project, inspiring inmates of prisons to use their time there for spiritual practice, and the Living/Dying Project and Dying Center, which teach people conscious approaches to dying. Ram Dass has also been instrumental in the work of the Seva Foundation, a nonprofit organization dedicated to manifesting compassion in action on a global scale. It helps to raise and distribute funds and to create and staff a variety of service projects throughout the world.

During the last twenty-five years Ram Dass has become a cultural archetype of a true spiritual seeker, devoting most of his time to practice and service. The following is adapted from a talk on the promises and pitfalls of the spiritual path that he gave at the Tenth

*International Transpersonal Conference in Santa Rosa, California, in
October 1988. In it he draws on his profound personal experience as
well as his work with countless people in the United States and abroad.*

In the 1960s, we underwent a major shift away from absolute reality.
We realized that what we saw and understood was only one kind of
reality and that there were other kinds of reality. William James said
many years before that "our normal waking consciousness is but one
type of consciousness, whilst all about it, parted from it by the
filmiest of screens, there lie potential forms of consciousness entirely
different. We may go through life without suspecting their existence,
but apply the requisite stimulus and at a touch there they are in their
completeness."

Up until the 1960s, the primary containers of spirituality and
ethical constraints in our culture were organized religions. These
institutions motivated people to ethical behavior through fear and
internalized superego. The mediator between you and God was the
priest. And what the 1960s did, through the use of psychedelics
initially, was blow that whole system apart. That era once again made
the relationship to God a direct experience of the individual. Of
course, the Quakers have had a history of such experience, as have
other traditions. But in terms of the mainstream, a new concept was
coming into the culture, one that was spiritual and not formally
religious.

Most of the time prior to the 1960s, mystical experience had been
denied and treated as irrelevant in our culture. I was a social scientist,
and I also spurned it. Rainer Maria Rilke said of that period:

> The only courage that is demanded of us, is the courage for the most
> strange, the most singular, the most inexplicable that we may encoun-
> ter. Mankind has in this sense been cowardly, has done life endless
> harm. The experiences that are called visions, the whole so-called spirit
> world, death, all these things that are so closely akin to us, have by
> daily paring been so crowded out of our life, that the senses with
> which we could have grasped them are atrophied, to say nothing of
> God.

But in the 1960s many of us recognized something in ourselves that
we had never known before. We experienced a part of our being that
was not separate from the universe, and we saw how much of our

behavior was based on the desire to alleviate the pain that came from our own separateness. For the first time many of us broke out of the alienation that we had known all of our adult lives. We began to recognize the health of our intuitive, compassionate hearts, the health that had been lost behind the veil of our minds and the constructs we had created about who we were. We transcended dualism and experienced our unitive nature with all things.

But it is interesting how mainstream those ideas have gotten in the twenty-five years since that time. When I was lecturing in those days, I was speaking to an audience between the ages of fifteen and twenty-five, the explorers of that time. These lectures were like meetings for the explorers club, and we were comparing maps of the terrain of our travels. Today when I speak in a place like Des Moines, Iowa, there are fifteen hundred people, and I am saying roughly the same thing that I was saying back then. I would say 70 to 80 percent of those people have never smoked dope, have never taken psychedelics, have never read Eastern mysticism, but they are all shaking their heads in agreement. How do they know? Of course the reason they know is that these values—the shift from our narrow view of reality into a relative reality—have permeated the mainstream of the culture. We now have many more options about reality, reflected in the many new kinds of social institutions for education.

To understand what was happening to us twenty-five years ago, we started looking for maps, and the best ones available to us at that time seemed to be Eastern maps, particularly Buddhism and Hinduism. In most of the Middle Eastern religions, the maps about the direct mystical experience were part of the esoteric rather than the exoteric teachings, and were guarded. The Kabbalah and Hassidism were not as popular as they are now. So in those early days we were going to the Tibetan *Book of the Dead,* the Upanishads, and the Bhagavad Gita. We turned to varied forms or practices in order to further experience or to integrate what had happened to us through psychedelics.

In the early 1960s, Tim Leary and I had a chart on our wall at Millbrook, a geometric curve that showed just how fast everyone would get enlightened. It did involve LSD being put in the water supply, but other than that it was not very dramatic. Collective enlightenment seemed so inevitable and irrevocable, because of the power of the psychedelic experience. We surrounded ourselves with other people who had experienced transformation and were soon considered a cult at Harvard, due mainly to the fact that people who had not experienced this type of breakthrough could no longer communicate with us. Having gone through the experience to the other side, our language had changed, thereby creating an unbridgeable gulf.

On another level, there was a kind of naive expectation that the process was going to be over immediately. This expectation was negated by the information that we read, but we felt that psychedelics were going to work where Buddhism and Hinduism fell short.

When the Buddha described how long humanity had been on the journey, as he spoke of reincarnation he talked of a mountain six miles wide, six miles high, six miles long. Every hundred years a bird would fly with a silk scarf in its beak and run it over the mountain once. The length of time it takes the scarf to wear away the mountain is the length of time you have been on the path. If you apply that to this life, you begin to see that it is less than a blink of the eye, each birth being a moment, much like still-frame photography. With that kind of time perspective, you relax and take the chart off the wall.

Yet at the same time, much of the spiritual literature speaks of urgency. Buddha says, "Work as hard as you can." Kabir said:

Friend, hope for the guest while you are alive.
Jump into experience while you are alive . . .
What you call "salvation" belongs to the time before death.
If you do not break the ropes while you are alive,
do you think
ghosts will do it after?
The idea that the soul will
join with the ecstatic
just because the body is rotten—
that is all fantasy.
What is found now is found then.
If you find nothing now,
you will simply end up with an
apartment in the city of death.
If you make love with the Divine now, in the next life you
will have the face of satisfied desire.
So plunge into the truth, find out who the teacher is,
Believe in the great sound!

So there was this desire to get on with it, which we interpreted as taking the entire spiritual journey and turning it into an achievement course. There is a lovely story of a boy who goes to a Zen master and says, "Master, I know you have many students, but if I study harder than all the rest of them, how long will it take me to get enlightened?" The master said, "Ten years." The boy said, "Well, if I work day and night, and double my efforts, how long will it take?" The master said, "Twenty years." Now, the boy talked of further achievement and the master said, "Thirty years." The boy replied, "Why do you keep adding years?" and the master said, "Since you will have one eye on the goal, there will only be one eye left to have on the work, and it will slow you down immeasurably."

In essence, that was the predicament we found ourselves in. We got so attached to where we were going that we had little time to deepen our practice to get there. But over the years we have grown. We have developed patience, and as a result, we have stopped counting. That in itself is great growth for a Western culture. I do my spiritual practices because I do my spiritual practices; what will happen will happen. Whether I will be free and enlightened, now or in ten thousand births, is of no concern to me. What difference does it make? What else do I have to do? I cannot stop anyway, so it does not make any difference to me. But one concern is to watch that you do not get trapped in your expectations of a practice.

There is a lovely story about Nasrudin, the Sufi mystic slob and bum. Nasrudin goes over to his neighbor's to borrow a large cooking pot. His neighbor replied, "Nasrudin, you know that you are very undependable and I really treasure this big pot. I don't think I can give it to you." And Nasrudin said, "My family is all coming, I really need it. I will bring it back tomorrow." Finally, begrudgingly the neighbor gave him the pot. Nasrudin took it home very appreciatively and the next day he was at the door with the pot. The neighbor was delighted and said, "Nasrudin, how wonderful." He took the pot, and inside the big pot was a little pot. He said, "What's that?" Nasrudin said, "The big pot had a baby." So the neighbor of course was very pleased. The next week Nasrudin came and said, "I would like to borrow your pot. I am having another party." The neighbor said, "Of course, Nasrudin, take my pot." So he did, and the next day Nasrudin did not appear. The day after that, still no Nasrudin. Finally, the neighbor went to Nasrudin and said, "Nasrudin, where's my pot?" Nasrudin said, "It died." See how you can get sucked in by your own mind?

Starting in the 1960s, there was an influx of Eastern spiritual teachers into the West. I can remember going to the Avalon Ballroom in the company of Sufi Sam to hear Alan Ginsberg introduce A. C. Bhaktivedanta, who was going to chant this weird chant called Hare Krishna. The Beatles were jetting with Maharishi Mahesh Yogi. At one point, I went with a group of hippies from the Haight Ashbury to meet with the elders of the Hopi in Hota Villa. This was to arrange a Hopi/hippie be-in in the Grand Canyon. We were honoring them as our elders, but they did not really want to be honored by us, I do not think. Because when we went there we made terrible mistakes, we gave feathers to the children and some of us made love by the well. We did not know how to honor lineages properly.

Over the years we learned how to honor lineages through our connection with Eastern traditions. Our problems with lineages came from the question of how much of them we would incorporate as they were, and how much we would modify them. You must modify traditions from within, not from without. What many Westerners started to do was take a tradition from Mahayana Buddhism and say, "That is fine for Tibetan Buddhists, but really what we should do is . . . " We attempted these modifications before fully understanding the practice from the deepest place within both ourselves and the lineage. Carl Jung writes about Richard Wilhelm in his preface to the I Ching. He calls Wilhelm a Gnostic intermediary, saying that Wilhelm had incorporated the Chinese being into his blood and his cells. Wilhelm had transformed himself in the fashion that is necessary to properly approach lineage.

Many of us were so eager to get ahead that we thus did violence to a number of the lineages. We went to the East and brought them, but kept modifying them for our own convenience and comfort. In the West, we are a cult of the ego. We are more focused on "what *I* want, what *I* desire, what *I* need." This attitude is not equally true of Eastern cultures. Many of the Eastern spiritual practices are not focused around personality and therefore are not immediately transferable to the West.

At first, I did not really understand the importance of lineage. I remember doing a television show with Chögyam Trungpa Rinpoche; we were talking about nonattachment as a highly desirable quality of mind. I said to him, "Well, if you are so nonattached, why don't you give up your lineage?" He said, "I am not attached to anything but my lineage." And I said, "Well, you have a problem." My judgment came from my lack of appreciation for the intimate love affair one has with a method. One goes into method as a dilettante, becomes attached to it in a rather fanatic way, and then emerges from the method and "wears" it without being attached to it.

In the 1960s, we gathered together around our newfound spiritual awakenings and all the ways we knew about how to get high. You would find groups gathered around sexual freedom, drugs, chanting, and meditation. We used Eastern names like the satsang and the sangha, but eventually our activities formed boundaries around them. Often there was a sense of elitism, a concern with who was and was not a part of our group. There was a common assertion that "our way" was the only way. Many of us recognize how much violence can be done with this attitude of exclusivity.

I am reminded of the story of God and Satan walking down the street, and they see this brilliantly shiny object on the ground. God reaches down, picks it up, and says, "Ah, it's truth." And Satan says, "Oh, yes. Here, give it to me and I'll organize it." That is roughly what it felt like, when "truth" started to become institutionalized and structured in the 1970s. It became fashionable to be part of these large spiritual movements (which were beautiful and got people incredibly high).

The predicament came from the fact that many of the Eastern teachers that came over had come from primarily celibate, renunciate paths. They were not ready for Western women, who were in the middle of experiencing sexual freedom and feminism. The teachers were absolutely vulnerable and fell like flies.

These people were teachers, not gurus. A teacher is pointing the way, while a guru is the way. A guru is a cooked goose: the gurus are done. We, however, took the concept of guru and limited it with our need for a good father in a psychodynamic sense. We wanted the guru to "do it to us," when the guru in fact is rather a presence that facilitates or allows you to do your work. Depending on your karmic predispositions, you "do it" to yourself.

We eventually brought our judging mind into the spiritual scene. I, personally, was surrounded by gossip about this spiritual teacher or that one. It seemed as if everyone was becoming a connoisseur of clay feet. Many of us were busy deciding whether or not we could afford to take a teaching from someone who was impure in our eyes. We misunderstood the concept of surrender. We thought that you surrender to someone else as a person, when what you do is surrender to the truth. Ramana Maharshi says, "God, guru, and self are one and the same thing." So what you are surrendering to is your higher truth or higher wisdom in the guru. Surrender is an interesting issue. We in the West see it as a very unpleasant idea. We associate surrender with images of MacArthur and the showing of the neck in vulnerability. The fact that surrender is such an important facet of the spiritual path is something that we have had to stretch to understand.

As we learned more about the traditions, we realized that if we were to incorporate what happened to us through psychedelics, we were going to have to do a great deal of purification. At first we were reluctant, but we began to see that we would have to stop creating karma to get ourselves into a place where we could get high and not come down. There was a big push for renunciate practices. There was a feeling that this earth-plane was the illusion and the source of the problem. There was a consensus that it was an error that we had ended up here anyway. The best thing to do was to get "up there, out there," where it was all divine. People began to feel that if they gave up worldly possessions, they would become purer and better able to have deeper experiences. Many did, but the problem again was that such experiences were collected like achievements.

Meister Eckhart said, "We are to practice virtue, not to possess it." We tried to wear our virtue like marks on our sleeves to show how pure we were. Nonetheless, our practices and rituals affected us and we started to have many more spiritual experiences, leading to a time when everyone was in a state of spiritual bliss.

We reacted to that experience by becoming enamored of all the phenomena that occurred as a result of our practices, meditation, and spiritual purification. We were very vulnerable to spiritual material- ism. If we had a Ford in the garage, we had an astral being in the bedroom. The traditions warned us about this attitude; Buddhism, for example, cautions against getting stuck in the trance states, be- cause you will experience omniscience, omnipotence, omnipresence. Buddhism advises that we simply acknowledge these states and move on. But the temptation to cling to such experiences as achievements persists. It is very hard to understand that spiritual freedom is ordi- nary, nothing special, and that this ordinariness is what is so precious about it.

With all these powers came a tremendous amount of energy, because when you meditate and quiet your mind, you start to tune into other planes of reality. If you were a toaster, this experience would be like sticking your plug into 220 volts instead of 110 volts, and everything fries. Many people have had incredible experiences of energy or shakti, or what is often called Kundalini, the cosmic energy rising up the spine. I recall the first time it happened to me; I thought I had damaged myself, because it was violent. As it started up my spine, it felt like a thousand snakes. As the Kundalini reached my second chakra I ejaculated automatically and it continued to rise. I remember being really frightened, mainly because I had not expected anything so horrendous.

I get phone calls all the time, as I imagine the Spiritual Emergence Network does, from people who are having Kundalini experiences. For example, a therapist from Berkeley called and said, "This thing is happening to me and I am riding my bike six hours a day, I don't get tired, I can't sleep, I cry at the strangest moments, and I think I'm going insane." I said, "Let me read you a list of all the symptoms, I have a Xerox." And she said, "I thought I was the only one having this experience." I said, "No, it's Xeroxed. Swami Muktananda published it a long time ago, and it is just mother Kundalini at work. Don't worry, it will pass. Just breathe in and out of your heart and keep it soft."

These phenomena started to happen to us, and they scared or excited or trapped or enamored us, and we stopped to smell the pretty flowers. Many people brought their egos up with them when they went to experience this plane; they claimed the power available in these realms as their own. They then went into a messianic journey, trying to convince everyone that they were "the One." These episodes were very painful for everyone.

I remember a moment with my brother when he was in a mental institution, because he thought he was Christ and he was doing terrible things as Christ. There was a point where the doctor, my brother, and I met in a hospital ward. The doctor would not let my brother see anyone without being present himself.

I came in with a beard, robe, and beads, while my brother was in a blue suit and a tie. He was locked up and I was free, the humor of which did not escape any of us. We talked about whether the psychiatrist would become convinced that my brother was God. All the while, the doctor was writing on his clipboard, obviously uncomfortable, because my brother and I were really out there floating. Then my brother said, "I don't understand, why am I in a hospital and you are out there free? You look like a nut." I said, "You think you're Christ?" He said, "Yeah." I said, "Well, I'm Christ, too." He said, "No, you don't understand." I said, "That's why they're locking you up." The minute you tell someone *they* are not Christ, watch out.

Many people, when the energy became so intense from their spiritual practices, lost their grounding on this plane. The Spiritual Emergence Network has been assisting people in the process of getting back to a grounded place. In India, people who experienced this type of separation were called "God-intoxicated." Anandamayi Ma, one of the greatest saints of all times, was a very dignified Bengali woman who spent two years doing cartwheels in her front yard. She was known to have thrown off her sari during that time as well. In our culture, such behavior is Bellevue material. In Indian culture, they say, "Ah, there's a God-intoxicated saint. We must take care of him at the temple."

In our culture, we do not have a support system for this kind of transformative loss of ground, the process of which you need to go through at times. Of course, a great many people have just gone into outer space and not come back. The complete process is one of losing ground and then moving *back* to this plane. In the early days the whole game was to get people out there, to get them to let go of their minds and the heaviness they had taken into their lives. Then you looked out and everyone was floating. I look at half the audience and I want to say, "Hey, come on up for air, it's okay. It's not so heavy in life." To the other half, I feel like saying, "Come on, get your act together, learn your zip code, go get a job."

When spiritual practices work a little bit, but you are not stable in your transformative experience, your faith flickers and the mosquitoes of fanaticism breed strongly. Most disciples fall victim to this kind of fanaticism, whereas their teachers have long ago left it behind. When you meet a spiritual master in any tradition—Zen, Sufi, American Indian, Hindu, Buddhist—you recognize another mensch. They do not sit around saying, "Well, you're not following my way, so you are lesser." But all the disciples right under them usually do; they have not gone deep enough in their faith, or come out the other end.

For a method to work, it has to trap you for a time. You have got to become a meditator—but if you end up a meditator you have lost. You want to end up free, not a meditator. There are many people who end up meditators: "I have meditated for forty-two years . . . " They look at you with earnestness, the golden chain of righteousness having caught them. A method must trap you, and if it works, it will self-destruct. You will then come through the other end and be free of method.

That is one of the reasons Rama Krishna's gospel is so wonderful; you get to see him go through Kali worship, come out the other end, and then explore other methods. Once you come through your method, you see that all methods lead you to the same thing. People say, "How come you are a Jew, do Buddhist meditation, and have a Hindu guru?" I say, "I don't have any problem, what's your problem? There is only one God, the One has no name, so there's no form and that is nirvana. I don't have any problem with that."

The way in which we were approaching the spiritual path had an element of righteousness to it, and there were teachers who assisted us in moving through that dilemma. The one who probably helped me most was Chögyam Trungpa Rinpoche. What you look for in a really good teacher is that quality of rascalness. Not scoundrelness, but rascalness. I remember when I was teaching at Naropa that first summer, I was having a hard time with Trungpa Rinpoche. One of the problems was that he had all of his students drunk all the time, busy gambling, and on heavy meat diets. I thought, "What kind of a spiritual teacher is this?" I came out of a Hindu renunciate path. The Hindus are always afraid of falling over the edge. Yet here was this man taking them all down the path to hell, as far as I was concerned.

Of course, I was sitting in judgment. When I looked at those same students several years later, I saw them deep in the Hundred Thousand Prostrations and the heaviest spiritual practices. Trungpa Rinpoche had taken them through their obsessions and on to deeper practices. He was not afraid, while most of the other traditions avoided such risks for fear that someone would get lost along the way. A Tantric teacher is not afraid to lead us through our own dark side. Thus you never know whether the Tantric is an exquisite teacher or hung up on his or her own obsessions. There is no way that you can know. If you want to be free, all you can do is use these teachers as hard as you can, and their karmic problems will remain their own. That is the secret you finally find out about teachers.

You get to the point where you see that you can proceed on the spiritual path only so fast, because of your own karmic limitations. Here you begin to recognize the timing of spiritual work. You cannot get ahead of yourself, or be phony-holy, because it comes back and hits you in the head. You can get very high, but you may fall.

So many people say that they have "fallen off the path." I say to them, "No, you didn't fall off the path. The impurities have had their karmic effect. This is all the path, and once you have begun to awaken, you can't fall off the path. There's no way. Where are you going to fall to? Are you going to make believe it never happened? You can forget for a moment, but what you think you have forgotten will keep coming back to you. So, do not be upset, just go ahead and be worldly for a while."

One of our expectations was that the spiritual path would get us healthy psychologically. I was trained as a psychologist. I was in analysis for many years. I taught Freudian theory. I was a therapist. I took psychedelic drugs for six years intensively. I have a guru. I have meditated since 1970 regularly. I have taught Yoga and studied Sufism, plus many kinds of Buddhism. In all that time I have not gotten rid of one neurosis—not one. The only thing that has changed is that, whereas previously my neuroses were huge monsters, now they are like these little shmoos. "Oh, sexual perversity, I haven't seen you in days, come and have some tea." To me the product of the spiritual path is that I now have another contextual framework that makes me much less identified with my known neurosis, and with my own desires. If I do not get what I want, that is as interesting as when I get it. When you begin to recognize that suffering is grace, you cannot believe it. You think you are cheating.

Along the way on the spiritual path, you begin to get bored with the usual things of life. Gurdjieff said, "That's just the beginning." He said, "There's worse to come. You have already begun to die. It is a long way yet to complete death, but still a certain amount of silliness is going out of you. You can no longer deceive yourself as sincerely as you did before. You have now gotten the taste for truth."

As this growth happens, friends change and you do not grow at the same rate. Thus you lose a great many friends. It can be very painful when people you have loved, even in marriage, are not grow-ing along with you. It is a pitfall that caught many of us feeling guilty about letting go of friends and realizing that we needed new kinds of relationships.

Along the way, when you can no longer justify your existence with achievements, life starts to become meaningless. When you think you have won and find that you really haven't won anything, you start to experience the dark night of the soul, the despair that comes when the worldliness starts to fall away. Never are we nearer the light than when darkness is deepest. In a way, the structure of the ego has been based on our separateness and our desire to be comfort-able, happy, and at home. Trungpa Rinpoche said in his rascally way, "Enlightenment is the ego's ultimate disappointment."

That is the predicament. You see the fact that your spiritual journey is an entirely different ball game than the path you thought you were on. It is very difficult to make that transition. Many do not want to. They want to take the power from their spiritual work and make their life nice. That is wonderful and I honor it, but that is not freedom and not what the spiritual path offers. It offers freedom, but that requires complete surrender. Surrender—of who you think you are and what you think you are doing—into what *is*. It is mind-boggling to think that spirituality is dying into yourself. But there is a death in it and people grieve. There is a grief that occurs when who you thought you were starts to disappear.

Kalu Rinpoche said, "We live in illusion, the appearance of things. But there is a reality, and we are that reality. When you understand this, you see that you are nothing, and being nothing, you are everything." When you give up your specialness, you are part of all things. You are in harmony, in the Tao, in the way of things.

Mahatma Gandhi said, "God demands nothing less than complete self-surrender as the price for the only freedom that is worth having. When a person loses himself/herself, they immediately find themselves in the service of all that lives. It becomes their delight and recreation. They are a new people never weary of spending themselves in the service of God's creation."

I am reminded of the story of the pig and chicken that are walking down the street. They are hungry and they want breakfast. They come to a restaurant and the pig says, "I am not going in there." And the chicken says, "Why not?" "Because there's a sign that says 'ham and eggs.'" The chicken says, "Oh, come on, we'll have something else." The pig says, "That's okay for you, 'cause from you all they want is a contribution. From me they want total surrender."

One of the things we develop along the way is the witness. The ability to quietly observe the phenomena, including our own behavior, emotions, and reactions. As you cultivate the witness more deeply, it is as if you are living simultaneously on two levels. There is the level of witness, then the level of desire, fear, emotion, action, reaction. That is a stage in the process, and it gives you a great deal of power. There is another stage beyond that, which is surrender. As a Buddhist text states, "When the mind gazes into the mind itself, the train of discursive and conceptual thought ends, and supreme enlightenment is gained." When the witness turns in on itself, when it witnesses the witness, then you go in behind the witness and everything just is. You are no longer busy with one part of your mind watching another. You are not busy watching, but rather just being. Things become simple again. I am having the most extraordinary experience these days. I have tried so many years to be divine, and lately I have received an enormous amount of letters saying, "Thank you for being so human." Is that not far out?

One of the big traps we have in the West is our intelligence, because we want to know that we know. Freedom allows you to be wise, but you cannot *know* wisdom, you must *be* wisdom. When my guru wanted to put me down, he called me "clever." When he wanted to reward me, he would call me "simple." The intellect is a beautiful servant, but a terrible master. Intellect is the power tool of our separateness. The intuitive, compassionate heart is the doorway to our unity.

The spiritual path at its best offers us a chance to come back to the innate compassionate quality of our heart and our intuitive wisdom. The balance comes when we utilize our intellect as a servant but are not ruled by, or trapped in, our thinking mind.

What I have done here is try to show that the spiritual path is a graceful opportunity for us. The fact that you and I have even heard that there is such a path is such grace from a karmic point of view. Each of us must be true to ourselves to find our unique way through. If you get phony-holy, it will end up kicking you in the butt. You must stay true to yourself.

We have the chance to become the truth we are all yearning for. One of Gandhi's strongest lines is, "My life is my message." The rabbi said, "I went to see the Sadic, the mystic rabbi in the other village. I did not go to study the Torah with him, but rather to see how he ties his shoes." St. Francis says, "It doesn't pay to walk to preach, unless our preaching is our walking." We must integrate the spirituality into our daily life, bringing into it equanimity, joy, and awe. We must take with us the ability to look suffering in the eye and embrace it into ourselves, without averting our glance.

When I work with AIDS patients and I am holding someone, my heart is breaking, because I love this person and they are suffering so much. Yet within me at the same time is equanimity and joy. The paradox is almost too much for me to be able to handle. But this is what real helping is all about. If all you do is get caught in the suffering, then all you are doing is digging everyone's hole deeper.

You work on yourself, spiritually, as an offering to your fellow beings. Because, until you have cultivated that quality of peace, love, joy, presence, honesty, and truth, all of your acts are colored by your attachments. You cannot wait to be enlightened to act, so you utilize your acts as ways of working on yourself. My entire life is my path, and this is true for every experience I have. As Emmanuel, my ghostly friend, said to me, "Ram Dass, why don't you take the curriculum? Try being human." All of our experience, high and low, is the curriculum, and it is exquisite. I invite you to join me in matriculating.

Part Four

HELP FOR PEOPLE IN SPIRITUAL EMERGENCY

Christina Grof and Stanislav Grof

ASSISTANCE IN
SPIRITUAL EMERGENCY

We shall not cease from exploration
And the end of all our exploring
Will be to arrive where we started
And know the place for the first time.

T. S. ELIOT, *Four Quartets*

There are many forms of spiritual emergency involving varying degrees of intensity. The extent of assistance required thus depends upon the situation. In some instances, treatment can be limited to specific support for the person in crisis; at other times it can be extended to involve relatives and friends, or supportive groups. However, if the process is especially dramatic, professional therapeutic help might be necessary around the clock. The approach to people in crisis has to be flexible and creative, based on the assessment of the individual nature of the crisis, and utilizing all the available resources.

The most important task is to give the people in crisis a positive context for their experiences and sufficient information about the process they are going through. It is essential that they move away from the concept of disease and recognize the healing nature of their crisis. Good literature and the opportunity to talk to people who understand, particularly those who have successfully overcome a similar crisis, can be invaluable.

Being surrounded by people who have at least a general understanding of the basic dynamics of spiritual emergency is of great help to a person in psychospiritual crisis. Whether the attitudes and interactions in the narrow circle of close relatives and friends are nourishing and supportive or fearful, judgmental, and manipulative makes a considerable difference in terms of the course and outcome of the episode.

Ideally, family, partners, and important friends should be included in the support network from the beginning and offered as much information about the situation as possible. Exactly who should be included, at what time, and how depends on individual circumstances. The quality of the relationship with the person in crisis, the general compatibility of the personality characteristics of the potential helpers, and their attitude toward the process are among the most important criteria on which we base our decisions. Besides books and discussions of the subject of spiritual emergency, experiential therapy groups can be an important source of understanding of nonordinary states and their positive potential for those in the position of helping someone in crisis.

In many instances, a good spiritual teacher who knows the inner territories from his or her experiences or a local spiritual group can be very helpful. Such individuals might be able to provide an opportunity to discuss some unusual experiences and offer understanding and support for someone in spiritual emergency. Guided individual or group spiritual practice can provide a good context for work with the emerging experiences, if the process is not too overwhelming.

It would be ideal to have a network of support groups specifically designed for people experiencing spiritual emergencies and their families and friends, similar to the already existing programs in the addiction field, such as Alcoholics Anonymous. To our knowledge, no groups of this kind exist at present in the area of spiritual emergency, but with a little effort, such a network could develop quite rapidly.

For spiritual crises that are not extreme, the above resources might be sufficient. Many people who have unusual experiences are puzzled and bewildered by them, but they can manage to function adequately in everyday life. Access to the right information, occasional supportive discussion, and a good context for spiritual practice are all they need.

Under favorable circumstances, if good support systems are available, it is possible to handle even more challenging experiences that the person in crisis would not be able to confront without assistance. However, if the process becomes overwhelming and seriously interferes with everyday functioning, more specific therapeutic measures have to be undertaken. While many of the judgments and procedures described in the following text require therapeutic experience, the basic rules and strategies we will discuss can be helpful for anyone with a desire to help.

The first and most important task for someone working with people in crisis is to establish an open and trusting relationship. Initially, this rapport will help to get an account of what is happening that is as honest and accurate as the person is able to give under the circumstances. Later, trust will be the most critical factor in actual psychotherapeutic assistance.

In addition to the usual qualities that invite trust, such as genuine human concern, personal integrity, and basic honesty, a solid knowledge of nonordinary states of consciousness from personal experience and from work with others is essential. The person in crisis is very sensitive and will immediately recognize whether the approach of his or her helper is based on true empathic understanding or on a professional routine stemming from the medical model. Intimate knowledge of the cartography of nonordinary states can be of great help in this process.

The next step for the helper is to decide whether using the strategies of transpersonal psychotherapy is appropriate for the particular case or whether conventional medical treatment is indicated. A good medical examination is an absolutely necessary part of this decision. We do not want to miss, and therefore neglect, conditions that can be diagnosed by today's clinical and laboratory techniques and require medical attention, such as infections, tumors, or circulatory diseases of the brain.

When medical tests are negative, we have to evaluate the person's attitude and "experiential style." It is essential that the individual in crisis is open to the idea that the problem resides in his or her own psyche and that this person does not "project" and blame everybody and everything else in the world for his or her own difficulties. And, naturally, he or she has to be willing to confront powerful experiences.

Once the therapeutic work begins, it is important that the facilitator and the person in crisis share certain basic concepts. They must agree that the difficulties are not manifestations of a disease, but of a process that is healing and transformative. They accept all the emerging experiences—biographical, perinatal, and transpersonal—as normal constituents of the human psyche. They must agree that the condition is not pathological per se, although it can be extremely inconvenient and inappropriate under ordinary life circumstances. Confrontation with such unusual experiences has to be limited, as much as possible, to situations where it does not create problems and where there is support.

The conscious world of consensus reality and the archetypal world of the unconscious are both authentic and necessary aspects of the human psyche. They complement each other, but are two separate and very different realms that should not be confused. While it is important to acknowledge both of them and respect their requirements with good discrimination, each at appropriate places and times, responding to both of them simultaneously is confusing and can be detrimental to functioning in everyday life.

This general understanding of the process leads to a combination of two alternative strategies. In the first category are various approaches that facilitate the process and cooperate with its healing potential; these are definitely preferable whenever it is possible to use them. In the second are various measures that can be used to slow it down; these should be employed only in situations where the person in crisis has to attend to demands of everyday life and the circumstances are not favorable for experiential work.

Among the gentle techniques that facilitate and accelerate the transformative process are various types of meditation, movement meditation, group chanting, and other forms of spiritual practice. A more radical approach is to create situations where one can go within oneself, preferably with the use of music, and give full expression to emerging emotions and physical energies—by crying, screaming, shaking, or full body movements—following the natural trajectory of the process. Working with dreams, expressive dancing, drawing and painting, and keeping a diary can also help in assimilating the inner experiences. The disturbing emotional and physical energies can also be dissipated in various physical activities, such as hard manual work, swimming, or jogging.

The next option in the facilitating strategies is systematic work with a trained therapist, either individually or in a group. Various approaches developed by humanistic and transpersonal psychology can be useful in spiritual crisis, such as Jungian active imagination, Fritz Perls' Gestalt practice, Assagioli's psychosynthesis, various neo-Reichian approaches, Dora Kalff's sand-play therapy, and others. Since the experiences often have an important psychosomatic component, good bodywork should be an integral part of a comprehensive approach to spiritual emergencies. Also, acupuncture has its place here; it can be extremely effective in removing energy blockages in various parts of the body and can equalize difficult emotions.

For optimal results, the general therapeutic strategy has to meet certain basic criteria. It should not be limited to talking and should allow full experience and direct release of emotion. It is absolutely essential to respect the healing wisdom of the transformative process, to support its natural course, and to honor and accept the entire spectrum of human experience, including the perinatal and transpersonal range. The therapist, of course, has to be open to the spiritual dimension and recognize it as an important part of life. Without this condition, the therapeutic process will be skewed and awkward and will not be able to reach its objectives.

We have developed an experiential technique that includes all the above criteria. This approach, known as Holotropic Breathwork, combines controlled breathing, evocative music, and focused body-work. It can activate the psyche and bring important unconscious material into consciousness, which makes it available for the necessary therapeutic work. In situations such as spiritual emergencies, where the unconscious is already active, this technique can facilitate and accelerate this process. It is beyond the scope of this paper to discuss this method any further; all of its various aspects have been described in Stanislav Grof's book *The Adventure of Self-Discovery.*

Creating special situations in one's life where it is possible to confront and process the emerging unconscious material helps to clear the rest of the day from unwelcome intrusions of its disturbing elements. This requires a place where one can fully express—by loud noises, if necessary—these emerging emotions. When the circumstances do not allow such an approach and one has to attend to urgent practical tasks, it is possible to resort to techniques in the second category—those that inhibit the process and slow it down. It should be emphasized that these are the second choice and should be used only as a temporary measure. As soon as the situation allows it, one should return to facilitating strategies, since expressive work expedites the process and facilitates its successful completion.

To slow down the process, one should temporarily discontinue all meditation and other forms of spiritual practice. Changing diet is usually very effective; shifting from a light vegetarian diet to heavier meals, including meat and cheese, and drinking beverages containing honey or sugar can have a very grounding influence. A warm bath and simple manual work in the house or in the garden can also be helpful. If one has identified situations that tend to activate the process, they should be avoided at this time, if possible. For some people, this could be complex social situations or crowded areas; for others, loud music and the noisy atmosphere of large cities, or even a specific type of vibration, such as the hum of the engines in a jet plane. In especially demanding situations, the occasional use of minor tranquilizers might be necessary.

At this point, a word of caution seems appropriate and necessary. People in spiritual emergencies might find that regular use of alcohol and sedatives can make the experiences more manageable by slowing down the process and suppressing difficult physical and emotional symptoms. However, those with an unidentified problem of chemical dependency are subject to the great danger of addiction. For this reason, one has to exercise utmost caution. The fact that some of these drugs might be prescribed by a physician rather than self-administered does not make them any safer.

The situation is much more complicated when the crisis becomes extreme and the individual develops self-destructive tendencies or presents management problems by being agitated, noisy, or otherwise difficult. Under these circumstances, psychotherapeutic work can be continued only if supervision around the clock is available. Unfortunately, there are very few facilities that offer support 24 hours a day and do not routinely use suppressive medication.

There are many obstacles that currently stand in the way of the establishment of such centers. Some of them are legal, political, and economic in nature; others are related to the inflexibility of insurance policies. Until such retreats are established and readily available, it will be difficult to use new approaches with people in acute spiritual emergencies. They will have the choice between hospitalization with traditional suppressive therapies, and various ad hoc improvisations and compromises. In spite of all the obstacles and difficulties, the creation of such centers is an absolutely necessary condition for successful treatment of acute psychospiritual crises.

Bruce Greyson and Barbara Harris

COUNSELING THE NEAR-DEATH EXPERIENCER

Here comes this white light. It didn't blind me. It was just the whitest white and the total area was filled with it . . . . It was just like you looked out into a total universe and there was nothing but a white light. The most brilliant thing in the world, and it was not the kind of white that hurt a person's eyes like looking at a light bulb . . . . Then I said to myself as plainly as I'm saying to you, "So I'm dying. I don't want to, but I'm not going to fight it. If this is death, I'll accept it." I had a very, very pleasant feeling.

NEAR-DEATH EXPERIENCE OF A MAN DURING
EMERGENCY SURGERY IN *Recollections of Death*
BY MICHAEL SABOM

C osmologies of all the ancient and preindustrial cultures describe biological death as a transition, rather than the irreversible end of human existence. Funeral mythologies of all times and countries, as well as the ancient books of the dead, contain elaborate accounts of the adventures of the soul during the posthumous journey. Modern Western science considered all these reports to be wishful fantasies of primitive peoples until the 1970s, when careful investigation of near-death experiences brought unexpected support for these claims.

It became clear that a large percentage of contemporary Westerners, when suddenly confronted with death, experienced a colorful visionary adventure resulting in a profound spiritual opening and personality transformation. Until recently, this often led to a profound psychospiritual crisis, since the reality of these experiences was not accepted by professionals and our culture at large.

In recent years, much careful research was conducted by pioneers in the field of thanatology, a young discipline concerned with death and dying. The remarkable results of this research have been widely publicized in professional journals as well as the mass media. This is extremely important, since the number of people having near-death experiences is rapidly increasing due to advances of medical resuscitation techniques. This topic is represented in our collection by a paper written specifically for this purpose by Bruce Greyson and Barbara Harris, researchers in the field of thanatology.

Bruce Greyson, M.D., is a board-certified psychiatrist who has done pioneering work in the area of death and dying. He received his medical degree from the State University of New York and completed his psychiatric residency at the University of Virginia Medical Center in Charlottesville, Virginia. He is currently associate professor of psychiatry at the University of Connecticut Medical School in Farmington, Connecticut, and director of the inpatient service at the John Dempsey Hospital, also in Farmington.

Among Greyson's publications are many papers in professional journals and books focusing on various problems in the fields of *thanatology and emergency psychiatry, as well as the book* The Near-Death Experience: Problems, Prospects, Perspectives, *coauthored with C. P. Flynn. He is also the recipient of the 1976 William James Award from the University of Virginia and the 1976 William C. Menninger Award, as well as associate editor of the* Journal of Near-Death Studies.

Barbara Harris, R.T.T., C.E., received her education at Oakland University in Rochester, Michigan, at the Respiratory Therapy Institute in Miami, Florida, and at the Connecticut Center for Massage Therapy in Newington, Connecticut. She is currently associate director of research at the International Association for Near-Death Studies (IANDS) in Storrs, Connecticut. Harris has been involved for many years in research on near-death experiences; she has lectured on this subject at various hospitals and has published articles in professional journals.

While this paper focuses on ways in which professionals can help those who have undergone near-death experiences, the general principles elucidated shed light on the nature of spiritual emergency and can be of use to anyone in close contact with someone in transformational crisis.

When some people come close to death, they go through a profound experience that involves leaving their bodies and encountering some other realm or dimension, and that permanently and dramatically alters their attitudes, beliefs, and values. These near-death experiences, or NDEs, are often the seeds that either immediately or eventually flower into profound spiritual growth. Thanks to medical technology, the NDE may become our most common doorway to spiritual development. But it is perhaps unique among doorways in that it opens to people regardless of whether or not they are seeking enlightenment. And precisely because it often occurs to people who are not looking or prepared for spiritual growth, it is particularly likely to lead to a spiritual crisis.

The growing literature on the aftereffects of the NDE has focused on the beneficial personal and spiritual transformations that often follow. Despite the fact that, according to the 1980–1981 Gallup Poll, about 8 million Americans have had NDEs, we know very little about the emotional and social problems NDEers often face. Although NDEers might naturally feel distress if the NDE conflicts with their previously held beliefs and attitudes, the emphasis in the popular press on the positive benefits of NDEs inhibits NDEers who are having problems from seeking help.

Sometimes people who were totally unprepared to face a spiritual awakening, as in an NDE, may doubt their sanity; yet they are often afraid of rejection or ridicule if they discuss this fear with friends or professionals. Too often, NDEers do receive negative reactions from professionals when they describe their experiences—which naturally discourages them even further from seeking help in understanding the experience.

Many NDEers gradually adjust on their own, without any help, to their experience and its effects. However, that adjustment often requires them to adopt new values, attitudes, and interests. Family and friends may then find it difficult to understand the NDEer's new beliefs and behavior. On the one hand, family and friends may avoid the NDEer, whom they feel has come under the influence of some evil force. On the other hand, family and friends who have seen all the popular publicity about the positive effects of NDEs may place the NDEer on a pedestal and expect unrealistic changes. Sometimes, friends expect superhuman patience and forgiveness from the NDEer, or miraculous healing and prophetic powers. They may then become bitter and reject the NDEer who does not live up to the new role as a living saint.

Common emotional problems following NDEs include anger and depression at having been returned, perhaps against one's will, to this physical dimension. NDEers may find it difficult to accept that return, and experience "reentry problems" much like those of an astronaut returning to Earth. They often have problems fitting the NDE into their traditional religious beliefs, or into their traditional values and lifestyles. Because the experience seems so central to their "core," and seems to set them apart from other people around them, NDEers may identify too strongly with the experience and think of themselves first and foremost as an NDEer. Since many of their new attitudes and beliefs are so different from those around them, NDEers can overcome the worry that they are somehow abnormal only by redefining for themselves what is normal.

The NDE can also bring about social problems. NDEers may feel a sense of distance or separation from people who have not had similar experiences; and they may fear being ridiculed or rejected by others—sometimes, of course, with good reason. It can be difficult for the NDEer to reconcile the new attitudes and beliefs with the expectations of family and friends; as a result, it can be hard to maintain the old roles and lifestyle, which no longer have the same meaning. NDEers may find it impossible to communicate to others the meaning and impact of the NDE on their lives. Frequently, having experienced the unconditional love of the NDE, the NDEer cannot accept the conditions and limitations of human relationships.

Above and beyond these problems, which all NDEers may face to one degree or another, people who have had unpleasant or frightening NDEs have additional concerns about why they had that kind of experience, and may be troubled by terrifying flashbacks of the experience itself. Similarly, additional problems may follow NDEs arising out of a suicide attempt or in young children.

The way a counselor or therapist—or a friend—responds to an NDEer can have a tremendous influence on whether the NDE is accepted and becomes a stimulus for further growth, or whether it is hidden away—but not forgotten—as a bizarre experience that must not be shared, for fear of being labeled mentally ill.

While many of the notions described in this paper apply uniquely to helping the near-death experiencer, others reflect common sense or approaches that would be helpful in any spiritual crisis.

APPROACHES DURING OR IMMEDIATELY AFTER THE NEAR-DEATH EXPERIENCE.

Professional staff involved in resuscitating a patient should avoid insensitive comments and actions. Patients who seem to be unconscious may be aware of what is going on around them, and may later remember offensive actions or statements. When during a resuscitation you have to say or do things that can be misinterpreted, explain to patients what you are doing, even though they appear unconscious; if you do not, you may have to help them untangle frightening memories after they awaken. During and immediately after being unconscious, physical touch is very helpful in orienting a patient. Talking to unconscious patients while touching them, outlining their bodies with your hands while you describe what you are doing, may help them refocus their attention on their bodies after an NDE.

When talking with people immediately after a close brush with death, be alert for clues that they have had an NDE. People often drop subtle hints to test your openness to listen before they risk sharing the experience with you. Do not push for the details of an

NDE, but wait for clues that the person wants to talk further. NDEers may not want to share the details until they trust you. Let them describe their experiences at their own pace, while watching for those subtle hints—tests of how open you are—that they want to tell you more.

Before approaching an NDEer, you should explore your own attitudes toward the NDE. Be aware of your own prejudices, both positive and negative, about what NDEs mean and about the people who have such experiences. You should not press your own beliefs or interpretation of the experience on the NDEer, but let your conversation be guided by the individual's own account and understanding of the experience. Listen for clues as to how he or she makes sense of the experience, and help the experiencer clarify that interpretation using his or her own words. You each have to develop your own personal ways of encouraging talk about the NDE. Using your own personal style of communicating, both verbally and nonverbally, is the best way to get across your willingness to listen openly.

Whatever you think of the ultimate meaning or cause of the NDE, you must respect it as an extremely powerful agent of transformation. If you ignore the NDE's profound potential to bring about both positive and negative changes in personality, beliefs, and bodily activity, you ignore what is often the individual NDEer's most pressing concern. You must respect not only the experience but the experiencer as well. All types of people have NDEs, and the NDEer's rich personal and spiritual background should not be ignored by focusing solely on that person's role as an NDEer.

Labeling the NDE, or giving the NDEer a clinical diagnosis based on having had an NDE, is more likely to get in the way of understanding and to push the NDEer away than it is to help. When an individual NDEer does seem to have a mental or emotional disease, both you and the NDEer must be clear that that disease is not related to the NDE itself. Trying to label the experience as a symptom of illness is not accurate or helpful.

Honesty is critical in establishing an NDEer's trust. If it seems appropriate, you can share your own reactions to the NDE, without discrediting the NDEer's own perceptions and interpretation. You must reassure the NDEer that you can treat what you are told confidentially; the NDEer must be able to trust that you will not tell others about the NDE without permission. People are often cautious about sharing something as unusual and intimate as an NDE until they are sure you will respect it, and they will have reasonable concerns about the respect or attitudes of other people with whom you might share information about the NDE.

The most helpful thing you can do after an NDE is to listen carefully to whatever the person wants to say. People who seem to be upset by an experience usually feel pressure and urgency to understand it. They often become *more* frustrated if you tell them *not* to talk about it, or if you sedate them into silence. Allowing NDEers to talk lets them share and get rid of frightening feelings. Unlike hallucinating patients, who may become more upset by talking about their fears and confusion, NDEers are usually relieved if you allow them to struggle until they find the right words to describe their experiences.

You should encourage the NDEer to express whatever emotions were brought on by the experience. Most NDEs include very intense emotions, and the NDEer might still have those unusually intense feelings afterward. Mirror the person's feelings, but do not analyze them. Feeding back to NDEers their own descriptions and emotions will help them clarify what at first may seem like unexplainable feelings, while analyzing and interpreting those emotions prematurely may only increase the NDEer's fears of being misunderstood.

In hospitals or other places where people often come close to death, it might be helpful to rotate listeners to prevent burn-out. NDEers are often excited about their experiences and might need fresh listeners who can take the time, and have the patience, to hear them out.

One of the most helpful things you can provide an NDEer is accurate information. Facts about NDEs and their aftereffects, shared in a straightforward, nonjudgmental way, will greatly reduce the experiencers' immediate concerns about the implications and consequences of the NDE. Near-death experiencers are usually relieved to learn how common NDEs are. On the other hand, no matter how universal the experience is, it is unique for each individual, and you must guard against using the NDE's commonness to trivialize any individual's experience or its unique impact on his or her life.

When NDEers seem upset immediately following the experience, help them identify exactly what it is about the NDE that is causing the problem. Explore the possible problems listed in the opening section of this paper, using the individual NDEer's understanding of his or her own personality and situation. Once the specific problem is identified, tailor the solution to that specific person and problem. No two NDEers have the same experience, the same personality, or the same life situation to return to.

Finally, NDEers may need help immediately after the experience in dealing with what brought them close to death. Focusing on the NDE itself and its meaning, they may find it hard to arrange practical medical and social details. For concerns centered on the experience itself, put them in touch with other NDEers or with local professionals who have worked with other NDEers. Many cities have Friends of IANDS support groups, in which NDEers and their families and friends regularly discuss issues around the experience; you can get the address of the nearest support group from the International Association for Near-Death Studies (IANDS), Box 7767, Philadelphia, PA 19101.

LONG-TERM APPROACHES AFTER THE NEAR-DEATH EXPERIENCE

If you expect to work with an NDEer past the initial contacts, you must be prepared for the NDE to raise issues about life and its purpose that may not come up in other clinical relationships. The profound aftereffects of an NDE may affect your own psychospiritual growth as much as the NDEer's. Decide whether you want to accept that risk before starting to work with an NDEer on an ongoing basis.

Once you have made that decision, you need to clarify what you expect from the work, and what the NDEer expects. Make sure you understand what help the NDEer wants from you, and what the NDEer hopes will come out of your work together; and make sure the NDEer understands what you want from him or her, and what you hope will come out of the relationship. Be especially careful of jumping to conclusions about people you knew before their NDE, particularly clients you may have helped prior to their NDE. Do not assume that work you began before the NDE will continue on the same course after the experience. Even though the person's underlying problems and personality may be the same, the NDE may dramatically change his or her goals and priorities in life and in your work together.

You may need to limit the areas you will address in your work together. Taking into account the NDEer's personality and situation before the experience, clarify what problems are new as a result of the

NDE. You may find it impossible to help someone both with NDE-related problems and also with unrelated emotional or psychological problems; the techniques and the goals of one kind of counseling may conflict with those of the other. For example, helping your client adapt to social norms may reduce his or her long-standing psychological problem, while helping that same client to adapt to values that no longer have meaning after the NDE might increase his or her problems dealing with the experience. If you choose to work with someone around NDE-related problems, you may need to refer that person's problems that are not related to the NDE to someone else.

You and the NDEer must continually work toward mutual trust. Because the NDE is so different from daily reality, it may take longer than usual for an NDEer to trust even the most sensitive helper with some parts of the experience and its aftereffects. The otherworldly reality of the NDE also makes it hard for even the most open-minded helper to trust some of the NDEer's recollections and interpretations of the experience.

Do not be too concerned about traditional clinical roles; rigid adherence to form and appearances may undermine your relationship with the NDEer. Since many of our labels and definitions lose their meaning after an NDE, you must rely more on your direct experience with the NDEer and less on your formal training and knowledge of clinical techniques. Labeling the NDEer's problems and separating yourself from the NDEer for the sake of objectivity are more likely to interfere with your understanding of his or her problems than they are to help. In particular, be flexible with how long and how often you see an NDEer you are helping. Since the NDE is so different from other experiences and is very difficult to describe in words, exploring it may take unusually long sessions, and may unleash overwhelming emotions and thoughts that require frequent sessions.

Be prepared to stick with NDEers. They often feel frustrated in trying to describe the NDE and its aftereffects, and may give up trying if they see you as giving up. Particularly, those who feel they were "sent back" to this life against their will may feel rejected and undeserving of the NDE, and may be on the lookout for rejection from you.

It is not helpful to think of the NDEer as a passive victim of the experience. Helping the NDEer see his or her active role in creating or unfolding the NDE will help in understanding and dealing with problems arising from the experience.

Remember that parts of the ego that may have died in the NDE need to be grieved for. Even though NDEers may be happy to be rid of parts they transcended or were freed from, they still need to deal with that loss.

The major features of an individual's NDE may give you clues as to the sources of problems continuing after the experience. For example, if the NDE was composed largely of a life review, or of precognitive visions, or of certain strong feelings, exploring those particular features with the NDEer may shed light on continuing problems. Particularly explore details of the NDE that seem bizarre or unexplainable, as well as the NDEer's mental and emotional associations to those details. You can interpret NDE imagery on many levels, just as you can with dream imagery.

Any techniques that you use for inducing altered states of consciousness may help the NDEer recall further details of the experience, and may help the NDEer learn to shift at will between different states of consciousness. Any techniques you use for integrating the left and right hemispheres in particular may help NDEers find practical ways to apply what they learned in the experience. Imagery, projective techniques, and nonverbal expressions such as art, music, and dance may help uncover and express feelings that are hard to put into words.

Explore the NDEer's sense of a specific purpose or mission after surviving death. The "unfinished business" of that mission may be a source of continuing problems. Those NDEers who chose to return to this life may feel ongoing regret or mixed feelings about that decision. On the other hand, NDEers who chose *not* to return to this life may feel ongoing guilt or anger at having been "sent back." Some NDEers feel manipulated by a higher power in being sent back, and that feeling may cause continuing problems.

Explore fully the NDEer's fears about unwanted aftereffects. Whether or not fears about the consequences of an NDE are realistic, they can cause continuing problems. It is important to distinguish the NDE from its aftereffects. The NDEer must feel free to reject or resist unwanted aftereffects without having to devalue the NDE itself. While the NDE is going to be a permanent part of the individual's life from now on, various aftereffects may come and go in a natural course, or may be developed or eliminated through counseling.

The changes in values and attitudes following an NDE often lead to subtle changes in family interactions that can cause continuing problems. Meeting with the NDEer and the entire family together, ideally in their home, may be the only way to understand how the family has changed, and to get the reactions of family members to the NDEer. If the family dynamics have been greatly changed, family therapy may help.

Avoid glorifying or idealizing the NDE and its aftereffects. The newness and uniqueness of the experience may lead both you and the NDEer to see it—and sometimes the NDEer as well—in unrealistically romantic ways. Similarly, it is tempting to see the remarkable aftereffects—physical, emotional, and mental—as more important than they are, simply because they are so dramatically different from the way the NDEer was before the experience. The NDEer must learn to see the striking aftereffects in the greater context of the entire NDE. Paranormal effects in particular may capture your interest and the NDEer's simply because of their novelty, and blind you to other important parts of the experience or other aftereffects that are more important in fostering psychospiritual growth.

In the same way, the NDEer must learn to see the NDE in the greater context of his or her entire life. Obviously, you cannot ignore the experience and its aftereffects, but neither should you allow the NDEer to focus on them to the exclusion of other parts of his or her life. The overwhelming need to understand the meaning or message of an NDE can lead the experiencer to overvalue its content or its aftereffects. If the NDEer overidentifies with the experience, he or she may not be able to deal with any issues not directly related to the NDE. While talking with other NDEers is very helpful in normalizing the experience, identifying *only* with other NDEers can lead to feeling alienated from people who have not had the experience, to feeling that the physical realm is not meaningful or important, and to ignoring basic problems of living in the physical world.

You may need to help those who become "addicted" to the NDE or its aftereffects to withdraw from it gradually. It may help to point out that problems often cannot be solved on the level that created them. NDEers often say that physical-plane problems they had for years were resolved only by what they learned in the NDE. By the same token, problems created by the NDE may be resolved only by working on the physical plane.

Some NDEers have to relearn how to handle daily responsibilities that no longer seem relevant since the NDE but are still necessary. The timeless quality of the NDE makes it hard for some NDEers to remain grounded in the present once they return. After a profound life review, NDEers may remain focused on the past, while after profound precognitive visions, they may fixate on the future.

You may need a very firm here-and-now focus to help the NDEer function in the present.

On the other hand, you cannot expect NDEers to take up life as usual after an NDE; their outside circumstances may have to be changed to meet their internal changes. If the NDEer's new attitudes, beliefs, and values do not fit with old roles and lifestyle, then he or she needs to find a new role and lifestyle that will meet the new goals and priorities. You may need to help the NDEer through major changes in careers and relationships.

Finally, your ultimate usefulness to the NDEer may be in helping to channel what he or she learned in the NDE into practical use. The same new attitudes, beliefs, and goals that create problems in the NDEer's surroundings can also be important in changing those surroundings for the better. The best way for many NDEers to feel comfortable with the experience and its aftereffects is to use what they have learned to help others. Your work is finished when the NDEer finds a way to bring into daily life the love that he or she received in the NDE.

Paul Rebillot

THE HERO'S JOURNEY: RITUALIZING THE MYSTERY

A hero ventures forth from the world of common day into a region of supernatural wonder: fabulous forces are there encountered and a decisive victory is won: the hero comes back from this mysterious adventure with the power to bestow boons on his fellow man.

JOSEPH CAMPBELL, *The Hero with a Thousand Faces*

Mythology is becoming increasingly relevant for our everyday life. It is reaching large audiences through popular television programs and best-selling books, and its impact is particularly profound in the area of modern depth psychology. Since the discoveries of C. G. Jung and his followers, a knowledge of mythology has become an indispensable tool for understanding the human psyche and for effective psychotherapy. The concept of the collective unconscious and its universal organizing principles, or archetypes, have created an entirely new basis for the understanding and treatment of mental disorders, particularly psychoses.

However, in the past, practical work with mythological elements was mostly indirect, as it is in the analysis of dreams. California psychologist and actor Paul Rebillot has developed a unique ritual form whereby the mythological psyche can be accessed and expressed directly in a psychodramatic way. His approach can be used for self-exploration, for training mental-health professionals, or as a therapeutic tool.

We have chosen Rebillot's article for this anthology for several reasons. His use of mythology in combination with music and drama for healing purposes is particularly effective. It is a beautiful example of how in the future, healing skills, ritual, art, and human support might replace or at least complement the often unimaginative and dry repressive routines of contemporary psychiatry. Furthermore, we have included this essay because Rebillot has undergone a particularly dramatic emotional and spiritual crisis that he sees today as very transformative and healing. This episode provided the single most significant inspiration for his current work. Here is an extraordinary example of how a gifted individual can use a very disturbing and upsetting experience in a way that is highly creative and that many other people can benefit from.

Rebillot was born in 1931 in Detroit, Michigan. He received his B.A. in philosophy from the University of Detroit and his M.A. in theater arts from the University of Michigan. For many years, he had been strongly attracted to the dramatic arts—directing, acting, and designing—and his academic studies helped him to crystallize and focus the theoretical and practical aspects of this passion.

His military service took him to Japan for a year, where he worked at the army's Far East Radio Network. His exposure to an esthetically refined culture with an ancient cultural tradition had a profound impact on his personal as well as professional life. He was particularly impressed by the Japanese Kabuki and No theater. After his return to the United States, he incorporated various elements of these Oriental dramatic arts into his own work.

Suddenly his life took an unexpected turn. Rebillot experienced a profound existential crisis followed by what we would call a spiritual emergency. In the middle of a play in which he was performing the leading role, he was struck by serious doubts and questions concerning the meaning of his life and of life in general and felt a strong need to embark on a journey of self-discovery.

He left the dramatic arts and went into seclusion, where he practiced intensive meditation. This period culminated in a two-month episode during which he experienced profound nonordinary states of consciousness. He emerged with an entirely new understanding of the potential of theater at its best—its healing, ritual, magical, and spiritual power. His personal experiences gave him a new appreciation of the roots of European theater in the Greek tragedy, with its cathartic effect.

Rebillot felt compelled to explore the experiences that so profoundly transformed his life and to give them some expression in his work. His quest took him to the Esalen Institute in Big Sur, California. During his long stay there, he met Fritz Perls, the founder of Gestalt therapy, and became one of his closest and most dedicated disciples. Gestalt practice is a unique experiential approach to psychotherapy that uses intense focus of awareness on the emotional and physical processes occurring in the here and now to psychologically complete various unfinished traumatic issues in one's life.

Another influential thinker and teacher whom Rebillot met at Esalen was the late Joseph Campbell, generally considered the greatest mythologist in the world. Campbell's book The Hero with a Thousand Faces, describing the universal myth of the hero's journey, became for him an extraordinary source of inspiration. Drawing on his background in theater, his unusual musical talent, his personal experiences of nonordinary states, Gestalt therapy, and Campbell's mythological insights, he created an original form of therapeutic ritual *called* The Hero's Journey, *which was originally designed to give mental-health professionals insight into the world of their psychotic patients.*

We have been fortunate enough to work with Rebillot several times and have been very much impressed by the depth of experience and self-exploration that participants reach in this amazing amalgam of theater, ritual, music, song, mask making, therapy, and exquisite entertainment. After exploring our attitudes and feelings about ourselves, home, work, and the beloved, the Hero's Journey takes us into our inner world to identify our heroic self and our demon. Under his guidance, we experience a confrontation of these two aspects of ourselves, a resolution, and an integration. Upon return to everyday reality, we explore how this inner transformation has changed our feelings about ourselves, our home, our work, and our beloved.

For many years, Rebillot has been offering workshops all over the United States and Europe. He also uses a similar format for his seminars Death and Rebirth, The Lovers' Journey, Owning the Shadow, *and others. Supported by a generous grant from Laurance Rockefeller, he is working on a book entitled* The Hero's Journey. *It will be a handbook for those interested in learning the techniques necessary to guide others on this amazing inner adventure.*

I created the process for *The Hero's Journey* several years ago after experiencing my own spiritual emergency. Originally it was designed as an opportunity for people in the helping professions to go through an experience that resembles, in an organized way, an episode of schizophrenia. My hope was that in their contact with people going through the same kind of episode, they would then have an experiential framework in addition to an academic one. I was working with the psychiatric staff of a hospital, and I wanted to teach them how to be with people in extraordinary spaces, how to be secure enough in themselves to allow their patients to complete their process without interfering out of fear.

The Buddhists say that one of the basic fears is the fear of unusual states of mind. We fear these in ourselves, and we fear them in others. A way to deal with that fundamental fear is to experience an unusual state of mind in a safe situation, in order to discover how to go into it and, most important, how to come out of it. Trance-dancing, breath meditation, certain forms of yoga, and dervish twirling techniques are some of the different ways to enter altered states voluntarily. For me, the most interesting and familiar is ritual-drama. The value of such a form is that it allows people to realize that they can both enter into and come out of an extraordinary space with full consciousness.

The Hero's Journey is a chance to play out a story of transformation in such a way that it has the order and control of ritual. Ritual is an event in which eternity and chronological time interpenetrate. By taking an archetypal structure and acting it out in the here and now, the daily life of the individual is illuminated by the eternal. This creates the possibility of an interchange between the two dimensions; a doorway is opened through which the archetypal world can enter the person's life, thus bringing new energy and form into the everyday world. This interpenetration of the two worlds is the essential nature of ritual-drama.

When I created the process, the first step was to discover a pattern, a plot that I might use to construct the ritual-drama. In Joseph Campbell's *The Hero with a Thousand Faces* such a plot is outlined. And Campbell, working with John Perry, discovered that many of the elements that exist within the heroic mythology seem to occur in episodes of schizophrenia as well—perhaps not in the same proportion or order, but similar images do arise. By using the plot line of the hero monomyth, I designed a process to guide a group of people through the archetype of transformation so they can then apply what they experienced to their own lives. Whether the change be of home, partnership, job, or point of view, all seem to go through a similar process. By experiencing the pattern of *The Hero's Journey*, many people have found that they know the form of transformation, so that, when change happens in their lives, it no longer threatens them. They know it will have a certain sequence. They have the map.

THE STORY

The story of the hero's journey follows a basic pattern. The hero is someone who hears the call to adventure and follows it. Generally this person, man or woman, is reasonably well adapted to the sociocultural environment but has a yearning toward the extraordinary. At some point, this inclination is intensified into an experience of a call. This call may come from outside in the form of an invitation or a suggestion from another, or it may come in the form of an inner voice. In either case it says, "There could be more to life than that which you are living." However it comes, the call sinks deeply into the person's being and remains there until it is either acted upon by the hero or killed by one who will not follow the striving of his or her own heart.

The call sets up the first level of resistance: whatever in the present life situation supports or depends upon the status quo, such as one's job, one's home, one's responsibilities, or one's pattern of relationships. These must be recognized and dealt with before the hero can begin the journey.

Along the way, helpers appear, people who give encouragement, guides, or friends who point out the dangerous places. A spirit guide gives the hero an instrument of power to arm him for the battles at the threshold and for the tests within the Mysterium. King Arthur is given a sword, Excalibur, by Merlin; Athena gives Perseus her own shield; Cinderella receives the ball gown and entourage from her fairy godmother.

Thus armed, the hero proceeds to the point of no return, called the threshold of adventure. It generally appears as a gate, a cave mouth, the entrance to a forest—the passageway to another world. When the hero arrives, he encounters a dragon, a castle guard, a three-headed dog, some threshold guardian that refuses admittance. This guardian is the second level of resistance, representing all the self-sabotaging forces within the personality.

A confrontation takes place between the hero and this guardian, which I call "the demon of resistance," until a resolution is reached. The hero, sometimes accompanied by the demon, now transformed, then proceeds into the mysterious inner world.

This is an extraordinary place, an enchanted forest of supernatural wonders. The hero continues along his way, encountering the new and the strange. But armed now with the knowledge of his confrontation at the threshold, as well as with his instrument of power, he feels ready to deal with any situation. Soon the hero encounters his supreme ordeal, a monumental struggle with his basic fear.

Finally, the hero has earned the reward of the journey. It is the Grail, the treasure, or the inner marriage for which this particular hero has been searching. This is the gift of life that comes after the long night of death, the healing with which the hero returns home. The magical aspects of the Mysterium are left behind when the hero once again departs beyond the threshold, but the awareness and the fullness of the voyage remain to enhance or change the situation at home. Thus the journey is complete.

THE PROCESS

The Hero's Journey is developed around the theme of the hero and his counterpart, the demon of resistance. It consists of a series of calibrated challenges—risks that, if taken, release creative expression and so develop a broader base for fuller self-realization. I have done the process of *The Hero's Journey* in a month, in two weeks, and in as short a time as a weekend. The preferred time is seven days, and the process described here takes place over that period of time.

The participants become a tribe, a group of people who have agreed to work through this particular ritual together. The main function of the group is to support the evolution of each individual. As each person works through the stages of his own process, the group supports him in a variety of tribal ways—with music, with dancing, with shouts and cheers of encouragement. This creates a powerful feeling of *ensemble* which, in turn, creates the sense of a safe space, essential if a person is to look deeply into his or her own process. Even though we are working on the hero story, the whole first part of the journey is devoted to group-building and bonding.

Every journey begins with a point of departure: the place that physically, psychologically, and spiritually feels like home. Thus, "home ground" is the takeoff point. The people experience the home-ground situation with their bodies, their hearts, and their minds as fully as possible. Through a dance movement-meditation they imagine themselves looking at four aspects of their lives: their home, their lifework, their love, and themselves.

Then they are guided to a golden throne, "the throne of miracles." They are told to let rise up from their deeper selves an image of what would fulfill them, of what would heal or complete any of the discrepancies and discomforts they have found in their lives. They let this image emerge, without necessarily knowing what it means. It becomes the vision that calls them to their journey.

After that, they select a spirit guide. This concept is very important, for the spirit guide transcends both hero and demon. If the hero and the demon are the thesis and the antithesis, the spirit guide is not the synthesis but the overseer who does not take one side or the other, seeing the two aspects of the personality as being just that—

two aspects rather than two enemies. For their spirit guide they choose a tarot card that images some archetype they feel drawn to, some being that might be helpful to them in achieving their miracle. They keep this inner guardian with them throughout the whole journey. Sometimes they even sleep with their chosen card to inspire their dreams. Later, it is this spirit guide who gives them their instrument of power.

Now they begin to build the hero by recalling images of childhood heroes, animals, movie stars, important figures in their lives, images of adventurers and gods or goddesses. Through these ideals they discover the qualities and powers they have envisioned. However, they also discover what they are lacking; they find the particular quality that most needs support. At this point, the group becomes helpers who offer encouragement to get in touch with that most needed quality.

This support process is the most primitive and tribal of all the structures within the journey. A circle is formed. The person then goes into the center and the rest of the group surrounds him, playing various kinds of rhythm instruments such as tambourines or drums. The person describes what it is he wants to feel more of, such as power or tenderness. The group then supports him with the rhythms and feelings appropriate to that quality, creating a song from the phrase "You are powerful" or "You are tender." He, in the center, expresses his resistance to this message until it is exhausted.

Gradually, then, he is able to allow the rhythmic impulse of the group into his body and into his whole being, adding the words "I am powerful" or "I am tender" and sharing them with the others.

The next step is meeting the hero. In a guided fantasy, the people imagine going to the house somewhere in a forest where their own heroic presence might live. They have been acting out images of heroic qualities. Now, as they open the door of the house of the hero, they experience how the psyche takes all of these qualities and unites them into one figure who becomes their own personal and unique heroic presence. They spend time with this figure, feeling the connection. They discover the hero's secret name and mission. Finally, as they embrace the hero to say good-bye, they imagine their bodies melding and merging. They have become their own heroic selves.

At this point, they put on costumes and makeup and hold a grand banquet in which everyone proclaims himself to be the hero of his or her own journey. This is a very special event; the images in their minds, the feelings in their hearts, and the movements of their bodies come together to dramatize existentially their heroic selves. The celebration of the hero combines several elements of medieval ritual. Frequently, before a knight went on a quest, he spent the night meditating in a chapel. In the morning, the priest came and said the first Mass, during which the knight was consecrated and anointed to awaken in him a sense of the spiritual aspect of his mission, thus connecting his individual task with the species task of the human race. If a knight came to court and asked its members to join him on his quest, the court's agreement was expressed by the queen's ceremonious presentation of a glass of wine. This symbolized the seal of good friendship between the court and the knight. So, after the hero has been anointed, someone is selected to bring him or her the ceremonial cup. These two rituals, with many people getting up and speaking in front of an audience for the first time, make this celebration a grand, frightening, and very touching event.

The next stage is the discovery of the instrument of power. Here, however, the necessities of the ritual-drama deviate from the line of the story. It is necessary now to evoke the character of the demon, the saboteur who stands at the threshold of the Mysterium and confronts the hero with his own resistances. To find this, the people become aware of all the tensions and holding they experience as they meditate on their call:

"You're not good enough!"
"You shouldn't do that!"
"You're too fat."
"You're too thin."
"You're too old."
"You're too young."

The demon exists on all levels—physical, emotional, and intellectual. It is the archetypal "No!" This is the inner limitation we always confront whenever a new situation presents itself, a situation that we want to experience and that we know will not physically or emotionally harm us, and yet one that still frightens us—in short, a situation of potential growth.

The demon evolves out of the physical and emotional blocks to self-expression as they are manifested in the body armor. By examining the bone structure of the body, finding where it is balanced and mobile and where it is restricted, we discover a pattern of resistance. "What muscles do you have to tighten in order to maintain that immobility in the chest, and how does that connect to the angle of the head and the retraction of the pelvis?" Soon enough a full picture emerges that, as each tension is exaggerated, creates in the body a paralysis of intensified body armor. People begin to see how it is that they both keep themselves in and keep the rest of the world out.

Safe techniques are taught to allow for discharge of any violent emotions that may be triggered. This discharge is encouraged and provided for, but the primary focus is on the completion of the archetype. The expression of pent-up negative emotions in a safe situation gives people a chance to learn various ways of dealing with their own hostilities and fears. The development of the demon teaches how to change these feelings into assertiveness and excitement.

Through a series of theater games, the demons have a chance to play out all the thwarted malevolence of childhood with both the humor and the full emotional investment of a child playing monster.

Now that participants have developed and experienced, emotionally and psychologically, both the heroic and the demonic aspects of themselves, they must prepare for the confrontation. However, after the group has come in contact with the more primordial aspect of themselves, the identification frequently shifts from hero to demon. Consequently, it is necessary to bring the identification back to the hero so that the confrontation will be equally balanced; thus the return to the instrument of power at this stage of the journey.

The instrument of power is some physical object that the group members endow with an otherworldly power. For the heroes, who are about to cross over from the ordinary world to the world of the miraculous, it is important that they have something with which they can encounter the forces they might meet there. They discover this by imagining that their spirit guides lead them through the outer environment and present them with some object that they find on their path. Thus, from the intense inner experience of resistance and the physical-body experience of the demon, they now go out into the open air. When they find the object, they sit in front of it and do an active meditation in which they call up the image of the spirit guide and ask the name of the instrument of power and the magic of which it is capable. In this way, they attain an understanding of how this instrument can be used when they reenter the fantasy of the confrontation between the hero and the demon. They then bring the object back to the group room, and in a ritual they dedicate their instruments of power to the accomplishment of their missions, to the illumination of their lives, and to the great work of the human species.

Following this, in a guided fantasy, each hero imagines himself finding the threshold, on the other side of which he can accomplish his mission or realize the miracle he wished for on the golden throne. But the hero also knows that before entering into this magical place, he must confront the demon of resistance. So he calls out and demands that the demon appear. Thus the confrontation can take place. At this point, the person becomes an initiate, because the confrontation at the threshold is performed by both aspects, or many aspects, of the psyche, and the entrance into the Mysterium is really the initial step into the new dimension of self. Therefore, the person is no longer referred to as hero or demon, but as initiate.

The confrontation is done in the Gestalt mode, with the initiate playing out all the roles in his or her own drama. Small subtribes of four or five people are formed, who work together. The initiate puts on a blindfold and imagines the scene in which the hero and the demon stand confronting each other. The other members of the tribe play guides, substitutes, and protectors. Their purpose in the drama is to heighten the sense of inner theater. When the initiate plays the hero, one of the members of the subgroup plays the demon. The guide suggests when to change roles and reminds the initiate of his or her resources. The protector makes certain that the environment is safe. The use of the blindfold intensifies the experience and allows the initiate to plunge more deeply into the inner dimension. The hero and demon confront each other until a resolution is reached that is satisfactory to both.

Earlier, the form of the drama is "outer theater." It is presentational, requiring participants to risk manifesting both the heroic and the demonic aspects of themselves to an audience. As the journey progresses toward the Mysterium, the focus shifts to "inner theater," where the drama is enacted not for an audience but for the deepest self. Here, the challenge is to surrender to and trust one's own internal process of healing and evolution.

After the conflict between the hero and the demon has been resolved, the initiates enter the land of miracles. Lying down blindfolded, they imagine crossing the threshold and then following the path on which they find themselves. A partner sits with each initiate and records his story, asking him to elaborate on or to communicate with any images that occur as he explores the magical place. A musical environment is provided to stimulate the imagination as they all follow their paths down into the depths of themselves.

After they have wandered about in the Mysterium for about an hour, they are asked to let go of words and just follow their images in silence. Gradually the idea of the supreme ordeal is introduced. They are asked to imagine that they come upon a cave on their path. Over the cave they see written, "The supreme ordeal of breath." They enter the cave and discover a black velvet couch in the darkness. They lie down on the couch, and then, step by step, they are guided with music into an intensive breath meditation. Whenever a period of time is spent meditating intensely on breath, it is likely that birth, death, or near-death experiences will be recalled, since these are the moments at which breath is most crucial. Therefore this process can call upon the initiates to confront their basic fears and, by doing so and passing through them, perhaps achieve a transpersonal dimension.

The last phase of the journey is the discovery of the reward. The reward is the symbolic gift that their psyches present to them as a statement of the resolution of their journey. In a movement meditation, they imagine receiving this gift from their spirit guides, who explain its meaning and its use for their lives. They express this reward in song and dance, and bring it back to the place of the beginning. They explore how the images of home, lifework, love, and self change with the addition of the reward. They contract with themselves to take simple concrete steps to bring this reward into manifestation after they leave. This is a way of grounding the material, because the initiate knows that he or she is the only one who can manifest the reward in life; it is going to come not from outside, but from the self. So, if love is the gift, a concrete step is designed to aid in that manifestation. The step out of the mythic world into the everyday world is the step of taking responsibility for manifesting the reward.

As the last part of the meditation, participants imagine that the gift they have received becomes a tiny light that they place in the center of their hearts, a light they can carry with them, symbolizing their new self-awareness. It is very important that they leave the magical powers behind in the land of the other world. To bring the magical powers across the threshold is to attempt to impose on other people the initiate's relationship to the archetypal world by failing to recognize the unique relationship that each person has to that world. It is also to deny the reality of and the difference between the two worlds. The metaphor or symbol belongs to the archetypal world and expresses the individual's relationship to that world. Those who attempt to bring the magic back risk either being looked at as crazy or being dealt with as saints.

In either case, they cannot be in compassionate contact with other human beings. So, to protect themselves against personal ego inflation, they leave the magical powers behind in their land of miracles and come back with the awareness of what they have lived. Their hero's journey is finished. Their new journey is about to begin.

INSIGHTS FROM *THE HERO'S JOURNEY*

What have I learned from *The Hero's Journey* now that I have been guiding people through it for fifteen years? That it is possible to find terror within the human psyche: monsters, ghouls, "things that go bump in the night." But I have also learned that looking long enough and deeply enough into the eyes of the most frightening inner monster can transmute it into treasure. Frequently I suggest to people, as they are about to enter into the confrontation between their heroic and their demonic selves, that they look deeply into the demon's eyes, because if they can look deeply enough, the demonic mask may fall away and they can then discover what is behind it. There is always something behind the resistance. If the hero asks, as Parsifal did, "What is troubling you?" he can, perhaps, experience the healing that comes with the awakening of compassion. And compassion toward others begins with the loving acceptance of the maligned or wounded inner self. Often one discovers that what one experienced as the apocalyptic war to end all wars is really nothing more than a lovers' quarrel.

I have also learned that we can approach the experience of chaos with more security if there is a form around it. And all change requires passage through chaos. *The Hero's Journey* gives structure to what is essentially a destructuring experience—an experience in which old forms and points of view are being destroyed in order for new ones to emerge. So it is a fragmenting experience, and this can be very frightening. The structure of ritual can provide the security of orderly unfoldment. Knowing that after this there is something else enables people to confront even the most frightening of images; they know this is not the end. Since change is the one thing we can be sure of in the world and in our lives, it is important to be able to move through the chaos toward our future selves. For as Fritz Perls said, "The only way out is through."

THEATER OR THERAPY?

Many people have asked me if this is theater or therapy. I am not sure if there is a clear-cut difference. After all, the roots of our theater are in the ritual-drama of ancient Greece. Aeons ago, people traveled miles in donkey carts or on foot to share in what I imagine was a kind of tribal exorcism. They did not go to find out what happens to Electra or Medea; they already knew the myths that today form the basis of much psychological speculation. Something beyond suspense brought those people. It was called enthusiasm, *en theos,* the God within. The intense identification with the hero at his or her moment of catharsis must have been similar to the release felt during the discharge of a primal scream. I think, however, that more than therapy, there was a kind of transcendence—an awakening of the God within. The chaos of creative energies was released in the form and structure of art. And that is what I believe *The Hero's Journey* to be: a chance for people to create a work of art out of the basic materials of their own lives.

Jeneane Prevatt and Russ Park

THE SPIRITUAL EMERGENCE NETWORK (SEN)

I shot to a place beyond words, beyond symbols, beyond imagery—a place of nothingness, but a nothingness in which all the knowledge of what is and what can be and what will be lay, a nothingness in which I was light waiting to shine, sound pulsating to be born.

. . . As I passed through the levels of reality between the material world and pure energy, I saw my body encapsulated in words, defined, restricted, limited by words. And in going where I went I burst out of these word bonds into an infinity of wordlessness and timelessness, an infinity of love, of ecstasy, of bliss, of "the peace that passeth all understanding." I was—and am—one with the universe; I am the universe; God and I are one.

DEANE BROWNE,
Psychosis as a Transformational Experience

T*he clarification of the concept of spiritual emergency and the development of new strategies of treatment are the first important efforts in the approach to evolutionary crises. The next and more difficult step is the creation of a broad supportive framework to implement these new strategies. Although such a network was started in 1980, it is still moving out of its infancy, and an enormous amount of work remains to be done before it can meet the urgent need. In this essay Jeneane Prevatt and Russ Park, both intimately involved with the Spiritual Emergence Network in Menlo Park, California, discuss its history and functioning.*

Jeneane Prevatt, M.A., the coordinator of the Spiritual Emergence Network, is a counselor with a transpersonal and Jungian perspective, specializing in work with children, adolescents, and adults experiencing psychospiritual crises. She is an educator, adviser, administrator, and developer of programs that encourage the empowerment of the individual. For the last thirteen years, she has been involved in psychological and psychiatric services for the abused and neglected. After a three-year stay in Zurich, Switzerland, studying at the Jung Institute, she began her most recent work with the Spiritual Emergence Network.

Russ Park, M.A., is currently a doctoral student and intern at the Institute of Transpersonal Psychology in Menlo Park, which hosts the SEN. He uses an integrative approach to psychology, combining bodywork, process-oriented psychotherapy, dreams, and Jungian and transpersonal perspectives. His interests include the relationship as a spiritual path, drug addiction, personal empowerment, spiritual emergence, the role of spirituality in everyday life, and research in transpersonal methods. His background lies in clinical laboratory medicine, alternative healing, computers, and environmental issues.

The Spiritual Emergence Network (SEN) was founded in 1980 as a grass-roots response to an increasing need for recognition, information, and support for those undergoing spiritual emergencies. Individuals experiencing such nonordinary states of consciousness had, in the past, often been labeled as psychotic, drugged, and locked up in hospital mental wards. As an alternative to the traditional mental-health system, SEN was formed by Christina Grof at the Esalen Institute, in Big Sur, California. SEN volunteers began gathering a list of people, SEN "helpers," who were exploring the frontiers of human consciousness and spiritual experiences. Some of these people had themselves been through transformational crises.

It is SEN's goal to provide a network for individuals in spiritual emergencies, or psychospiritual crises, through which the proper information and support can be found. SEN "helpers" are friends, psychotherapists, medical doctors, bodyworkers, spiritual leaders, and community members who are willing to help others through this inner crisis in a supportive, nurturing manner. It is through this information and support that individuals can begin to integrate their experiences and resume normal, often healthier lives.

Currently located at the Institute of Transpersonal Psychology, in Menlo Park, California, SEN is a nonprofit international organization operating a free information-and-referral service. SEN works to inform the lay and professional communities about the forms, incidence, and treatment of spiritual emergencies.

After nine years, SEN is alive and responding to an ever-increasing populace. SEN has grown into an international organization with a mailing list over 10,000 strong. Currently, SEN handles 150 callers a month, of which 46 percent are in need of "helper" referrals. Our last analysis of 501 calls and 117 letters, from November 1986 through July 1987, revealed that a "typical caller" was a forty-year-old female (69 percent) experiencing some form of Kundalini awakening (24 percent).

SEN "helpers" consist of over 1,100 people, from professionals to laypeople, who have volunteered to assist those in psychospiritual crises. Besides providing referral services, SEN offers current theoretical information, bibliographies, trainings, and monthly seminar programs that address the concept and experience of spiritual emergency. SEN serves as a supporting network among many psychological, human-potential, and spiritual/religious organizations throughout the United States and the world.

HOW SEN WORKS

One of the main services that SEN offers is listening to and validating the experiences of people who reach us by telephone. Based upon the belief system expressed by a caller, SEN's volunteers or staff will attempt to select at least three "helpers" located in the caller's geographical region who have expertise in the type of crisis at hand. SEN's approach to assisting those who contact us is eclectic, since its staff and helpers have many different spiritual and psychological orientations.

We encourage SEN callers to communicate with the suggested helpers and to determine for themselves whether a particular helper is appropriate. This encourages those who need help to strengthen their own autonomy and participate in the healing process. If these referrals prove dissatisfying to the caller for one reason or another, we encourage him or her to call back for additional names. In some cases, the person contacting us may need more than one type of referral. The caller then has a pool of resources to draw upon that can facilitate his or her individual process. We might also offer the name of SEN's regional coordinator in the person's area. SEN's forty-three regional coordinators provide additional resources and helpers in their regions and personalize the assistance given from our office.

In addition to the information-and-referral service, SEN also offers an education-and-training program to professionals and laypeople who are actively assisting others in spiritual emergencies. The educational component of SEN provides an ongoing speakers' program dedicated to presenting varied ways of understanding mental and spiritual crises. We offer these programs out of respect for the richness and variety of the human experience, in the hope of furthering appropriate and compassionate treatment.

To educate, we must define. Therefore, in addition to our speakers' program, we offer trainings, which address some of the following questions:

1. What is a spiritual emergency? What does it look like, and how does one respond to it?
2. What is the difference between psychosis and mystical states? How do we diagnose and treat them?
3. How can the community best respond to and support such happenings, both for the individual undergoing the crisis and for his or her family?
4. How can therapists support one another in such cases? What modalities can be developed to best contain and support the process?

Training in the field enhances our ongoing program by allowing us to gather personal stories and new case material. This allows SEN to keep current, reviewing people's needs in order to facilitate a more responsive dialogue with the public. And finally, such programs provide a growth-oriented base for training interns referred to us by local colleges and universities.

We attempt to encourage the inclusion of a transpersonal intervention strategy in mainstream psychology, rather than excluding or antagonizing the already established field. The exploration and description of psychospiritual crises and their differentiation from other mental states have only just begun. Fundamental psychological and spiritual questions remain to be formulated, even prior to beginning the quest for answers. It is with this in mind that we have begun a research program.

Below are some of the questions that arise as we begin to explore the picture that emerges from our callers' individual experiences:

1. Are spiritual emergencies states or experiences that are measurable using current psychological testing techniques?
2. What patterns are collectively emerging? For example, one-fourth of our callers are experiencing manifestations of Kundalini awakening. Does this hold true in other parts of the world? If so, what does this imply? Why on a given day do we receive calls from a number of people in the same city who independently report experiencing the same type of phenomena? What is the correlation between the phenomena being experienced and the place in which they happen? Are there collective triggers? If so, what are they?
3. Are these psychospiritual crises a result of normal individual human development, or do they represent a collective evolutionary event?
4. Are there other categories of spiritual emergency yet to be characterized?
5. Does the description of spiritual emergencies as manifested through the contemporary Western psyche conform to classical religious descriptions?
6. Does the contemporary Western experience of these psychospiritual crises, as seen through the "window" offered by the Spiritual Emergence Network, add any new dimensions to the classical understanding of these phenomena?

7. With what efficacy can conventional treatment modalities address these experiences, and what new therapeutic techniques are needed in order to understand and integrate these experiences into everyday life?

SEN's growing data base can be of great help to researchers as they begin to explore some of these questions. Currently, SEN collects information regarding each client's demographic profile, services provided, phenomena experienced, therapeutic and spiritual orientation, and referrals given. This information is collected via a computer system and added to a data base. From this resource, SEN maintains its helper and resource files, from which referrals are given. SEN also maintains its mailing list from this data base, using it to disseminate important information and funding requests.

SEN's data base and information are raw and, in some cases, incomplete. A more in-depth research program is currently being implemented to better support investigators in their quests.

WHERE IS SEN GOING?

As the number of people needing support in spiritual emergency grows, we explore new avenues of service. We get many calls requesting a referral for residential care, for a place where people can allow their process to unfold completely, unimpaired by the demands of daily living. We have only a few referral sources that can meet such a need. We would like to see SEN become a vehicle for the development of 24-hour residential centers.

Too often, the traditional mental-health system requires an individual to conform to existing treatment modalities rather than allowing the treatment to arise from his or her own process. It is our belief that each person holds an existing map to his or her own healing. If we can provide a container that allows creative intervention, as well as safety and nurturing care, the outcome for the clients can be invaluable.

In addition, SEN proposes to develop training for teams that can administer care in people's homes. Such home care facilitates the family's understanding and its involvement in the individual's care and recovery, so that family members can become part of the healing process. This encourages them to participate rather than assume the role of helpless victims of an uninvited event.

In order to make the continuum of available care more complete, SEN would like to foster support groups through our training program. These would provide an arena for individuals to both talk about their experiences and come to some understanding of their "deep dive" into the unconscious. Support groups can be developed that not only nurture and validate the individual going through the process but also allow for healing within the family and in daily life. In addition, psychotherapists treating psychospiritual crises may also find value in forming support groups with other therapists. This allows not only a forum for creative exploration and exchange of ideas but also a place for integrating their own personal issues arising out of deep psychological work with their clients.

Another need that will have to be addressed relates to the adolescent. Our Western culture fails to acknowledge the rite of passage of the adolescent into adulthood. By ignoring this process, we invalidate the visionary experiences that many of our young people go through during this transition. Some of these states are induced by drugs, while others are spontaneous. SEN is beginning to receive many calls regarding people in this age group, and we have very few appropriate referral sources. Therefore, in the near future, SEN hopes to promote services by teens for teens.

Finally, we at SEN are beginning to realize how spiritual emergence experiences seem to seek expression through the arts. Often, the symbolism inherent in dance, painting, music, and the written word allows us to learn and speak the language of the soul. In beginning to gather material related to creative expression, a living archive could be established that would reflect what the transition during a transformative crisis has meant to the individual. SEN also hopes to establish a working library of videotapes, audio recordings, pertinent literature, and any mythological material relevant to transitional and nonordinary states of consciousness.

SEN is in a unique position to observe various forms and manifestations of spiritual and psychological phenomena occurring around the world. As such, SEN serves as a "window" to these unique and often intense psychospiritual experiences. Through this window, we can begin to gain some insight into the individual, social, and even global patterns and significance of spiritual emergence.

Stanislav Grof and Christina Grof

EPILOGUE: SPIRITUAL EMERGENCE AND THE GLOBAL CRISIS

One morning I woke up and decided to look out the window, to see where we were. We were flying over America and suddenly I saw snow, the first snow we ever saw from orbit. Light and powdery, it blended with the contours of the land, with the veins of the rivers. I thought—autumn, snow—people are getting ready for winter. A few minutes later, we were flying over the Atlantic, then Europe, and then Russia. I have never visited America, but I imagined that the arrival of autumn and winter is the same there as in other places, and the process of getting ready for them is the same. And then it struck me that we are all children of our Earth. It does not matter what country you look at. We are all Earth's children, and we should treat her as our Mother.

SOVIET COSMONAUT ALEKSANDR ALEKSANDROV IN
The Home Planet

Modern science has all the knowledge necessary to eliminate most diseases, combat poverty and starvation, and generate an abundance of safe and renewable energy. We have sufficient resources and manpower to realize the wildest dreams humanity has ever had.

However, in spite of all this progress, we are further than ever from a happy, sorrow-free future. The greatest technological triumphs—atomic energy, cybernetics, space-age rocketry, laser technology, electronics, computers, chemistry, and bacteriology—have been turned toward the purposes of warfare, unleashing unimaginable destructive power. Hundreds of millions of people are dying of starvation and disease, both of which could be remedied by the billions of dollars wasted annually on the insanity of the arms race. Furthermore, several plausible doomsday scenarios, from gradual environmental destruction of various kinds to sudden and immediate devastation by nuclear holocaust, leave us with the dubious privilege of being the first species in the history of the planet that has developed the potential to commit collective suicide and, what is worse, destroy all other forms of life by this act.

In view of this dangerous situation, it is vital that we recognize the roots of the global crisis and develop effective remedies to relieve it. Most of the existing approaches of governments and other institutions focus on military, political, administrative, legal, and economic measures that reflect the same strategies and attitudes that created the crisis, address symptoms rather than causes, and therefore yield, at best, limited results.

When we have the means and technological know-how for feeding the population of the planet, guaranteeing a reasonable standard of living for all, combating most diseases, reorienting industries to inexhaustible sources of energy, and preventing pollution, what prevents us from taking these positive steps?

The answer lies in the fact that all of the critical developments mentioned above are symptoms of one fundamental crisis. In the last analysis, the problems we are facing are not merely economic, political, or technological in nature. They are all reflections of the emotional, moral, and spiritual state of contemporary humanity. Among the most destructive aspects of the human psyche are malignant aggression and insatiable acquisitiveness. These are the forces that are responsible for the unimaginable waste of modern warfare. They also prevent a more appropriate division of resources among individuals, classes, and nations, as well as a reorientation toward ecological priorities essential for the continuation of life on this planet. These destructive and self-destructive elements in the present human condition directly reflect the alienation of modern humanity from itself and from spiritual life and values.

In view of these facts, one of the few hopeful and encouraging developments in the world today is the renaissance of interest in ancient spiritual traditions and the mystical quest. People who have had powerful transformative experiences and have succeeded in applying them to their everyday lives show very distinct changes in their values. This development holds great promise for the future of the world, since it represents a movement away from destructive and self-destructive personality characteristics and an emergence of those that foster individual and collective survival.

People who are involved in the process of spiritual emergence tend to develop a new appreciation and reverence for all forms of life and a new understanding of the unity of all things, which often results in strong ecological concerns and greater tolerance toward other human beings. Consideration of all humanity, compassion for all of life, and thinking in terms of the entire planet take priority over the narrow interests of individuals, families, political parties, classes, nations, and creeds. That which connects us all and that which we have in common become more important than our differences, which are seen as enhancing rather than threatening. In the attitudes characteristic of spiritual emergence, we can see the counterpoint to the intolerance, irreverence toward life, and moral bankruptcy that are the root causes of the global crisis. Thus we hope that the growing interest in spirituality and the high incidence of spontaneous mystical experiences herald a shift in the consciousness of humanity that will help to reverse our current self-destructive course.

We have seen repeatedly that people experiencing spiritual emergencies benefit greatly from approaches that support the transformative potential of these states. The new strategies can also have very beneficial effects on their immediate human environment—family, friends, and acquaintances. It is exciting to consider that such activity might, in addition, have relevance for human society as a whole, in helping to alleviate the crisis faced by all of us.

APPENDIX

FURTHER READING

ALTERNATIVE UNDERSTANDING
OF PSYCHOSES

One of the major obstacles to acceptance of the idea of spiritual emergency is the indiscriminate use of the concept of disease for all nonordinary states of consciousness. Among the most articulate critics of the way the medical model is applied to psychiatry is Thomas Szasz, particularly in his most famous book, *The Myth of Mental Illness.* Additional important representatives of this critical trend are the controversial psychiatrist R. D. Laing, author of *The Politics of Experience,* and Kazimierz Dabrowski, who in his book *Positive Disintegration* emphasized the healing potential of many states traditionally mistaken for mental diseases.

PSYCHOLOGICAL APPROACHES
TO PSYCHOSES

There is rich psychoanalytical literature attempting to explain various psychotic states through psychological mechanisms and treat them by psychotherapy rather than biological therapies. Significant contributions to these efforts can be found in the works of Sigmund Freud, Karl Abraham, Viktor Tausk, Melanie Klein, Harry Stack Sullivan, and many others. Here belong also the studies of family structures and interactions conducive to psychoses that can be found in the writings of Theodore Lidz, Gregory Bateson, and others. Efforts to conduct psychotherapy with psychotic patients culminated in the work of Frieda Fromm-Reichmann. A great limitation of all such attempts is the narrow conceptual framework, which lacks genuine understanding of the transpersonal dimension and reduces spirituality to unresolved problems from early childhood.

TRANSPERSONAL UNDERSTANDING OF NONORDINARY STATES OF CONSCIOUSNESS

A rare exception to the dismissal of spirituality in the field of depth psychology is the work of C. G. Jung; he expanded the model of human personality far beyond biography and introduced the transpersonal dimension into psychiatry. His work revolutionized the theory of nonordinary states of consciousness; his concepts of the collective unconscious, archetypal dynamics, the ego and the self, synchronicity, and many others are the cornerstones of the modern understanding of psychoses. Passages that are very relevant from the point of view of spiritual emergency can be found throughout Jung's books and the work of his followers. Jung has also written studies specifically focusing on this problem area, such as *The Psychogenesis of Mental Disease*. An excellent, easily readable synopsis of the principles of Jungian theory and practice is contained in June Singer's book *Boundaries of the Soul*.

The person who has most creatively developed Jung's ideas on psychosis is John Weir Perry, the author of *The Far Side of Madness*, *Roots of Renewal in Myth and Madness*, and many other writings on the subject. His books based on intense psychotherapeutic work with clients in acute episodes are a rich source of information on the role of archetypal dynamics in transpersonal crises. They also describe the therapeutic approach that he developed in his private practice and at Diabasis, an innovative treatment center he founded in San Francisco.

Jungian psychology demonstrated the paramount significance of the study of mythology for the understanding of the human psyche in general, and psychoses in particular. The best resources in this respect are the books of the late mythologist Joseph Campbell, such as *The Mythic Image* and *The Masks of God*. He quite specifically addressed the problem of the relevance of mythological understanding for spirituality and psychoses in his books *The Hero with a Thousand Faces* and *Myths to Live By*. A unique source of Campbell's ideas is *The Power of Myth*, a series of his discussions with Bill Moyers, available on commercial videotapes. Many of his brilliant insights are directly applicable to the crises encountered during the transformation process.

Roberto Assagioli, the late Italian psychiatrist and founder of the psychological system called psychosynthesis, originated many valuable ideas related to the psychological importance of spirituality and to the concept of spiritual emergency. They are summarized in his book *Psychosynthesis*.

The four classics of spiritual literature, *Cosmic Consciousness* by Richard Bucke, *Ecstasy* by Marghanita Laski, *Varieties of Religious Experience* by William James, and *Mysticism* by Evelyn Underhill, are rich sources of information directly applicable to the problems of transpersonal crises. We should also mention in this context Anton Boisen's book *The Exploration of the Inner World* and Wilson van Dusen's *The Natural Depth in Man* and *The Presence of Other Worlds*, the latter inspired by the philosophical writings of Emanuel Swedenborg.

Among the important sources of transpersonal psychology that have led to a new understanding of spirituality is the research of Abraham Maslow, the author of the books *Religions, Values, and Peak Experiences, Toward a Psychology of Being*, and others. He demonstrated beyond any doubt that mystical experiences, or "peak experiences," as he called them, should not be confused with mental illness.

Clinical research of nonordinary states of consciousness induced by psychedelics and nondrug techniques has many implications for an alternative understanding of psychotic states. Much of this information is summarized in Stanislav Grof's books *Beyond the Brain, The Adventure of Self-Discovery*, and *Beyond Death*, the last coauthored by Christina Grof.

Among recent contributions to the problem of spirituality and psychosis is the work of Ken Wilber. In a series of articulate and comprehensive books, particularly *The Spectrum of Consciousness* and *The Atman Project*, he outlined the principles of his encompassing theory of human personality, which he calls spectrum psychology. Of particular interest for the subject of spiritual emergency is the book *Transformations of Consciousness*, coauthored by Wilber, Jack Engler, and Daniel Brown; it applies the concepts of spectrum psychology to the understanding of psychopathology, including various spiritual crises.

We should also mention two studies specifically focusing on the problem of spiritual emergency: Emma Bragdon's practical guidebook *Helping People in Spiritual Emergency* and Bonnie Lee Hood's doctoral dissertation "Transpersonal Crisis: Understanding Spiritual Emergencies." Interesting personal accounts of spiritual crisis are Flora Courtois' *An Experience of Enlightenment*, Irene Tweedie's *Daughter of Fire*, Naomi Steinfeld's article "Surviving the Chaos of Something Extraordinary," and Christina Grof's chapter from our forthcoming book on spiritual emergencies, *The Stormy Search for the Self*.

SPECIFIC INFORMATION ON VARIOUS FORMS OF SPIRITUAL EMERGENCY

For the type of spiritual emergency that shows a great similarity to shamanic crisis, the best sources of basic information are Mircea Eliade's classic book *Shamanism: The Archaic Techniques of Ecstasy* and Joseph Campbell's book *The Way of the Animal Powers*. Michael Harner's excellent book *The Way of the Shaman*, drawing on shamanic wisdom from many different cultures, offers practical guidelines for working with shamanic techniques and experiences. Additional sources of information are Stephen Larsen's *The Shaman's Doorway*, Joan Halifax's *Shaman: The Wounded Healer* and *Shamanic Voices*, Holger Kalweit's *Dreamtime and the Inner Space: The World of the Shaman*, Gary Doore's *Shaman's Path*, Roger Walsh's forthcoming *Cosmic Travelers: A Psychological View of Shamanism*, and Julian Silverman's article "Shamans and Acute Schizophrenia." The best-selling books by Carlos Castaneda, in spite of their poetic license, are a gold mine of information about shamanism.

The form of transpersonal crisis that has the characteristics of Kundalini awakening has been thoroughly described in ancient Indian Tantric literature. Among the best modern sources are Swami Muktananda's *Kundalini: The Secret of Life* and *Play of Consciousness*, Ajit Mookerjee's *Kundalini: The Arousal of the Inner Energy*, the books by pandit Gopi Krishna, particularly *Kundalini: The Evolutionary Energy in Man* and *Kundalini for the New Age*, Lee Sannella's *The Kundalini Experience: Psychosis or Transcendence*, and John White's compendium *Kundalini: Evolution and Enlightenment*. A detailed scholarly discussion of the subject can be found in Sir John Woodruffe's *The Serpent Power*.

Abraham Maslow's books on "peak experiences" and John Perry's writings on the crises involving renewal by return to the center have already been mentioned. The original literature on reincarnation and past-life experiences is vast and of varying quality. The corresponding passages in the Buddhist psychological text *The Path of Purification* will provide a good classical introduction to the subject. Among modern treatises, Ian Stevenson's *Twenty Cases Suggestive of Reincarnation* and Roger Woolger's *Other Lives, Other Selves* might be of interest.

Where nonordinary states of consciousness have a significant component of psychic phenomena, such as out-of-body experiences, mediumistic states, precognition, telepathy, and remote viewing, modern parapsychological literature can be very useful. The realm of out-of-body experiences has been described in Robert Monroe's autobiographical book *Journeys Out of the Body* and objectively studied by Charles Tart. Among the books that offer important information on various aspects of psychic phenomena are Tart's *PSI: Scientific Studies of the Psychic Realm*, Stanley Krippner's *The Song of the Siren: A Parapsychological Odyssey* and *Human Possibilities*, Russell Targ and Harold Puthoff's *Mind Reach: Scientists Look at Psychic Ability*, and Russell Targ and Keith Harary's *The Mind Race*. Those who want to know more about channeling should read Jon Klimo's excellent book *Channeling: Investigations on Receiving Information from Paranormal Sources*. More data about synchronicity can be found in C. G. Jung's original study, entitled *Synchronicity: An Acausal Connecting Principle*, and David Peat's *Synchronicity: The Bridge between Matter and Mind*.

More information on near-death experiences can be found in Raymond Moody's *Life after Life*, Ken Ring's *Life at Death* and *Heading toward Omega*, and Michael Sabom's *Recollections of Death*. In the vast literature on the UFO phenomenon, the best general information can be found in Jacque Vallee's *UFOs in Space*. In addition, C. G. Jung's study *Flying Saucers: A Modern Myth of Things Seen in the Skies* offers fascinating psychological insights into the subject.

The most interesting source of information relevant to the problem of possession states is the modern literature on the closely related subject of multiple personalities, which has recently been receiving great attention. A good introduction would be R. Allison's book *Minds in Many Pieces*.

NOTES AND REFERENCES

Assagioli: "Self-Realization and Psychological Disturbances"

1. One of Assagioli's major interests, and an important theme in his unpublished writings, was the social correspondences to the patterns of the individual's journey. Looking at society as if it were a person (see Donald Keys, "The Synthesis of Nations," *Synthesis* 2, p. 8), the symptoms of the individual crisis described in the last paragraphs are familiar: indeed, they characterize much of the behavior and collective states of mind of present-day society. Taken together, these social symptoms can be seen as the manifestation of an existential crisis in society itself. This crisis points to a spiritual awakening of society as a whole—an awakening observed by an increasing number of people. Viewed from this perspective, it may be of value to consider the many social difficulties with which we are all so familiar in the light of the patterns and suggestions that Assagioli outlines for the individual in this article.

2. This is why a certain amount of psychosynthesis—the integration of the personality around the center of identity, or "I"—needs to be undertaken before or concurrently with

spiritual psychosynthesis—the fusion of the personality with the superconscious energies, and of the "I" with the Transpersonal Self.

3. This distinction between the "I" and the "Self" and the relationship between them is discussed in Betsie Carter-Haar's article "Identity and Personal Freedom," *Synthesis* 2, pp. 89–90, 1977.

4. Additional information on the concept of levels of organization can be found in "Drive in Living Matter to Perfect Itself" by Albert Szent-Gyoergyi, *Synthesis* 1, p. 14, 1977.

5. This process of evoking an ideal model is often used intentionally by spiritual teachers to foster the growth of those whom they are guiding. See also *Synthesis* 2, p. 40, 1977.

6. See Assagioli, *Psychosynthesis, A Manual of Principles and Techniques*, Viking Press, New York, 1971, pp. 267–277.

7. Often the situation is complicated by the fact that there is an admixture of "regressive" and "progressive" factors. In such cases, individuals may reach a high level of development with some parts of their personality and yet be dominated by unconscious conflicts or handicapped by certain infantile fixations.

8. The entire process is necessarily complex and lengthy, and I have dealt with it in more ample detail in my other writings.

Perry: "Spiritual Emergence and Renewal"

Grof, S. *Realms of the Human Unconscious: Observations from LSD Research*. New York: Dutton, 1976.

Grof, S. *Beyond the Brain: Birth, Death, and Transcendence in Pyschotherapy*. Albany, N.Y.: SUNY Press, 1985.

Perry, J. W. *The Self in Psychotic Process*. Berkeley: University of California Press, 1953.

Perry, J. W. *Lord of the Four Quarters: Myths of the Royal Father*. New York: Braziller, 1966.

Perry, J. W. *The Far Side of Madness*. Englewood Cliffs, N.J.: Prentice-Hall, 1974.

Perry, J. W. *Roots of Renewal in Myth and Madness*. San Francisco: Jossey-Bass, 1976.

Kalweit: "When Insanity Is a Blessing: The Message of Shamanism"

1. Diószegi, V. *Tracing Shamans in Siberia*. Oosterhaut, 1968, p. 58.
2. Ibid., p. 57.
3. Ibid., p. 279.
4. Diószegi, V. "Der Werdegang zum Schamanen bei den nordoestlichen Sojoten." *Acta Ethnographica*, no. 8, 1959, pp. 269–291.
5. Diószegi, V. "Zum Problem der ethnischen Homogenitaet des tofischen (karagassischen) Schamanismus." *Glaubenswelt und Folklore der sibirischen Voelker*. Budapest, 1963, p. 267.
6. Boas, F. *The Religion of the Kwakiutl Indians* (part 2). New York: AMS Press, 1930, p. 41.
7. Ibid., p. 46.
8. Loeb, E. M. "Shaman and Seer." *American Anthropologist*, no. 31, 1929, p. 66.
9. Callaway, C. H. *The Religious System of the Amazula*, no. 15. London: Publications of the Folk-Lore Society, 1884, p. 259.
10. Good, C. M., et al. "Gūkunūra mūndū: The Initiation of a Kikuyu Medicine Man." *Anthropos* 75, no. 1–2, 1980, pp. 87–116.
11. Harvey, Y. K. "Possession Sickness and Women Shamans in Korea." *Unspoken Worlds: Women's Religious Lives in Non-Western Cultures*, edited by N. A. Falk and R. M. Gross. San Francisco: Wadsworth Publishing, 1980.
12. Sich, D. "Ein Beitrag zur Volksmedizin und zum Schamanismus in Korea." *Curare*, no. 4, 1980, pp. 209–216.
13. Beuchelt, E. "Zur Status-Persoenlichkeit koreanischer Schamanen." *Sociologus* 25, no. 2, 1975, pp. 139–154.
14. Lee, J. Y. *Korean Shamanistic Rituals*. The Hague, Netherlands: Mouton, 1981, p. 173.
15. Sharon, D. *Wizard of the Four Winds: A Shaman's Story*. New York: Free Press, 1978, p. 11.
16. Ibid., p. 12.
17. Sieroszewski, W. "Du chamanisme d'apres les croyances

des Yakoutes." *Revue de l'Histoire des Religions*, no. 46, 1902, pp. 299–338.

18. Shternberg, L. J. "Shamanism and Religious Election." *Introduction to Soviet Ethnology*, vol. 1, edited by S. P. Dunn and E. Dunn. Berkeley, 1974, p. 476.

19. Sancheyev, G. "Weltanschauung und Schamanismus der Alaren-Burjaeten." *Anthropos*, no. 23, 1928, pp. 967–986.

20. Harva, U. *Die religioesen Vorstellungen der altaischen Voelker*, no. 52. Helsinki: Folklore Fellows Communications, 1938, p. 453.

21. Boshier, A. K. "African Apprenticeship." *Parapsychology Review* 5, no. 4., 1974.

22. Watson-Franke, M. B. "Guajiro Schamanen (Kolumbien und Venezuela)." *Anthropos*, no. 70, 1975, pp. 194–207.

23. Hung-Youn, C. *Koreanischer Schamanismus*. Hamburg: Hamburgisches Museum fuer Voelkerkunde, 1982, p. 28.

Thompson: "The UFO Encounter Experience as a Crisis of Transformation"

Campbell, Joseph. *The Hero with a Thousand Faces*. Princeton, N.J.: Princeton University Press, 1949.

Hillman, James. *Re-Visioning Psychology*. New York: Harper & Row, 1975.

Hopkins, Budd. *Intruders*. New York: Random House, 1987.

Jung, C. G. *Flying Saucers: A Modern Myth of Things Seen in the Skies*. Princeton, N.J.: Princeton University Press, 1978.

Streiber, Whitley. *Communion*. New York: Beach Tree/Morrow, 1987.

Turner, Victor. "Betwixt and Between: The Liminal Period in Rites of Passage." *Betwixt and Between: Patterns of Masculine and Feminine Initiation*, edited by L. C. Mahdi, Steven Foster, and Meredith Little, 3–19. La Salle, Ill.: Open Court, 1987.

BIBLIOGRAPHY

Allison, R. *Minds in Many Pieces*. New York: Rawson and Wade, 1980.

Boisen, A. *The Exploration of the Inner World*. New York: Harper & Row, 1962.

Bragdon, E. *Helping People in Spiritual Emergency*. Los Altos, Calif.: Lightening Up Press, 1988.

Bucke, R. *Cosmic Consciousness*. New York: Dutton, 1923.

Campbell, J. *The Masks of God*. New York: Viking Press, 1968.

_____. *The Hero with a Thousand Faces*. Cleveland: World Publishing, 1970.

_____. *Myths to Live By*. New York: Bantam, 1972.

_____. *The Mythic Image*. Princeton: Princeton University Press, 1974.

_____. *The Way of the Animal Powers*. New York: Harper & Row, 1984.

Campbell, J., and Moyers, B. *The Power of Myth*. New York: Doubleday, 1988.

Castaneda, C. *Teachings of Don Juan: A Yaqui Way of Knowledge.* Berkeley: University of California Press, 1968.

―――. *A Separate Reality: Further Conversations with Don Juan.* New York: Simon and Schuster, 1971.

―――. *Journey to Ixtlan: The Lessons of Don Juan.* New York: Simon and Schuster, 1973.

Courtois, F. *An Experience of Enlightenment.* Wheaton, Ill.: Theosophical Publishing House, 1986.

Dabrowski, K. *Positive Disintegration.* Boston: Little, Brown, 1966.

Doore, G. *Shaman's Path: Healing, Personal Growth, and Empowerment.* Boston: Shambhala, 1988.

Eliade, M. *Shamanism: The Archaic Techniques of Ecstasy.* New York: Pantheon, 1964.

Greeley, A. *The Sociology of the Paranormal.* Beverly Hills, Calif.: Sage, 1975.

Grof, S. *Beyond the Brain.* Albany: State University of New York Press, 1985.

―――. *The Adventure of Self-Discovery.* Albany: State University of New York Press, 1987.

Grof, S., and Grof, C. *Beyond Death.* London: Thames and Hudson, 1980.

Halifax, J. *Shamanic Voices: A Survey of Visionary Narratives.* New York: Dutton, 1979.

―――. *Shaman: The Wounded Healer.* London: Thames and Hudson, 1982.

Harner, M. *The Way of the Shaman.* New York: Harper & Row, 1980.

Hastings, A. "A Counseling Approach to Parapsychological Experience." *Journal of Transpersonal Psychology* 15 (1983): 143–167.

Hood, B. L. "Transpersonal Crisis: Understanding Spiritual Emergencies." Ph.D. diss., University of Massachusetts, Boston, 1986.

James, W. *Varieties of Religious Experience.* New York: Collier, 1961.

Jung, C. G. *Collected Works*. Bollingen Series XX. Princeton: Princeton University Press, 1960.

_____. *Flying Saucers: A Modern Myth of Things Seen in the Skies*. Vol. 10, *Collected Works*. Bollingen Series XX. Princeton: Princeton University Press, 1964.

_____. *Synchronicity: An Acausal Connecting Principle*. Vol. 8, *Collected Works*. Bollingen Series XX. Princeton: Princeton University Press, 1980.

_____. *Psychological Commentary on Kundalini Yoga*. New York: Spring Publications, 1975.

Kalff, D. *Sandplay: Mirror of A Child's Psyche*. San Francisco: Hendra & Howard, 1971.

Kalweit, H. *Dreamtime and the Inner Space: The World of the Shaman*. Boston: Shambhala, 1988.

Klimo, J. *Channeling: Investigations on Receiving Information from Paranormal Sources*. Los Angeles: Jeremy P. Tarcher, 1987.

Krippner, S. *The Song of the Siren: A Parapsychological Odyssey*. New York: Harper & Row, 1977.

_____. *Human Possibilities*. Garden City, N.Y.: Anchor/Doubleday, 1980.

Krishna, G. *Kundalini: The Evolutionary Energy in Man*. Berkeley: Shambhala, 1970.

_____. *Kundalini for the New Age*. Edited by G. Kieffer. New York: Bantam, 1988.

Laing, R. D. *The Divided Self*. Baltimore: Penguin, 1965.

_____. *The Politics of Experience*. New York: Ballantine, 1967.

_____. "Metanoia: Some Experiences at Kingsley Hall." In *Going Crazy*, edited by N. Ruitenbeck. New York: Bantam, 1972.

Larsen, S. *The Shaman's Doorway: Opening the Mythic Imagination to Contemporary Consciousness*. San Francisco: Harper & Row, 1976.

Laski, M. *Ecstasy: A Study of Some Secular and Religious Experiences*. New York: Greenwood, 1968.

Lukoff, D. "Diagnosis of Mystical Experiences with Psychotic Features." *Journal of Transpersonal Psychology* 17 (1985): 155–181.

Lukoff, D., and Everest, H. "The Myths of Mental Illness." *Journal of Transpersonal Psychology* 17 (1985): 123–153.

Maslow, A. *Toward a Psychology of Being.* Princeton: Van Nostrand, 1962.

_____. *Religions, Values, and Peak Experiences.* Cleveland: Ohio State University, 1964.

Monroe, R. *Journeys Out of the Body.* New York: Doubleday, 1971.

Moody, R. *Life After Life.* Atlanta: Mockingbird, 1975.

Mookerjee, A. *Kundalini: The Arousal of the Inner Energy.* New York: Destiny, 1982.

Mosher, L., and Menn, A. *Soteria: An Alternative to Hospitalization for Schizophrenics.* Vol. 1, *New Direction for Health Services.* San Francisco: Jossey-Bass, 1979.

Muktananda, Swami. *Play of Consciousness.* South Fallsburg, N.Y.: SYDA Foundation, 1974.

_____. *Kundalini: The Secret of Life.* South Fallsburg, N.Y.: SYDA Foundation, 1979.

Peat, D. *Synchronicity: The Bridge between Matter and Mind.* New York: Bantam, 1987.

Perry, J. *The Self in Psychotic Process.* Berkeley: University of California Press, 1953.

_____. *Lord of the Four Quarters.* New York: Braziller, 1966.

_____. *The Far Side of Madness.* Englewood Cliffs, N.J.: Prentice-Hall, 1974.

_____. *Roots of Renewal in Myth and Madness.* San Francisco: Jossey-Bass, 1976.

Rappaport, M., et al. "Are There Schizophrenics for Whom Drugs May Be Unnecessary or Contraindicated?" *International Pharmacopsychiatry* 13 (1978): 100.

Ring, K. *Life at Death.* New York: Coward, McCann & Geoghegan, 1980.

_____. *Heading toward Omega*. New York: Morrow, 1984.

Sabom, M. *Recollections of Death*. New York: Simon and Schuster, 1982.

Sannella, L. *The Kundalini Experience: Psychosis or Transcendence*. Lower Lake, Calif.: Integral Publishing, 1987.

_____. "The Many Faces of Kundalini." *The Laughing Man Magazine* 4, no. 3 (1983): 11–21.

Silverman, J. "Shamans and Acute Schizophrenia." *American Anthropologist* 69 (1967): 21.

_____. "Acute Schizophrenia: Disease or Dis-ease." *Psychology Today* 4 (1970): 62.

_____. "When Schizophrenia Helps." *Psychology Today* (1971).

Singer, J. *Boundaries of the Soul: The Practice of Jung's Psychology*. Garden City, N.Y.: Anchor/Doubleday, 1972.

Steinfeld, N. "Surviving the Chaos of Something Extraordinary." *Shaman's Drum* 4 (1986): 22–27.

Stevenson, I. *Twenty Cases Suggestive of Reincarnation*. Charlottesville: University Press of Virginia, 1966.

Szasz, T. *The Myth of Mental Illness*. New York: Hoeber-Harper, 1961.

Targ, R., and Puthoff, H. *Mind Reach: Scientists Look at Psychic Ability*. New York: Delta, 1977.

Targ, R., and Harary, K. *The Mind Race*. New York: Villard, 1984.

Tart, C. *PSI: Scientific Studies of the Psychic Realm*. New York: Dutton, 1977.

_____. *States of Consciousness*. New York: Dutton, 1975.

Tweedie, I. *Daughter of Fire: A Diary of a Spiritual Training with a Sufi Master*. Grass Valley, Calif.: Blue Dolphin, 1986.

Underhill, E. *Mysticism: A Study in the Nature and Development of Man's Spiritual Consciousness*. New York: Meridian, 1955.

Vallée, J. *UFOs in Space: Anatomy of a Phenomenon*. New York: Ballantine, 1965.

Van Dusen, W. *The Natural Depth in Man*. New York: Harper & Row, 1972.

_____. *The Presence of Other Worlds: The Teachings of Emanuel Swedenborg*. New York: Harper & Row, 1974.

Walsh, R. *Cosmic Travelers: A Psychological View of Shamanism* (in press).

White, J., ed. *Kundalini: Evolution and Enlightenment*. Garden City, N.Y.: Anchor/Doubleday, 1979.

Wilber, K. *The Spectrum of Consciousness*. Wheaton, Ill.: Theosophical Publishing House, 1977.

_____. *The Atman Project: A Transpersonal View of Human Development*. Wheaton, Ill.: Theosophical Publishing House, 1980.

Wilber, K., Engler, J., and Brown, D. *Transformations of Consciousness*. Boston and London: New Science Library/Shambhala, 1986.

Woodruffe, Sir J. *The Serpent Power*. Madras: Ganesh, 1964.

Woolger, R. *Other Lives, Other Selves*. New York: Bantam, 1988.

ABOUT THE EDITORS

Christina Grof was raised in Honolulu, Hawaii, and graduated from Sarah Lawrence College in New York. Her original career as a teacher of art was interrupted when a powerful spiritual experience during childbirth launched her into many years of emotional turmoil, later identified as manifestations of Kundalini awakening. She taught Hatha-Yoga and was deeply influenced by Swami Muktananda Paramahansa, head of the Siddha-Yoga lineage; she was his student until his death in 1982.

Her own unusual experiences generated in her deep interest in nonordinary states of consciousness and transpersonal psychology. Together with her husband, Stanislav Grof, she has developed Holotropic Breathwork, an experiential technique of psychotherapy that combines controlled breathing, evocative music, and bodywork. She and her husband have also organized international transpersonal conferences in Boston, Melbourne, Bombay, and Santa Rosa, California.

Christina's particular area of interest is the relationship between mysticism and psychosis. In 1980 she founded the Spiritual Emergence Network, an international organization providing support for individuals undergoing transformative crises. More recently, her interest has extended into the area of the spiritual aspects of alcoholism and addiction. In the last decade she has conducted lectures and workshops in North and South America, Europe, Australia, and Asia. She is also coauthor of the book *Beyond Death*.

Stanislav Grof, M.D., is a psychiatrist with more than thirty years of research experience in nonordinary states of consciousness. He was born and educated in Prague, Czechoslovakia, and received an M.D. from Prague's Charles University School of Medicine, where he specialized in psychiatry. He was the principle investigator for a program at the Psychiatric Research Institute in Prague that explored the potential of psychedelic therapy. For his dissertation on this subject, he was awarded a Ph.D. (doctorate of philosophy in medicine) by the Czechoslovak Academy of Sciences.

In 1967 he was invited to Johns Hopkins University as a clinical and research fellow and to the research unit of Spring Grove State Hospital in Baltimore, Maryland, where he continued his psychedelic research. In 1969 he was offered the position of chief of psychiatric research at the Maryland Psychiatric Research Center and of assistant professor of psychiatry at Henry Phipps Clinic. The research team he headed systematically explored the value of psychedelic therapy in neurotics, alcoholics, drug addicts, and terminal cancer patients.

Stanislav continued these functions until 1973, when he moved to California and became scholar in residence at the Esalen Institute in Big Sur. Since that time, he has focused on exploring the potential of experiential psychotherapy without drugs, in addition to writing and conducting seminars worldwide. He one of the founders and chief theoreticians of transpersonal psychology and the founding president of the International Transpersonal Association. He has published more than ninety papers in professional journals and is the author of *Realms of the Human Unconscious, The Human Encounter with Death, LSD Psychotherapy, Beyond the Brain,* and *The Adventure of Self-Discovery.* He was also editor of the volumes *Ancient Wisdom and Modern Science* and *Human Survival and Consciousness Evolution.*